PIONEER COOKERY
AROUND OKLAHOMA

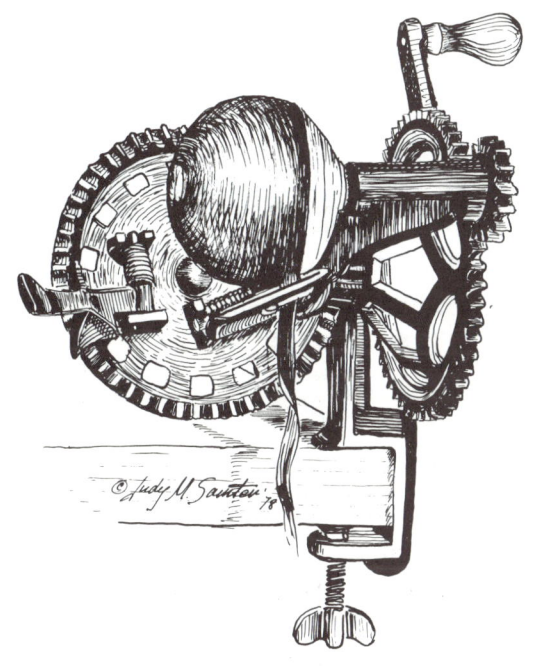

Compiled and Edited by Linda Kennedy Rosser

Illustrated by Judy Mideke Samter

Bobwhite Publications
ISBN - 0-929546-01-6

For additional copies, use the order blanks
in the back of the book or write directly to:

PIONEER COOKERY AROUND OKLAHOMA
Bobwhite Publications
Post Office Box 14641
Oklahoma City, Oklahoma 73113

Special rates available for retail outlets or
organizations for fundraising projects.

DAVID BOREN
OKLAHOMA

WASHINGTON OFFICE:
RUSSELL BUILDING
WASHINGTON, D.C. 20510

STATE OFFICES:
821 NORTH ROBINSON
OKLAHOMA CITY, OKLAHOMA 73102
440 SOUTH HOUSTON
TULSA, OKLAHOMA 74127
MUNICIPAL BUILDING
SEMINOLE, OKLAHOMA 74868

United States Senate

WASHINGTON, D.C. 20510

MEMBER:
COMMITTEE ON FINANCE
COMMITTEE ON AGRICULTURE,
NUTRITION AND FORESTRY
COMMITTEE ON SMALL BUSINESS

October 24, 1984

Dear Linda:

While a young State by some standards, Oklahoma has a rich culture and interesting history. The pioneers who built Oklahoma instilled in our citizens a sense of pride and accomplishment for a job well done.

It is a benefit to preserve this culture and history not only for today's Oklahomans but also for those of future generations. This book of pioneer cookery adds a new dimension to our State's recorded history and preserves a unique portion of the culture of that period.

Oklahomans appreciate the research effort represented by this historical cookbook.

Sincerely,

DAVID BOREN
United States Senator

3

INTRODUCTION

By wagon, by horse, by train, and by foot they came — some who were pioneers by choice, others whose destiny was ordained by treaty. The word pioneer usually calls to mind sunbonnets and covered wagons, but it literally refers to those who come first, preparing the way for others. So in the broadest sense, even the Indians were pioneers, and so were the cowboys on dusty and lonely cattle trails

Food was a common need of all who came to this land which would become Oklahoma. Tucked safely in the minds of the women were recipes taught them by their mothers in distant places. Others had carefully packed a cookbook into a corner of the big trunk with other family treasures. Cattle trail cooks relied on imagination to satisfy fellow cowmen.

Settling into her new home, whether tent, cabin, soddy, or pine house, the pioneer woman learned to make-do with what was available. The spicy aroma of gingerbread baking in the wood stove, a plate of biscuits swimming in gravy, the smell of camp coffee brewing on an open fire, and the fellowship of a taffy-pull made the struggles of life lighter.

Oklahoma's colorful heritage is like grandmother's patchwork quilt; a variegated assortment of cultures stitched together to form a warm and interesting pattern. The sadness and starvation of the Trail of Tears, traveled by the Five Civilized Tribes, was a far cry from the excitement and anticipation of later people lined up at the border awaiting the noon gun which would signal the first Run, a wild, dusty race to stake claims in the Unassigned Lands. The treaty removals begun in 1829 continued almost 60 years, bringing 65 tribes to Indian Territory. Several Runs and land allotments held between 1889 and 1901 brought thousands of settlers into Oklahoma Territory. The influx kept up until the Twin Territories, I.T. and O.T., became a single state in 1907.

The contrast in foods and the style of preparation were as varied as the homes from which they came: European immigrants seeking rich farmland, working the coal mines, and peddling merchandise; cowboys and ranchers herding cattle on the open plains; Northerners and Southerners coming as teachers, bankers, doctors, and farmers, bringing regional customs; blacks accompanying the Civilized Tribes Indians as slaves, later as freemen and cowboys; and the Indians, unwilling pioneers, hoping at last to find peace.

With this book we hope to preserve some of the legacy of those early Oklahomans. Recipes, as links to the past, are presented with family tales, historical anecdotes, and warm memories of days-gone-by. Similar recipes were included for variations and interesting sidelights. Though many are as practical today as in 1907, others are for reading enjoyment only, particularly the home remedies. Through years of family use, some updating has taken place, but we have tried to use only recipes for which ingredients were available prior to statehood. Remember that the railroad, which greatly influenced the opening of the Territory to settlers, also brought a surprising variety of groceries for the pioneer larder, and turn-of-the-century technology brought an unexpected degree of sophistication to the young territorial towns of Oklahoma country.

CONTENTS

ACKNOWLEDGEMENTS

Thanks to everyone who furnished pioneer recipes and anecdotes. We regret that not all could be included, and there are probably many popular dishes for which recipes were not received, or there wasn't space. Many individuals, organizations, and museums have provided invaluable assistance and encouragement in the research and development of this book: special thanks to the 1889er Society, R. E. Katigan, Pres., Pat Murphy and Alice Whitten, Past Presidents, for allowing use of excerpts from *Oklahoma The Beautiful Land* (which has recently been reprinted) and for the enthusiastic response of the Society members to this project; Mary Lee Ervin and the Oklahoma Historical Society, also Rocky Jones and Patricia Lester; the Overholser Mansion and Mable Krank; The Oklahoma Heritage Association and Dr. Paul Lambert; The Junior League of Oklahoma City and Midge Lindsey, Past President; The Guthrie Daily Leader and Dale Himes; the Guthrie Territorial Museum and Fred Olds; The Stroud Public Library and Miriam Horn; 1st Baptist Church of Oklahoma City and Mrs. R. K. Stapleton; Church of Jesus Christ Of Latter Day Saints and Elva Lindsey; Czech Festival Association of Yukon, Anna Smrcka, Mildred Stejskel and Paul Stejskel, President, for allowing use of several recipes from the *Festival Cookbook;* Daughters of the American Revolution, 14 Flags Chapter; Kirkpatrick Oil, John Kirkpatrick and Mrs. Darwin T. Maurer; Meyers-Samter Insurance Agency, Inc.; Manon Atkins, Oklahoma Historical Society Library; Cowboy Hall of Fame Library.

Thanks also to the following individuals for special favors: Betty Lou Fritsche, Wayne Mackey (Oklahoma City Times), Judy Morrison, Barbara Stanfield, Marta Reynolds, Harriet Carson, Janice Segell, Mrs. Joseph F. Rumsey, Bessie Jenkins, Catfish Henderson, Esther Rainey, Janie Russell, Frances Miller, Allison Stanfield, Laurie Carson, Linda Garrett, Peggy Haynes, Anita Poarch, Lisa Poarch, Mark Lindsey, Leslie Lindsey, Bea Milligan, Robin and Pendleton Woods, Jeanette Sias, Franci Hart, Susan Amis, Patty Saunders, Susan Wade, Patti Leeman, Joe Jerkins, Lee Bollinger, C. D. Ellison, Jack Conn, Pat Samter, Joan Mary Putnam, Mary and Monroe Parker, Don Lisle, Leslie & Jim Diggs.

Very special thanks go to Judy Samter for her imaginative and interesting illustrations which enhance the book so greatly.

$\mathcal{L}. \mathcal{K}. \mathcal{R}$

Overholser Mansion, Okla. City

SOUPS & STEWS

Mrs. Overholser's

CREAM OF CELERY SOUP

Take three or four heads of celery, cut in small pieces, cover with cold water; bring slowly to a boil. Then place in Caloric and leave two hours. Take from Caloric and drain. Take two tablespoons of butter and four tablespoon of flour; place on the stove and blend thoroughly. Add three-fourths pint of cold milk and cook. Then add drained celery water and if stronger flavor is desired press the cooked clery through a sieve. Season with salt and pepper.

1907 Caloric Cookbook

The Overholser Mansion still stands on N.W. 15th Street in Oklahoma City, preserved as a tribute to one of the city's greatest founding fathers. In the butler's pantry stands a Caloric Cooker along with the original cookbook, just as many original fine furnishings adorn other rooms of the main floor ... the dining room with its stately chandelier and typical victorian furniture, the living room with hand-painted walls.

The first Caloric Fireless Cookstoves came out about the time of statehood, 1907, as a successor to the "hay-box", in which the initial heat was supplied by boiling the liquid in which the food was to be cooked and then retaining heat with an insulation of hay. This method limited the cooking method to stewing and steaming since the temperature could not exceed 212° F. An early Caloric was not a real cookstove, but by 1907 an improvement had been made with the addition of steatite radiators which were first heated in conventional stoves, then placed into the well of the Caloric. A special container holding the food was then placed into the well and another radiator on top. Temperatures of over 400° could be obtained.

The Caloric was particularly suitable for soups, which could be kept warm while other dishes were being prepared on the stove. Included in this chapter are a number of soup recipes from Mrs. Overholser's Caloric Recipe Book.

Caloric Cooker

8

Grandmother's

PEA SOUP

Open a can of peas, pour into a saucepan adding a can of water. About 1 tsp. of finely minced onion a bit of garlic. Cook a little while, salt and pepper to taste. In the meantime make (Kapani) — Beat 1 egg, add 2½ tbsp. flour stir until smooth. Drop a little at a time into the boiling peas. Cover and cook 10 min.

Mildred Svoboda Stejskal
Yukon

Yukon, Oklahoma Territory, was established in 1891 attracting a large number of immigrants from Czechoslovakia and first generation Czechs from the northern U.S., looking for more pleasant farming conditions ... they brought with them traditional recipes still in use today.

Mrs. Foreman's

FRENCH SOUP

Slice thin one each of the foregoing vegetables: potatoes, tomatoes, onions, parsnips, carrot, celery and a bit of cabbage, cook in a quart of water to which stock has been added and a generous pinch of summer savory. When cooking add water as needed. Season with pepper, salt and worchestershire sauce or a little catsup. Serve unstrained.

1904 Tulsa Cookbook

In 1904 the Ladies Aid Society of the First Presbyterian Church of Tulsa, Indian Territory, compiled a cookbook containing popular and unusual recipes of that era. Susan Tague of Oklahoma City, has her grandmother, Mrs. James P. Boddy's, copy.

Mrs. Arthur White's

CORN CHOWDER

1 onion chopped	4 cups scalded milk
1½ inch cube salt pork	2 cups boiling water
2 cans corn	Salt and pepper
1 large potato diced	

Cut salt pork fine. Fry the salt pork. Skim out the meat and fry the onion in the fat. Simmer the corn in the boiling water for ten minutes. Add the milk and diced potato, pork, onion, salt and pepper. When well blended and the potato is done, serve with crackers.

5 O'Clock Tea Club Cookbook
Oklahoma City

The 5 O'Clock Tea Club was formed about 1907 as a very exclusive ladies' club in Oklahoma City but actually met for luncheons.

Mrs. Gladstein's

CABBAGE SOUP

Cut one onion in sauce pan and fry golden brown with two pounds of beef brisket, then add one head of cabbage cut fine. Cover with water. When meat is half done add several tomatoes. Season to taste. Add the juice of one lemon and several tablespoons of sugar according to taste. This requires a little more pepper than other soups. Cabbage should generally be salted and scalded before adding to meat. Cook slowly until meat is tender.

Harriet Goldberg Carson (Mrs. Joel)
Oklahoma City

Just as "Oklahoma Fever" was caught by people in other states seeking new opportunities, so it was with many Europeans immigrating to the U.S., including Jewish immigrants from eastern Europe who saw promise in the Twin Territories.

Juel Craver Butler's

TOMATO BISQUE SOUP

1 can tomatoes	1 Quart milk
2 T. sugar	⅓ cup butter
½ T. soda	

Scald milk (do not allow to boil). Cook tomatoes, sugar, salt & pepper. Heat milk, add butter, soda combine. (Do not let milk boil or it will curdle.)

Mrs. Leslie M. Voss (1889er)
Oklahoma City

Mrs. Voss is an active member of the 1889er Society. Her sister's recipe for Tomato Bisque Soup has won prizes and was popular in the early days.

Mrs. Brogan's

TOMATO SOUP

1 quart tomatoes	1 onion
1 quart water	salt & pepper
butter	

Boil 20 minutes, strain, then add salt, pepper, and butter. Thicken a little with flour.

1900 Stroud Cookbook

"Staple and fancy groceries; Queensware and Feed; country produce of all kinds" were available at F.E. Brogan's store in Stroud in 1900.

Mrs. F.M. Rinehart's

NOODLE SOUP

Sift a small quantity of flour into a pan, then make a hole in the center and break three eggs into it. Put in a small pinch of salt. Knead into a stiff dough, divide in half, and roll each piece separately as thin as paper. Then spread a cloth over the back of a chair and hang the dough on the cloth to dry. When it is about half dry or dry enough to not stick together take down and roll up into a tight roll and take a sharp knife and slice across the end very thin. The thinner it is sliced the nicer the noodles will be. Cook in clear beef soup with a dash of nutmeg grated in soup.

Capital City Cookbook
Guthrie, 1898

In December of 1898, the Ladies of the Christian Church of Guthrie, Oklahoma Territory published the Capital City Cookbook, so-named because one year after the Run of 1889, the land was organized as Oklahoma Territory with Guthrie as its capital ... which it remained until 1910, three years after statehood.

Grandma's

FADDLE SOUP

2 eggs
Pinch salt (½ tsp.)
1 cup flour
1 tsp. baking powder

1 T. melted shortening or oil
Milk to make thin batter, like
   pancake batter

Bake on greased griddle or in iron skillet like pancakes — Cut in strips and place in bowls of hot broth ... eat.

Mrs. Ova S. Hull
Oklahoma City

"Grandma Dobbs fixed Faddle Soup for us on her old wood stove ... it was so good on cold evenings for supper when we got home from the country school we attended."

Mrs. Gladstein's

BORSCHT

Four or five nice-sized beets cut into cubes cooked with a good marrow bone. Season with salt and pepper and the juice of one lemon. Add sugar to taste (about 1 T.) and boil until meat and beets are tender. Beat the yolks of two eggs with a little water and temper them with several spoonsful of beet soup. Add all to soup. Let boil up and serve with boiled potatoes. (a garnish of sour cream is often used)

Harriet Goldberg Carson (Mrs. Joel)
Oklahoma City

Mrs. B. Gladstein was a pioneer of McAlester, and this traditional Jewish recipe has been a popular recipe with her family and friends since long before statehood.

Mrs. W. D. Lindsey's

INDIAN BEEF SOUP

Take flank of beef, break in short pieces, so that marrow will cook into the soup. One pint corn grits, cover with water and boil; add salt and pepper to taste.

1904 Tulsa Cookbook

In 1904, Tulsa, Indian Territory was just beginning to grow ... oil had not yet been struck. Its name derived from an earlier name, Tulsey Town, and it was situated on land which had been part of the Creek Indian Lands assigned to them following the Trail of Tears.

PESHOFA

Use cracked corn (pearl hominy), approximately 2 cups to two pork chops and a small amount of beef. Cook with green chili peppers, salt, pepper, and water all day in a very large pot (it swells). Serve with corn bread or crackers.

Gillett Massey Conn (Mrs. Jack)
Oklahoma City

Mr. and Mrs. Conn both grew up in Pontotoc County, where many Choctaws and Chickasaws still cook this traditional dish, which contained whatever meat was available.

12

Traditional Jewish

CHICKEN SOUP

4 pound stewing hen	3-4 pieces of celery
6 quarts water	3-4 carrots
1 onion	salt & pepper to taste

Clean and cut up chicken, place in large pot with water, boil, skimming as necessary. After soup has boiled about 45 minutes, add whole carrots, celery, onion, salt and pepper. Allow to cook until chicken is tender and broth has rich flavor.

Among the most prominent citizens of early Oklahoma were Jewish families, many of whom were in the retail clothing business. Among the leaders in Oklahoma City were Solomon Barth and Joseph Meyer who established the B & M store in 1898 and the Gerson Brothers, whose store advertised "Men's and Boy's clothing and Gent's furnishings" in 1893. The Gersons were well known for their imaginative entertaining.

Mrs. Street's

RICH OYSTER SOUP

1 quart milk	1 pint oysters
3 T. butter	salt and pepper to taste

Heat milk, butter, and seasonings. While heating, butter a skillet, turn in the oyster liquid and bring to a boil. Pour in ½ teacupful of the hot milk liquid, turn the oysters into this and stir them a few seconds. Throw the contents of the skillet into the hot milk and serve immediately.

1900 Stroud Cookbook

Mrs. Street's husband, A. L. H., was a Stroud attorney and owner of the "Stroud Star", in 1900 "the oldest newspaper in the city", according to ads of the day.

The Ladies Society of the 1st Presbyterian Church of Stroud, Oklahoma Territory, published a cookbook in 1900 ... Miss Violet Sterrett of Oklahoma City still has her mother's time-worn and often-used copy.

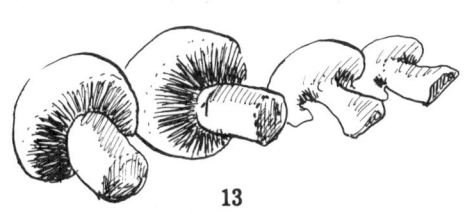

CLAM CHOWDER

1 cup chopped onion
½ cup diced salt pork or bacon
½ cup butter
1 cup diced raw potatoes
½ cup water

2 T. flour
2 cup milk
1 cup cream
2 8 oz cans of clams

Saute onion and pork in butter, cook til soft, not brown. Add potatoes and water. Cook til tender. Add flour, cook 2 minutes. Add milk. Cook 5 minutes, stirring constantly. Add cream and clams, cook til hot.

Linda Kennedy Rosser (Mrs. Ronald E.)
Edmond

At the turn of the century clam chowder was very popular ... almost always included in cookbooks published at that time.

Mrs. Overholser's

BEAN SOUP

Just as lean meat makes a better soup than fat, so does lean pork make a much finer flavored soup than fat, though either may be used. Soak one quart of navy beans for several hours. Place in kettle with two or three quarts of water and two to three pounds of pork-loin and a heaping teaspoon of salt and large pinch of black pepper. Boil ten minutes and remove to Caloric four hours, using one radiator. The lean pork may be lifted from soup and browned as a roast, or sliced cold makes a very fair meat, though of course not so rich as when cooked alone. Spanish onions sliced in vinegar make a fine side dish for bean soup.

1907 Caloric Cookbook

Henry Overholser made the Run of '89 into Oklahoma Station, invested in real estate, and arranged for prefabricated buildings to arrive by rail from Minneapolis within months after the run.

Otelia Hill Martin's

VEGETABLE SOUP

2 pieces center cut beef shank (about 1 pound)
(these are superior to the usual soup bones as
they contain the marrow)
1 lb. of stew beef for added richness
1½ quarts home-canned tomatoes
1 tsp. salt
4 grinds pepper (about ¼ tsp.)
1 onion about 4 inches in diameter, peeled
and cut in 1/8ths

Place all ingredients in a 4 quart or larger stock pot. Bring to a boil, reduce heat and simmer covered for 2 hours. Add 4 large spines of celery, cleaned, stringed, and cut into ½ inch pieces. Continue simmering for another hour, then hold (for later use) or add 4 cups peeled Irish potatoes cut in 1 inch pieces, one medium cabbage coarsely chopped (about 8 cups), 2 cups fresh okra. Simmer about 30 minutes or until potatoes are tender. Add salt and pepper seasoning or let each person season to taste. Very good served with buttered and warmed sour dough bread — a true meal in one.

Mary Lee Martin Ervin (Mrs. John W.)
Oklahoma City

"At the age of 6 Mother came with her parents, the George H. Hills, from Arkansas to Oklahoma in February, 1903 ... they settled on a farm near Hydro, where her maternal grandparents, the William Cullens, were living."

Mrs. R. A. Vose's

CHICKEN GUMBO

1 Chicken (frying size)
1 onion (chopped)
1 medium sized potato
(cut up)
1 green pepper (chopped)
1 can okra (or 1 pt. fresh)
1 qt. tomatoes
1 cup rice
2 T. chili powder
Salt and pepper to taste

Cut up chicken and fry in hot fat until browned. Remove and in the same fat, fry the onion, potato, pepper and okra. When these are done, turn into a kettle with the chicken, and the rest of the ingredients, adding enough water to cook the rice. This should simmer for several hours.

5 O'Clock Tea Club Cookbook
Oklahoma City

Mrs. Vose, wife of a prominent Oklahoma City banker, was well-known in social circles around the time of statehood.

Dan Cullin's

SONOFAGUN STEW

¼ beef liver, cut in small pieces
½ beef heart, cut in small pieces
All the marrow gut, cut in small pieces
All the sweetbread and brains, cut in small pieces
1 cup of chopped tallow
1 small onion, chopped
1 small red pepper, chopped in small pieces
½ tsp. pepper
1 tsp. salt

Place all the ingredients except the brains in an iron pot. Add 1 cup water and bring to boil. Skim and continue cooking until all meat is tender. Add the brains and cook very slowly until the natural gravey becomes thick. Stir often and cook as slowly as possible from the beginning.

David E. Raines
El Reno

When this stew was made out on the range by the camp cook feeding hungry cowboys, it had a more raucus name, "Sonofa..." Stew. To be absolutely right, according to James Neill Northe of Oklahoma City, "it should contain the tube connecting the two stomachs of a cud-chewing animal, preferably an unweaned calf". The stew would be made in camp right after slaughtering ... was considered a real treat with sourdough biscuits.

The Pioneer Woman, Ponca City

BISCUITS & BREADS

BISCUITS & BACON

Over and over again references are made to the pioneers' dependence on biscuits and bacon during their trip to Oklahoma Country as reflected in this reminiscence by Eighty-niner, Alice Beitman Heaney, a single woman when she staked her claim near Britton:

"I came to Oklahoma the second week after the opening, and secured a claim near Britton. It was a new experience to camp out on the open prairie with few of the conveniences of life.

The first night out there I had biscuits and bacon for supper. One frying pan sufficed for both. The prairie sod was my bed, with a bit of canvas for the top and bottom sheets, and the stars were my friends. Oh, how much one comes to value these nightly visitors when other friends are few.

Next morning I was up bright and early, 'bacon and biscuits' this time for a change. I took a walk around my claim and posted notices on the stakes which I drove with my own hands, that 'This claim is taken.'

Now I was ready for a visit to the land office at Guthrie. I went up there on the afternoon train to file, but when I got there I found a long line of tired, dusty settlers ahead of me. They had brought their food with them, or had friends who would relieve them in line while they hurriedly visited a restaurant.

My chances of filing seemed extremely remote, and discouragement was settling down over me, when a cry of 'Let the lady file' went up from that big-hearted frontier throng."

Oklahoma–The Beautiful Land

Joanna Jerkins'
BISCUITS, SOUTHERN STYLE

Start with 1 quart flour, 1 teaspoon salt worked in to the center, a piece of lard the size of an egg, a pint of sour milk into which a teaspoonful of soda has been stirred just as you add all to the flour. Mix until soft dough is formed. Pinch off enough dough for a biscuit and roll into the palm of your hand. Pat flat, dip in melted grease of the baking pan which was placed in the oven while mixing biscuits. Continue until all dough is used up. Biscuits should bake about 10 to 12 minutes until they are a warm brown.

Ruth Nation Jerkins
Oklahoma City

"My mother-in-law, Joanna Jerkins, came to Lawton in the fall of 1901, bringing her family and belongings in a covered wagon from Texas, where they had lived 10 years after leaving Georgia. She, too, like my mother from the north, made her biscuits in a washpan — a gray granite one that also was never used for anything else."

BISCUITS, NORTHERN STYLE

To start, have at least 3 pint cans of flour in the pan. Make a "well", or hole, in the center into which 3 teaspoons baking powder and 1 teaspoon salt is placed. Mix through the flour, add lard the size of an egg. Make a well again in the center and add 1 cup sweet milk. Mix together until it forms a soft dough; sometimes you may have to add a bit more flour. Lift out the bread board — pat or roll out flat. Cut out with the usual biscuit cutter and bake in a quick oven on a greased pan until firm and brown on top.

These were usually placed on what was called "our bread pan", which held a lot of biscuits. There was almost always butter for them and sorghum molasses, sometimes honey. Once in a while there was enough sugar to make preserves, jam, or jelly.

Ruth Nation Jerkins
Irene Nation Van Sandt
Oklahoma City

"My mother, Cora Nation, came to Caddo County, 8 miles east of Binger from Iowa by way of Kansas (1870's) and on to Oklahoma in the fall of 1902 in a covered wagon. Mother Nation kept her flour in a 10 gallon lard can with a tight lid . . . the biscuits were mixed in a dark blue granite pan, actually a washpan never used for anything but mixing biscuits. If biscuits were mixed properly, and they always were, the pans were entirely clean of flour or anything else when finally mixed . . . the pan was placed carefully inside the lard can that held the flour and the lid reclosed tightly."

Pre-Civil War

SOUR MILK BISCUITS

1 qt. flour
1 T. salt

1 tsp. soda
1 pt. sour milk

Sift flour with salt and soda. Shorten with lard, size of a "banty" egg. Add milk.

Mrs. Martha J. Birchum (Mrs. J.W., Jr.)
Chickasha

"This recipe is written just as it was found, with no directions for cutting or baking. It belonged to my great-grandmother, who lived on a plantation near Atlanta, Georgia, which was burned out during the Civil War by General Sherman. My grandmother, Martha Frances Vandiver, and her brother hid in a cave in the woods with a cow and two horses. After the war they did as many other Southerners did, migrated to Texas. When lands opened up in Indian Territory they moved on."

19

SOUR DOUGH BISCUITS

Dissolve 1 cake yeast or 1 pkg. dry in 1 qt. warm water, 2 T. sugar, 2 pints flour. Mix in a crock and let rise until light and slightly aged, 24-48 hours. Do not let sponge chill.

Form a nest in a pan of sifted flour. Pour about 2 cups of "starter" in nest. Sprinkle over the sponge ½ tsp. salt, 1 T. sugar, 2 heaping tsp. baking powder. Mix to firm soft dough. Turn out on board and pat or roll ½" thick. Bake on well greased iron skillet. Grease tops of biscuits well. Cover, set out of draft and let rise 15 min. Cook 500° preheated oven.

Bessie Jenkins
Cresson, Texas

Vera Holding, of Norman, recently recalled her father's preparation of sourdough into what he called "Terrapin Biscuits" for their first Thanksgiving at Fort Cobb: "Papa placed his cow-camp dutch oven on a bed of glowing coals in readiness for his "terrapin biscuits" as he called them. He made them of sourdough, squeezed them into balls then flatted them between his hands, dipped them in hot grease and placed them in the oven, put the lid on and topped the lid with more hot coals. There was no taste on earth to compare with them. Especially when you'd make little lakes of sorghum in your plate where small islands of butter floated and you could sop it up with Papa's biscuits."

Mrs. Lindsey's

AHA IUKLIKE

(*Sweet Potato Bread*)

After paring, grate three raw potatoes. To one quart of grated potatoes, one and a half tablespoon flour, teaspoon of sugar, pinch of black pepper, mix and make into small cakes, and bake as biscuits, but more slowly.

1904 Tulsa Cookbook

Sweet potatoes were used in many recipes by Indians and white settlers. They could be kept through the winter and were sweet enough to use for dessert dishes as well as breads and vegetables.

Grandmother Eskridge's

BASIC BUTTERMILK BISCUITS

To each ½ cup of flour use:	1 T. Crisco
1 tsp baking powder	pinch of soda
¼ tsp. salt	¼ cup buttermilk
½ tsp. sugar	

Blend dry ingredients and Crisco with a fork until mixture resembles coarse crumbs. Add buttermilk and beat. Turn out on floured board. Roll to ½ inch thick. Cut with biscuit cutter. After turning once in grease, bake on greased pan in 450° oven 10-12 minutes.

Use 2 cups flour for 4-6 people; 3 cups for 8 people. Measure Crisco generously — almost 1½ T. to each ½ cup flour.

Franci King Hart (Mrs. William H.)
Oklahoma City

C.W. McQuown came to Oklahoma City in 1889 shortly before the opening, as a telegraph operator for the Santa Fe Railroad. On April 22nd, he staked the lots on the southwest corner of Third and Harvey and built one of the first fifty houses in the city. This location later became the home of the Oklahoma Gas & Electric Company. In the basement of this little house, Mr. McQuown made a studio where he mounted many specimens of the native animals and birds of Oklahoma. Frankie McQuown was born in this little house in May, 1892. She married Jake Eskridge, son of James Burnette Eskridge, who had the distinction of being the first President of Oklahoma A&M College in Stillwater to have a Doctorate.

Em Dobbs'

CORN MEAL BISCUITS

1½ cups flour	½ cup corn meal
1½ tsp. soda	⅓ cup shortening (lard)
Pinch salt (½ tsp.)	⅔ cup buttermilk

Mix dry ingredients, cut in shortening — add milk. Stir with fork, just to moisten flour and dry ingredients. Pinch off amount of dough for size of biscuit you want — roll gently in hands, flatten ball of dough — turn once in melted shortening in baking pan — Bake 450° for 12-15 minutes.

Mrs. Ova S. Hull
Oklahoma City

Mrs. Matt Peters'

CORN BREAD

1 cup flour	1 cup corn meal
1 T. sugar	¼ tsp. salt
1½ cups sour milk	1 egg beaten well
3 tsp. baking powder	4 T. melted lard

Sift first 6 ingredients, add beaten egg and milk to make a stiff batter. Add melted lard, beat till well mixed; pour into greased shallow pan, and bake in hot oven 425° for about 30 minutes.

Arthur E. Peters
Oklahoma City

"Grandpa Peters brought his family to Edmond, O.T., soon after the Run in four covered wagons from Topeka, Kansas ... Matt was 12. During those early years he helped his father who was a rock quarrier. Two buildings on which Grandpa was proud to have worked were the North Tower of Oklahoma Normal School (which still stands at Central State University) and the First National Bank of Edmond."

Great-Grandmother Quillen's

CORN PONE

2 cups milk	3 cups corn meal
4 tsp. baking powder	1 egg
1 can whole corn, drained	2 T. bacon grease
¼ tsp. salt	

Mix dry ingredients, add milk, egg, bacon grease and corn. Form in oval cakes or put in a well greased cast iron skillet or shallow baking pan. Bake in a hot oven until brown, serve hot. Fresh corn may be used if available.

Ron Capshaw
Oklahoma City

Ollie Campbell came to Osage County as a girl with her parents, who left the South (Tennessee) after the Civil War. They established a ranch outside of Ralston, Oklahoma and Pawhuska, coming to Oklahoma before the opening. Her husband, Quade Quillen, served for many years as Sheriff of Osage County.

Cora Goodrich Nation's

OLD FASHIONED INDIAN BREAD

Two pint cups of Indian meal
One pint cup of flour
Two pint cups of sweet milk
One pint cup of sour milk

One half pint cup of sugar
One teaspoonful of salt
One teaspoonful of soda
Mix and bake slowly 1½ hours

Ruth Nation Jerkins
Oklahoma City

"This recipe was among those of my mother, Cora Goodrich Nation, who travelled from Iowa to Kansas and then to Oklahoma. It was a worn and yellowed newspaper clipping, probably picked up in St. Joseph, Missouri, the cross-roads for pioneers heading west. One of her earliest recollections was of the fear that Santa Claus would never find a wagon out on the trail ... but he did. Soon after Christmas they arrived in Kansas after being on the trail since October. It hardly seems possible today that the trip could have taken that long."

Grandmother's

CORN PONE

(Johnny Cakes or Hoe Cakes)

1 cup cornmeal (preferably
   yellow)

1 cup boiling water
1 tsp. salt

Pour boiling water over salted meal. Stir well. Immediately wet your hands in cool water and make into cakes (approx. 5). Fry in hot fat with seasoned grease such as bacon grease. Fry to a golden brown on each side.

Mrs. George A. Waters
Pawnee

This recipe was brought to Oklahoma from Tennessee by Mrs. Waters' grandmother following the Civil War, in which her grandfather was wounded fighting for the confederacy. She and her cousins still use the recipe.

Sometimes the term, Corn Pone, also referred to these same ingredients with milk or molasses added and baked in the oven. In parts of the South these fried pones were referred to as hoe cakes because they were fried over open fires on hoes. Settlers who came to O.T. and I.T. from the North might have called these "Johnny Cakes", probably derived from journey cake.

Mother Pugh's

HOMINY GRIT SPOON BREAD

1 pint milk
1 tsp. salt
1 scant cup hominy grits

1 T. butter
3 well beaten egg yolks

Scald the pint of milk, stir in salt and hominy grits. Cook until mixture thickens. Add butter, remove and cool slightly, then stir in egg yolks. Whip the 3 egg whites until stiff, adding 1 teaspoon baking powder to them. Fold through the hominy grit mixture. Turn into buttered baking dish and bake about 40 minutes in 350° oven. (A later addition to this recipe — sharp grated cheddar cheese added to the top.)

Dorothy Pugh (Mrs. Pat)
Oklahoma City

"My mother-in-law, Lois Pritchard Pugh, was a Southerner. This recipe is typical of those brought to Oklahoma from the southern states by pioneers. She accepted me, even though I was a 'northerner'."

Mrs. Benjamin M. Turner's

SPOON BREAD

(*Batter Bread*)

1 pint milk
½ pint corn meal

1 tsp. salt
4 eggs

Scald milk, add corn meal, and cook to smooth mush, stirring constantly. Add salt and drop in egg yolks one at a time, while stirring. Fold in egg whites beaten until stiff and bake in a moderate oven for thirty minutes. Serve at once.

Junior League Cookbook
Oklahoma City, 1929

Mrs. Turner's father, Robert H. Gardner, was an early OKC real estate and insurance man; built an English half-timbered and stucco house on N.W. 15th the year of statehood, still in the family. The original hitching post stands in the front yard.

WHOLE WHEAT BREAD

1 cake FLEISCHMANN'S YEAST
1½ cups lukewarm water
1½ cups milk, scalded and cooled
3 T. brown sugar

3 T. lard or butter (melted)
7½ cups whole wheat flour
1½ tsp. salt

Dissolve yeast and sugar in lukewarm liquid. Add lard or butter, then flour, gradually, as whole wheat flour absorbs moisture slowly, adding enough to make dough that can be handled, and the salt. Knead thoroughly, being sure to keep dough soft. Place in well-greased bowl, cover and set aside in a warm place, to rise for about two hours. When double in bulk, turn out on kneading board. Mould into loaves, place in well-greased pans, cover and set to rise again for about one hour, or until light. Bake one hour, in a slower oven than for white bread.

If wanted for over night, use one-half cake of yeast and an extra half teaspoonful salt.

From early pamphlet of recipes put out by Fleishmann's Yeast, which became available to housewives in the Twin Territories prior to statehood.

"Fleischmann's Yeast is a plant which needs warmth, air and moisture for its growth, but it is killed by an excess of heat or cold. Anything too warm for the hand is too warm for the yeast, and anything which chills the yeast will stop its growth. For these reasons all liquids should be lukewarm and the flour also should be warmed in cold weather.

Our yeast contains Pure Tapioca Flour to better sustain its natural quality in distribution and use.

Guaranteed by The Fleischmann Co. under the Food and Drugs Act, June 30th, 1906."

Mrs. R. R. Carlin's

SALT RISING BREAD

Take a teacup of new milk, let it boil, then stir in two tablespoons of meal, set it where it will keep warm enough to lighten. Next morning thin with warm water, add two or three tablespoons of flour, one-fourth teaspoon salt, set it in warm water, and the rising will come quickly. Take two quarts flour, one tablespoon of lard, about one teaspoon salt, mix with warm water. Knead, set to lighten in a warm place, when it is quite light, put in to bake.

Capital City Cookbook
Guthrie, O.T. 1898

Guthrie was the destination of Ralph Richard Carlin when he left Dennison, Texas, to participate in the opening of the Unassigned Lands in 1889. He staked thirty acres at the edge of town, later selling off portions of it for town lots. Their home at 1301 West Noble stood in the heart of town within a few years.

OLD STYLE RYE BREAD

Night before baking, boil one large potato in 1 qt. water until it dissolves. Add enough cold water to make 1 qt. (some water boils away). Add ½ cup rye flour, 1 T. caraway seed, 1 cake yeast (or any dry yeast) and leave in warm place overnight.

In the morning put another cake of yeast in ½ cup warm water with 1 T. brown sugar and 2 tsp. salt. Dissolve well and add to the yeast from night before. Add 2 cups rye flour. Mix well. Let stand 20 minutes. Then add enough white flour to the mixture until dough will not stick to hand or spoon and let rise 20 minutes in a warm place. Roll it out on a well floured board and knead 5 minutes. Let rise another 20 minutes, again knead 5 minutes. Let rise another 20 minutes. When dough has risen double in bulk, remove from bowl and knead again a few minutes. Shape into loaves and put in well greased pans. Beat 1 whole egg and spread over the loaves. Let rise til double in size. Bake 375° for 1 hour. When done, grease tops of loaves.

Anna Stejskal Smrcka (Mrs. Ralph)
Yukon

Mrs. Smrcka's parents, Karolina and Frank Stejskal, were married in Oklahoma Territory in 1899. He came here from Czechoslovakia as a boy, she from Nebraska. Mrs. Stejskal is now 98 years old.

BUNS

Break 1 egg into a cup and fill with sweet milk: mix with it ½ cup yeast, ½ cup butter, 1 cup sugar, enough flour to make a soft dough. Flavor with nutmeg. Let rise very light then mold into biscuits with a few currants. Let rise a second time in the pan. Bake and when nearly done, glaze with molasses and milk.

FRENCH ROLLS: 1 qt. milk scalded, adding while hot ½ cup of sugar, 1 T. butter. When all is cool, add salt, ½ cup of yeast. Stir in flour to make stiff sponge and mix as soon as light. Let rise again, punch down with the hand and let rise again. Turn the dough on the board and pound with the rolling pin until thin enough to cut. Cut out with a tumbler brushing surface of each with melted butter and fold over. Let rolls rise in the tins. Bake and while warm brush the surface with melted butter.

1897 Chickasaw National Records

The Chickasaws and Choctaws were two of the most compatible of the Five Civilized tribes. The sophistication on the recipes found in the Indian Archives indicates why they were referred to as the Civilized tribes. They attained a high level of education, economics, and government.

Daniel Henry Cullins'

SOUR DOUGH STARTER

1 cake of yeast or
  1 pkg. dry yeast
  dissolved in 2
  pints (4 cups)
  warm water

2 T. sugar
4 cups flour
1 raw potato, cut in
  fourths

Mix all ingredients in a crock and let rise until very light and slightly aged. The time required for this depends on the temperature. If the weather is very hot, the starter will be ready for use in 10 to 12 hours. If the weather is cold, it will require more time for the starter to become ready for use. When the starter is light and bubbling, it is ready for use. Do not let the sponge get too sour because this will cause the water to rise to the top, and when this happens the bread will not rise properly.

David E. Raines
El Reno

"Keeping the starter warm enough to work good in the winter time is important, so I have wrapped the crock in a blanket and put a burning lantern in my teepee with my sourdough and myself. Sourdough Starter is as tempermental as a woman, so treat it like your wife — with tender loving care."

Daniel Henry Cullins, born 10 April 1862 in Texas, came to Greer County in 1885, driving a herd of cattle from the Jumbo Ranch of Borden County Texas. After the herd was delivered to the H-Y Ranch in Greer County, Dan decided to stay. While a cowboy there he made several trips 'up the trail' but only once as the cook, since this was a highly responsible job. Dan thought he was still in Texas, as he and so many others were caught in the Greer County boundary dispute. Texas wanted the north fork of the Red River as the boundary, and the U.S. said it was the south fork. They finally got it settled in 1906 and that made him an Oklahoman.

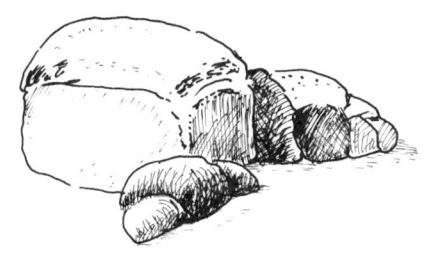

Callie Davis Hurt's

RAISED DOUGHNUTS

3½-4 cups flour
1 cup milk scalded
2 T. shortening
1 cake yeast
¼ cup warm water

¾ cup sugar
1 tsp. salt
1 egg slightly beaten
½ tsp. nutmg,

Cool milk. Make sponge with remaining ingredients added to milk. Let it rise til double. Roll out into a sheet. Cut with a doughnut cutter. Cover with a warm damp cloth. Let rise, then fry in deep fat.

Kay Oliver (Mrs. Gates)
Oklahoma City

The town of Davis, Oklahoma was founded by the father of Callie Davis Hurt. Doughnuts were very popular with the early settlers.
Isobel Armstrong of Midwest City recalls that her mother, Susie E. Wheeler, Omaha-Osage Indian, who came to the Osage Nation in 1888, would always use her wedding ring to cut out the holes.

Mrs. Claude E. Hensley's

DROP DO-NUTS

1 cup sugar
1 cup milk (sweet)
2 eggs
3 tsp. baking powder

3 cups flour
1 tsp. vanilla
dash of salt and nutmeg

Beat eggs until foamy, add sugar, salt, vanilla, and milk. Sift flour and baking powder and add to mixture. Stir until smooth. Drop by teaspoonsful into deep hot fat.

I prefer a small iron pot to cook them in and have fat about 4 inches deep. Test by dropping a small spoonful into the fat. It should rise and then turn over, when brown it should be done.

Save your fat it can be strained and used another time.

Hot grease is hard to handle, so use wisdom, it can easily get too hot so keep folks away from you while cooking.

Dorothy Hensley Keys (Mrs. Mott)
Oklahoma City

Mother's Hints — put a few whole cloves in the kettle of fat for a nice flavor. ¼ teaspoon of ground ginger added will keep do-nuts from absorbing fat. A piece of ginger root added to the hot fat will help too.

Mother's

EGG CAKE

5 eggs
1 cup sweet milk

1 cup flour (sifted)
1 tsp. baking powder

Beat the eggs. Add flour and baking powder alternately with milk. Stir until flour is moistened. Pour into skillet containing a few tablespoons of hot oil. Fry until the cake begins to brown. Cut and turn each piece; fry until done. Serve hot with butter and jelly.

Melvena Thurman
Oklahoma City

"This recipe has been in our family for at least five generations. Alma Jewett, who lived in Iowa, gave it to her daughter Mary (Jewett) Silsbey, who came to the Panhandle of the present state of Oklahoma in 1906. My grandmother, Marie (Silsbey) Tidrick, has shared it with my mother, Virgie (Tidrick) Thurman and me. The egg cake was used as a substitute for bread and was considered a treat when served with jelly or jam."

Brigham's

BUTTERMILK DOUGHNUTS

4 cups buttermilk
4 beaten eggs
2 cups sugar
10 cups flour
4 tsp. baking soda
2 tsp. baking powder

2 tsp. salt
2 tsp. nutmeg, grated
  or ground
½ cup melted butter or
  shortening

Combine buttermilk, eggs, sugar, and blend well. Sift flour baking soda, baking powder, salt, and nutmeg together and beat into buttermilk mixture. Stir in melted butter. Turn dough out on well-floured board, dust the top with flour and roll to about ¼ inch thickness. Cut with a floured 2½ inch doughnut cutter, rerolling scraps and cutting them too. Fry in hot fat until golden brown on both sides. Drain and sprinkle with sugar. Makes 5 dozen.

Dona McLain
Oklahoma City

The earliest Mormons in Oklahoma came to Indian Territory as traveling missionaries long before it opened for white settlement, going from place to place without purse or script (money). Their first Oklahoma City meeting was in 1912.

Harriet Colcord's
HOT CAKES

1 pint flour	½ cup sugar
2 eggs	½ cup melted butter
3 heaping tsp. baking	or salad oil
powder	about 1 pint milk
1 tsp. vanilla	

Cream butter and sugar. Beat eggs to froth, then add vanilla and baking powder. Add to sugar and butter mixture, then add flour and milk, alternately, beating after each addition.

Junior League Cookbook
Oklahoma City, 1929

In 1901 Charles Colcord, Harriet's father, began construction on an elegant Georgian Colonial home at 421 N.W. 13th in Oklahoma City. It was a copy of the Colcord family home in Kentucky from plans by Thomas Jefferson. In 1964, when the mansion was demolished by an insurance company, a movement began which created the Heritage Hills Preservation District, a protection for other fine homes built by early day leaders.

Arthur Ellis King's
CORN WAFFLES (for 2)

Break 1 egg in bowl ... Add salt ... 4 tablespoons bacon grease ... About 1 pint sour milk or buttermilk ... stir well ... Add 3 or 4 tablespoons flour ... then enough corn meal to make proper batter ... then a pinch of soda dissolved in a very small amount of water ... then about ¾ teaspoon full of baking powder ... Stir hell out of it all the time to get thoroughly mixed and no lumps ... The soda and baking powder should make batter raise and be very light. There is no substitute for bacon grease. (To be cooked on a waffle iron)

Patsy Eskridge King (Mrs. Arthur E., Jr.)
Oklahoma City

This recipe is verbatim from Mr. King's handwritten instructions. At 14, Arthur King worked in a cook tent selling soup prior to the Run of '89. Whenever the kettle would get low, they would add more water, which was of questionable quality and sold for $1.00 a gallon. He joined his father and brother in the run and staked a claim. The two boys were forced to protect the claim from a neighbor's rifle fire while their dad waited in line to file for it.

Grandma Dollie's

VINEGAR ROLLS

(Cinnamon Rolls)

Combine 2 cups sugar, ¾ cup vinegar, 4 cups of water. Bring to a boil and keep simmering all the time you are making up your dough. In a large mixing bowl put 3½ cups flour, 3 tsp. baking powder, 1/8 tsp. salt. Cut in 1 cup of shortening. Make a deep well in center of mixture and pour in 2 cups milk. Mix into a stiff dough. Roll out very thin on bread board. Spread soft butter (2 to 3 sticks) over dough. Just slither it on. Sprinkle well with sugar-cinnamon mixture (about 1½ cups sugar-4 tsp. cinnamon.) Roll up and cut in slices. Place cut side down into buttered 9½ x 11 inch pan. Pour the boiling hot vinegar mixture over the rolls and bake in 350° oven for some 30 minutes or until golden brown. Best flavor when served hot from oven.

Washington Jones
Oklahoma City

"In some instances, when baking powder was not available, the cooks would use soda and sour milk or buttermilk."

Annie Laurie Gossett's

WAFFLES

2 eggs
scant 1¼ cup milk
1½ cups sifted flour
1 tsp. baking powder

½ tsp. salt
heaping T. sugar
4 T. melted butter

Mix eggs and milk. Beat well, then add dry ingredients. Mix well, then add melted butter. Cook on hot greased waffle iron.

Linda Kennedy Rosser (Mrs. Ronald E.)
Edmond

"Na-Na made waffles for Granddaddy every morning of the world, keeping the batter going in the ice-box. One time when lots of relatives were visiting, she became confused and put batter into the waffle iron, not noticing one stuck to the upper part. That was the origin of a long-standing family joke about 'double-decker' waffles."

31

Annie's

FRITTERS

4 cups flour	1 cup sugar
4 tsp. baking powder	2 eggs
1 tsp. salt	1 cup milk
2 T. shortening	

Sift flour, add baking powder and salt. Cream shortening; add sugar, gradually; beat until light and fluffy. Add eggs, beating after each addition. Add milk and flour mixture, stir until blended. Drop by tablespoon into hot fat and fry until well-browned, turning fritters as they rise to the top. Drain and serve with syrup.

Mary Gray Thompson (Mrs. Homer)
Oklahoma City

"My parents, Annie Van Grinkle and George Gray, came to Hennessey from Pella, Iowa, in 1899, bringing one son, two daughters, and a grandfather who was a Union Veteran. I don't remember the trip ... but how well I recall Mama's fritters when we were growing up on our farm in Hennessey and later in Edmond."

Mrs. Roland's

SQUAW BREAD

1 pint sour milk	¼ tsp. soda
1 T. lard (shortening)	3 heaping tsp. baking powder

To these ingredients add enough flour to make a dough easily rolled. Knead smooth. Roll ½ inch in thickness, and cut about the size of a saucer with the center out. Fry in deep fat like donuts.
Serve with syrup:

1 qt. corn syrup	1 box brown sugar

Boil together then add 1 T. mapeline flavoring and ½ cup bacon drippings.

Mrs. Samuel R. Fryer
Oklahoma City

"This recipe was given to me many years ago by Mrs. George Earl Roland, wife of a Pawhuska dentist, and is the traditonal way of making Indian fried bread."

MATZO MEAL PANCAKES

½ cup Matzo meal
3 eggs

½ cup water
½ tsp. salt

Beat yolks and blend with water, salt and matzo meal. Fold in beaten whites and drop 1 large T. on to a greased griddle and brown on both sides. Serve with sour cream, jelly, etc.

Adeline Byers Fagin (Mrs. Max)
Oklahoma City

These are eaten anytime, but in particular, during the Passover Holiday. Matzo meal takes the place of flour, not eaten during this holiday. Tradition says it was like meal the children of Israel used when they fled from Egypt.

Aunt Pauline's

GRAHAM GEMS

3 cups sweet milk
salt to taste (1 tsp.)
Butter the size of a
hickory nut (1 T.)

½ tsp. soda
Graham flour to make stiff
batter (3½-4 cups)

Mix and drop into hot tins (black iron "gem pans" the best) and bake in a quick oven (hot) so they will be "crustee" (Add 1 or 2 well beaten eggs the last thing before baking if desired and if you have your own chickens.)

Note: ¼ cup-½ cup sugar optional. Some use half graham, ½ white flour (lighter). Do not overmix muffins, just moisten dry ingredients.

Dorothy DeWitte Wilkinson (Mrs. Jim)
Oklahoma City

Pauline Tyler Townsend (Mrs. Frank L.) was an artist, residing in Tulsa 1905-1957. She hand copied her mother's "best, everyday recipes" into blank pages of her teacher's class book which she bought when teaching drawing and writing in grade school in Ames, Iowa in 1894 (brought up on waste not, want not philosophy). This was prior to her marriage and honeymoon trip to Lamont, Ok. in 1900. Her parents, T.D. and Sarah Ann Wall Tyler, had moved to Newkirk, Okla. prior to 1895 with two other daughters, Nelle Gertrude, hat "trimmer", and Carrie, piano teacher.

Mittie Wright's

TEA ROLLS

2 cups hot water   ½ cup sugar
1 T. salt   2 T. melted shortening

Mix and add 2 beaten eggs. Use 2 cakes of yeast and 1 T. sugar dissolved in ¼ cup warm water. Use 8 cups flour.

Mrs. Wm. O. Green
Edmond

Mrs. Green's mother, Mittie McCain Wright, is an 89er and still lives in Edmond. She came as a baby with her parents after her father, J. C. McCain, had staked his claim on the county line near Piedmont. They lived in a sod house and the elderly grandmother who came with them assumed the duty of rocking the babies.

Mary Mullen Hensley's

GEMS

1 egg   about 4 T. melted
1 cup flour   shortening
1 tsp. baking powder   and enough sweet milk to
1 tsp. salt   make a stiff batter
1 heaping tsp. sugar

I do not even sift it together but stir the batter good.
Beat egg, add milk and then pour it onto the flour and other ingredients — and of course bake in greased gem pans.
This makes nine medium sized gems, or you could squeeze it all into a six hold pan.
When I want to make more I use only one egg for 1½ or 2 cups flour, but add the required amount of other ingredients for more.
After baking always turn gems over so the bottoms are crusty.

Dorothy Hensley Keys (Mrs. Mott)
Oklahoma City

"Grandmother Hensley was an accomplished writer and business woman and with her two sons managed the newspaper office established by her husband, Travis Franklin Hensley, who published the first newspaper in the Cherokee Strip (also called the Cherokee Outlet), the Westside Democrat of Enid, on the day the territory was opened for settlement in 1893. The story is told that Mr. Hensley loaded the press on a boxcar and printed the paper enroute to the opening."

Grandmother Rosinsky's

BLINTZES

Batter:
2 eggs, well beaten
¼ tsp. salt

1 cup water
1 cup flour

Add egg & salt to liquid and stir in flour gradually til smooth. Grease skillet slightly with vegetable fat, pour in about 2 Tablespoons of batter, make a thin pancake. Bake on one side til it blisters; toss in soft towel, fried side up.

CHEESE FILLING:
1 lb. dry cheese
  (well-drained)
1 egg yolk, beaten

1 T. sugar
1 T. melted butter
1 tsp. cinnamon

MEAT FILLING:
2 cups precooked meat,
  chicken, etc.
1 T. onion

1 egg, beaten
½ tsp. salt

Put meat and onion through food chopper. Place a rounded T. of either meat or cheese mixture in the center of each pancake. Fold over each side, then tuck in ends (envelope shape). Proceed in this manner until all the batter has been used. Before serving fry on both sides until golden brown (Cool pan slightly before frying filled blintzes). Serve the cheese blintzes with sour cream or preserves.

Adeline Byers Fagin (Mrs. Max)
Oklahoma City

Clara Rosinsky left St. Louis in 1895 as the bride of Ben Byers, a young merchant from Lehigh, Indian Territory. Raising six children in the Hebrew faith required importing teachers of the Torah, and every Passover Grandmother Rosinsky would send a big shipment of food from St. Louis, including whitefish, matzos, salami, corned beef, sugar, and wine for the Passover Sedar.

Libby Soward's

PUFFET

Two eggs, butter the size of an egg, one quart of flour, two tablespoons sugar, two and a half tablespoons baking powder, one pint sweet milk. This bread must be mixed together quickly, and baked in a hot oven. Beat eggs, sugar, and butter together, then add the milk; mix well the yeast powder with flour. Have your pan well greased and hot; bake quick. This is nice for tea.

Anita Ellis (Mrs. Marvin)
Guthrie

THE KANSAS HOME COOK-BOOK — Published by the Board of Managers for the Benefit of the Home for the Friendless, an institution to extend temporary relief to homeless women and children — recipes contributed by ladies of Leavenworth and other cities and towns — published at Leavenworth, Kansas; 1879. This book was owned by Mrs. Thomas E. Soward (Libbey) wife of Colonel Thomas E. Soward, first mayor of East Guthrie.

Bim-Bom's

STREUSEL KACHEN

(*Coffee Cake*)

¾ cup milk	½ tsp. nutmeg
¾ cup sugar	½ tsp. lemon extract
1 pkg. dry yeast	Rind of 1 lemon grated
¼ cup warm water	½ cup currants
3 cups flour, sifted with	½ cup almonds
1 tsp. salt	2 eggs

Scald milk with 1 T. sugar and cool. Soften yeast in warm water and add 1½ cups flour to first mixture. Beat well and let rise til light and bubbly.

Cream ⅔ cup butter and gradually ¾ cup sugar with nutmeg and lemon extract. Add eggs one at a time, beating well after each addition. Combine the first raised sponge with butter mixture and remaining flour, beating well all ingredients. Spread in three 8" layer pans and let rise til double in bulk. Brush with melted butter and put streusel topping on.

Streusel Topping: 1 cup sugar, ¾ cup flour, ¾ cup butter, crumble with fingers and mix until crumbly. Put on top with almonds. Bake 18-20 minutes at 400°.

Marta Frost Reynolds (Mrs. A. D.)
Oklahoma City

"This is served every Christmas, a traditional German recipe, which 'Bim-Bom', my grandmother Frost, brought from Germany."

Mother's

NUT BREAD

1 cup white flour
1 cup Graham Flour
1 cup sugar
1 cup sour milk (or
  buttermilk)

1 cup nuts
1 tsp. baking powder
½ tsp. soda
1 egg

Dissolve soda in sour milk, and sift baking powder with white flour. Beat egg and add sour milk, then gradually add dry ingredients. Pour into greased loaf pan and bake at 350° until done (About 40 minutes).

Ruth Vaught Thompson (Mrs. Wayman J.)
Oklahoma City

Edgar S. Vaught came to Oklahoma City in 1901 from Danbridge, Tennessee to take the principalship of Irving High School ... during his career in education he studied law and was admitted to the bar in 1906, the year before statehood.

Mrs. Peter G. Sinopoulo's

PINEAPPLE BACON MUFFINS

3 strips bacon
1 cup sifted flour
¾ tsp. soda
1 tsp. salt
1 cup cornmeal
2 T. brown sugar

2 eggs beaten
1½ cups buttermilk
1 tsp. baking powder
½ cup drained crushed pineapple
¼ cup reserved bacon srippings

Fry bacon crisp and reserve drippings. Crumble. Sift dry ingredients. Combine eggs, buttermilk, pineapple and ¼ cup bacon drippings. Add all at once to dry ingredients, mixing only til flour is dampened. Fill greased muffin tins ⅔ full, top with crumbled bacon. Bake in hot oven 425° for 20 to 25 minutes.

Pat Sinopoulo Gambulos (Mrs. Byron)
Oklahoma City

"My parents, Peter and Ruby Tate Sinopoulo were both excellent cooks. He and his brother John developed the popular Delmar Garden in 1903. The Delmar theater seated over a thousand people and was the scene of performances by Lon Chaney, John L. Sullivan, and Buster Keaton. The first streetcar line in Oklahoma City offered transportation to the hotel, restaurant, dance hall, theater, and park which made up the Garden."

Mrs. William Mee's

12 MUFFINS

1½ cups flour	3 tsp. baking powder
¼ tsp. salt	1 egg
¾ cup milk	1 large T. melted butter
¼ cup sugar	

5 O'Clock Tea Club Cookbook
Oklahoma City

Mr. Charles H. Mee recalls that his mother always had a cook, usually a young German or "Bohemian" (Czech) daughter of settlers on farms surrounding Oklahoma City. Many families in the finest residential sections had gardens, and if they owned an extra lot, would keep a cow, particularly if they had many children.

Mrs. Bearpaw's

BAKED BROWN BREAD

Mix with SPOON	1 cup whole wheat flour
⅔ cup flour	1 egg well beaten
⅓ cup sugar	⅔ cup dark molasses
1 tsp. baking soda	1 cup milk
½ tsp. salt	2 tsp. vinegar

Sift flour, sugar, baking soda and salt. Add whole wheat flour, mix. Combine, egg, molasses, milk and vinegar. Bake at 325° for 55 minutes. Cool on rack and wrap in foil.

Victoria Guidroz Davis (Mrs. Walker B.)
Oklahoma City

Some years ago, '89er John J. Wetzel recalled being one of the very first bakers in Oklahoma City, "On Main street in the 100 block we built the first hotel and named it the Hotel Weaver in honor of James B. Weaver, who did so much in getting the U.S. Government to open this wonderful country to settlement.

Being a baker by trade, I occupied one of the two lower rooms for my bakery and confectionery. While building the hotel, I cooked for nine carpenters, without a stove, out in the middle of Main street. While I occupied the store room in the hotel, I did my own baking and my brother-in-law, Mr. Chrisney, delivered the bread. During the year, I built a one-story frame store building and continued my bakery, confectionery, and ice cream business for ten years."

Grandmother Phelps'
BOSTON BROWN BREAD

1½ cups white flour	3 tsp. soda
1½ cups corn meal	1 tsp. salt
1½ cups whole wheat flour	1 cup raisins
9/8 cup sorghum	3 cups buttermilk
Nuts if desired	Nuts if desired

Sift together dry ingredients. Add sorghum and buttermilk, and mix well. Grease six # 202 cans and fill ⅔ full. Steam for two hours.

Marta Frost Reynolds (Mrs. A. D.)
Oklahoma City

Mrs. Reynold's maternal great-grandfather, Frank Warren, came from Indiana before statehood and was President of City National Bank. They bought a house on the most popular side of town at the time-the east side.

Marion Harland's
BUTTER CRACKERS

One quart of flour; two tablespoonfuls COTTOLENE (Shortening); one-half teaspoonful soda dissolved in hot water; one salt-spoonful salt; two cups sweet milk.

Rub the COTTOLENE into the flour, or, what is better, cut it up with a knife or chopper, as you do in pastry; add the salt, milk and soda, mixing well. Work into a ball, turning and shifting the mass often. Roll into an even sheet a quarter of an inch thick, or less, prick deeply with a fork, and bake in a moderate oven. Hang them up in a muslin bag in the kitchen for two days to dry.

Capital City Cookbook
Guthrie, O.T., 1898

"COTTOLENE is made of 80 per cent triple refined cottonseed oil and 20 per cent of choice beef suet, assuring users the purest possible shortening and frying fat, palatable and digestible. It can be used for many purposes in place of butter when it is impossible to use lard."

KOLACHE

½ cup milk
½ cup sugar
1½ tsp. salt
¼ cup butter
½ cup warm water

2 pkgs. yeast
2 eggs beaten
4½ cups flour (approx.)
grated lemon rind or vanilla
(if desired)

Scald milk; stir in sugar, salt, and butter; cool to lukewarm. Sprinkle yeast in warm water; stir until dissolved. Stir in lukewarm milk mixture, beaten eggs and half the flour; beat until smooth. Stir in remaining flour to make light dough. Turn dough out on lightly floured board. Knead until smooth and elastic. Don't work too much flour into dough. Place dough in greased bowl, turning to grease top. Cover; let rise in warm place, free from draft until double in bulk, about 1 hour. Punch down.

Form dough into 1½ inch diameter balls. (The size of balls will determine finished size of kolache) Place on greased sheet, allow room for rising (approx. 12 on 15½x10½" pan). Cover loosely and let rise until double in bulk.

Lightly brush raised balls with melted shortening. Then, with your fingers, starting in the center, press the dough out making a place to hold the filling. Put in the fruit filling of your choice. Then sprinkle a little mixture on top of filling.

MIXTURE: Equal parts of flour, sugar and enough melted butter or shortening to make crumbly.

Cover with waxed paper and let rise again until double in bulk. Bake in pre-heated oven 350° 20-25 minutes. Leave in pan. Brush dough with melted shortening. Put topping or glaze of cream and sugar on the fruit.

FILLINGS: (Must be thick or will run during baking)

Cooked prunes: Run through sieve, add lemon juice and sugar to taste. After baking, put coconut on top just before adding sugar and creme glaze.

Apricots: Cook dried apricots, add sugar, mash with fork to blend. Canned apricots may be used by draining juice and mashing well to form smooth paste.

Poppy Seed:

1 cup ground poppy seeds
½ cup milk
2 T. sugar

1 tsp. grated orange rind
1 tsp. honey or light corn
syrup

Cook seeds and milk slowly for five minutes, stirring constantly. Add honey or syrup and cook two minutes longer. Add orange rind.

Mrs. Richard Sestak
El Reno

Mrs. Sestak's husband's grandparents came to Prague, Okla. with many other Czechoslovakians prior to statehood. Kolaches have become popular with all Oklahomans who have attended annual Czech festivals in Prague established in 1902 and Yukon, 1891.

Simple Czech

KOLACHES

PART I:
Scald and cool to lukewarm 1½ cups milk, add 2 cakes yeast and 1 T. sugar. Let dissolve and add enough flour to make a batter (pancake consistency). Let rise until double in bulk.

PART II:
Cream ½ cup butter or oleo, ½ cup crisco and ½ cup sugar. Add 1 tsp. salt, 3 egg yolks and 2 whole eggs, add part I to part II and then add 2½ to 3 cups more flour. Beat until smooth. Put in refrigerator over night or chill for several hours. In the morning roll out on floured board, cut in rounds. Place on greased cookie sheets, brush with melted shortening. Let rise until double bulk. Press down middle, fill with fruit preserves, poppy seed or cottage cheese. Let rise 15 minutes longer. Bake 350° for 15 minutes, take from oven brush again with melted shortening.

Ethel Dobry (Mrs. Joe)
Yukon

Mrs. Dobry's in-laws came to Oklahoma Territory in 1890 from Nebraska along with many other Czechs.

Kolache

COTTAGE CHEESE FILLING

1 cup dry cottage cheese	lemon juice
1 egg yolk	sugar
¼ grated lemon rind	raisins

Mix 1 cup dry cottage cheese with one egg yolk. Add ¼ grated lemon rind and a few drops of lemon juice. Add raisins and sugar to taste.

Elizabeth Ambrose Stevens (Mrs. Ralph)
Oklahoma City

Elizabeth Ambrose came to Oklahoma City with her family in 1889, and grew up on Choctaw Street where the Union Station was later constructed. Her husband served as president of Capitol Iron and Steel Company.

Eugene Couch's

WHOLE WHEAT STICKS

1 cup Whole Wheat Flour
  (spoon into the cup)
2 T. Butter, Margarine or

shortening
⅓ cup whipping cream
½ tsp. Salt

Cut the butter into the flour. Make little wells in the flour and mix in a small amount of cream until all the flour is dampened with the cream. Pinch this stiff dough together. It must not be sticky but it must hold together.

Cut or pinch off small amounts of dough. Roll on a pastry cloth or between the palms of the hands to make sticks about ½ inch in diameter and 3 or 4 inches in length. Place on pie pan or cookie sheet, not touching each other.

Bake in 450° oven for 30 minutes until lightly brown. YUMMY.

Edna M. Couch
Norman

"This recipe was from my father's cooking school lessons about 80 years ago. We had these for breakfast very often when I was growing up in the Kickapoo country of eastern Oklahoma County. My brother liked to dip the end in WHIZZ, take a bite then dip again. WHIZZ was a mixture of soft butter and honey whizzed together."

When surplus land in the "Kickapoo Country" (near the present town of Choctaw) was opened for settlement in 1893, the Couch family moved out there. Edna Couch was later born in the house built by her grandmother in 1907 with income from the sale of town lots in Oklahoma City deeded to her after the death of her husband, Captain Wm. L. Couch, following a claim dispute.

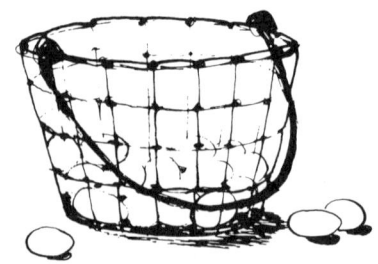

EVERLASTING YEAST

1 quart warm potato
water
½ T. dry yeast

1 tsp. salt
2 T. sugar
2 cups flour

Stir all ingredients well and put in warm place to rise until ready to mix for baking. Leave a small amount of the everlasting yeast (about 1 cup) for the start. Keep in cool place until a few hours before needed again. Add the same ingredients to this start, except the yeast, to build up supply for next baking. This way you always keep a bit of the everlasting yeast for future.

Dona McLain
Oklahoma City

Alice Baugus Whitten remembers that her mother, Daisy, kept her Everlasting Yeast going by returning about 3 tablespoonsful of the raw dough from the weekly baking to the yeast sponge in the fruit jar, which she then sealed tightly until needed the following week. This gave a finer textured bread than the sourdough bread. This was the only leavening she ever used in those early years after her husband, John Baugus, made the Run of '89.

YEAST CAKES

2 medium white potatoes
4 cups water
½ cup white flour
½ cup cornmeal

½ cup sugar
1 cake compressed yeast
extra white flour and
cornmeal

Peel and cook potatoes in water til tender. Drain well, (keeping water) and mash potatoes. Pour the reserved potato water over the dry ingredients and stir well. Add hot mashed potatoes, blend well and cool. Add enough water to make 2 quarts. Set aside in room temperature 12-14 hours. Stir it down, add enough flour to make stiff batter, then let rise til very light. Add enough cornmeal to make even stiffer, then pat into squares ½" thick. Cut squares into 2 inch cakes and spread to dry. Turn daily til thoroughly dry and hard. 1 cake makes 4 loaves of bread.

Viola Gulick Krob's mother made yeast cakes and sold them, 8 for 5c. "I delivered a lot of yeast to neighbors when she made it. The country had houses on every 160 acres then, and some 80 acres had houses. We celebrated our 55th wedding anniversary on February 15, 1978."

DOUGHNUTS

1 cup of sugar, 1 cup of milk,
Two eggs beaten fine as silk,
Salt and nutmeg (lemon will do)
Of baking powder teaspoons two,
Lightly stir the flour in,
Roll on pie board not too thin;
Cut in diamonds, twists or rings,
Drop with care the doughy things,
Into fat that briskly swells
Evenly the spongy cells;
Watch with care the time for turning,
Fry them brown just short of burning.

Mildred Svoboda Stejskal
Yukon

Mildred Stejskal's parents came to Oklahoma from Kansas. All Czech names have meanings: her father's name, Svoboda, meant "freedom".

GAME, POULTRY, & FISH

Bob White Quail

GAME

BAKED QUAIL

Dress and clean several quail. Lay in a baking dish, sprinkle with salt and pepper. Cover with slices of bacon, put lid on, and bake 30 minutes.

Mrs. W. D. Perkins
Edmond

By the time Mrs. Perkins' folks brought her to Edmond around 1902 as a baby, modernization was taking place with telephone lines and brick sidewalks replacing wooden ones.

Quail continued to be a popular game bird. Mrs. George W. Brauer, an '89er, reminisced about earlier Edmond times:

"The first Thanksgiving celebration in Edmond was a community game dinner held in a newly completed building. This money was used for school expenses. The men brought in venison, wild turkey, prairie chicken, and all kinds of game and helped cook and serve it. During the winter the ladies made a beautiful crazy quilt. The money derived from the sale of the quilt, $50.00, was used for the upkeep of the school."

ROAST DUCKS

Clean and truss them nicely, and fill bodies with a stuffing made of ½ mashed potatoes and half sage, and onions, well seasoned with salt and pepper. Baste them with slices of sweet fat pork in the pan and baste frequently. Make a rich gravy, into which put a tablespoon of Worcestershire sauce. Serve with applesauce. For a change, one of a pair of ducks may be stuffed with prunes.

Jennie June's Cookbook (1878)

It is interesting to see a reference to Worcestershire sauce as early as 1878 in this book belonging to Mrs. Warram. Another sauce of long-standing popularity is Tabasco Pepper Sauce, available commercially since 1868.

STEWED PRAIRIE CHICKEN

Prepare the chickens the same as for roasting. Put them in a stew pan with some stock or water, and a cup of cold gravy, a little lemon, a clove or 2 and some pepper and salt. Add after a while a few spoonsful of tomato sauce. Stew slowly for 2 hours, serve with a little tomato catsup added to the sauce, and a light thickening of butter and flour.

Jennie June's Cookbook (1878)

"This cookbook was used by the Davis family while Mother and Aunt Maggie were growing up in Lehigh, I.T.," according to Mrs. J. H. Warram, Oklahoma City. To prepare a prairie chicken, of which there were many (particularly in the western parts of the Twin Territories), it was suggested that they be skinned for added sweetness.

Prairie Chicken

Mrs. Oberholzer's

QUAIL

Dress them, split down the back; let stand in salt water a few minutes; wash, roll in flour, salt and pepper. Have a skillet hot, put equal parts lard and butter. Cross the legs back of the breast, lay in skillet with back down, use a cover that will fit inside of the skillet and set a sadiron on this to keep quail in a flattened form. When a light brown, turn, keep the weight on till they are tender. Make gravy of juice in skillet.

Capital City Cookbook
Guthrie, O.T. 1898

Calling on a new neighbor in the Territory might induce an invitation to dinner, as recalled by a pioneer meeting a little girl on the adjoining claim for the first time: "I hope you'll stay for dinner, she said hospitably. 'We are having venison, poke salad, hot corn bread, butter, cottage cheese, and wild dewberry pie. We had quail for breakfast and just as I had finished mine, a centipede fell from the ceiling right in my plate' ".

47

BROILED QUAIL ON TOAST

Everything, so to speak, is in the looks. It should not lie on the toast humped up and with the limbs pointing many different ways, but should lie flat, round, and compact. This is accomplished by flattening the quail, after opening and cleaning it sufficiently, with a few pats of the cleaver to depress the breast bone and loosen the joints, not to mash the meat or make splinters in it. Split the quail down the back to open it, rinse off in cold water, wipe it dry and brush over with butter. Broil it about 8 minutes, perhaps with the hot brick on top if in haste. Baste. Have ready a little melted butter, pepper and salt in a pan, press the quail down into it, dish on toast and garnish. To make a neat appearance the toast should be cut to shape. Cut a square slice of toast diagonally across, making two triangles, and place the broad ends together in the dish.

American Meat Cooking for Restaurants & Hotels (1901)

Indians from the Kickapoo Reservation just east of Oklahoma Territory often brought quail and other game into the nearby towns to trade for coffee, flour, and other supplies. The quail would be strung by the dozens in the open markets ... sometimes hardware merchants displayed them to promote the sale of guns.

Nettie Taylor Walker's

FRICASSEED RABBITS

The best way for cooking rabbit, is fricassee. Cut and disjoint, and put into stewpan; season with cayenne pepper, salt and some chopped parsley. Pour in a pint of warm water (or veal broth, if you have it) and stew it over a slow fire til tender; add when ½ done some bits of butter rolled in flour. Just before taking from fire, enrich gravy with a gill or more of thick cream with some nutmeg. Stir gravy well but don't boil after cream is in, lest it curdle. Put pieces of rabbit on hot dish and pour gravy over.

Joe Ellis
Bethany

When Mr. Ellis' grandmother married in 1886, she received the cookbook which contains this recipe.

Mrs. White's

POTTED VENISON

Put the venison into a baking dish, and spread over it a liberal quantity of butter; cover with a crust made of flour and water; bake until thoroughly done; remove from the oven, and, when cold, pound the meat in a mortar until a smooth paste, adding the butter with which it was baked, and more if required to make it sufficiently moist; season to taste with salt, pepper, cayenne and nutmeg. Pack very firmly in tiny jars; set in the oven for fifteen minutes; remove and, when cold, cover well with clarified drippings. Paste paper over the top of the jars. If properly done, potted meats will keep for months.

New Process Cookbook (1896)

R. C. White had been surveying in Norman, Oklahoma Territory, when he sent for his wife and children in Illinois. Mrs. White and her husband were both schoolteachers for many years after settling here. This book of hers now belongs to her granddaughter, Elizabeth Ann Patterson.

Creek Indian

SQUIRREL

Cut the squirrel in parts and season. Cook in shortening until tender (about an hour). Drain off shortening, leaving enough to make gravy. Add 1 or 2 Tablespoons flour into squirrel and drippings. Stir in a few minutes until smooth, add about 1 cup of water and simmer for few minutes. It's ready to eat.

The cooking time depends on whether the squirrel is young or old. If gravy is too thick add a little water and simmer.

Margie Fish Scott
Oklahoma City

Mrs. Scott is a Creek Indian, and this is the traditional way her family has fixed squirrel for many years.

VENISON PASTRY

Cut venison into pieces; line a dish with pie crust, place a layer of beef suet, cut up finely, in the bottom of the dish, then put in the venison. Season with salt and pepper, lay on butter, cover with crust and bake.

Jennie June's Cookbook (1878)

Included in this old cookbook belonging to Mrs. J. H. Warram is a recipe for "Rainy Days":
"Make the house look as bright as possible inside, have something good for tea, put on a pretty dress, light up early, romp with the children, tell them stories, and determine at least to have sunshine in the house, if you cannot have it outside."

WILD TURKEY WITH CRANBERRY JELLY

The most considerable part of the wild turkey is the solid dark meat of the breast. Cover that part, at least, with very thin bands of fat salt pork, tied on, cover the whole upper part of the turkey with a moveable sheet of thick paper well greased, and roast the turkey in the oven for nearly or quite 2 hours. Wild turkeys sometimes weigh as much as 25 pounds each, and even more, and in such cases needs longer cooking in a moderate oven with frequent basting. Let the water dry out at the last, increase the heat, take off the paper and the pork and brown the outside quickly.

Wild turkeys should not be stuffed as long as they are a rarity in any place and there is a curiosity to taste the natural flavor unalloyed with herbs and seasonings. The flesh of the wild turkey has more color and flavor than that of the domestic turkey.

American Meat Cooking for Restaurants & Hotels (1901)

Eighty-Niner, Mrs. J.M. Owen, recalled, "My father, Thomas Vaughn, staked a good claim one and a half miles south of Kingfisher, moving his family down the following August. The household furniture, and general merchandise store, were moved in covered wagons from Liberal, Kansas. On the trip my father killed a large number of young wild turkeys, and I helped my mother fry them and pack them in a 5-gallon lard can, pouring hot lard over them. They were good and furnished us meat on the trip."

ROAST VENISON

Trim and wash meat, put it in to bake in a baking pan containing salt, a little water or soup stock. Never let the pan be quite devoid of water while the venison is in, and there will never be any dry crust. Roll the meat over or baste frequently, but take care never to stick a fork in it. A leg of ordinary size will be done in an hour to an hour and a half. It should be slightly rare around the bone when cooked. A saddle or loin will cook in ¾ hour. Serve either with fruit jelly and natural gravy — which will of course, be scarcely a tsp. to moisten each slice — or with game sauce made by mixing currant or other fruit jelly with brown sauce. The expense of the currant jelly accompaniment to venison is in many places more onerous than the expense of the meat itself.

American Meat Cooking for Restaurants & Hotels (1901)

"Doubtless the best of wild meats and the best worth buying for hotel use. Every part is valuable, good soups being made from the neck and course pieces and stews and hunters' pies from the rough cuts. The English term haunch of venison seems never to have become Americanized, but remains an unfamiliar word and unsuitable for hotel bill of fare. Some seem to expect from it something peculiar and unusual like the hump of a buffalo. Saddle or leg of venison are common and well understood."

BAKED JACK RABBIT

Dress your jack rabbit and quarter it. Put in salt water for 6 to 8 hours to take away wild taste. Get a smooth yellow pine board about 12 by 14 inches. Sandpaper splinters off. Butter or tallow the board and place rabbit on it, leaving 2 inches space on outside. Put mashed potato wall around the rabbit about 2 inches high, cover rabbit with lemon peels, parsley, onion and salt entire mixture lightly. Place in oven. Bake moderate heat for 1½ to 2 hours. When done, take out of oven, give the rabbit to the dog and eat the board. NOTE: This same procedure may be used for carp, but give it to the cat.

A. B. Wiedle
Oklahoma City

This humorous "recipe" was typical of the frontier type of story, so we decided to include it.

BUFFALO

"Buffalo more nearly resembles beef than anything else, but is not so good. It is ordered by most people while still a novelty, but not sought after.

It will probably not be long before the buffalo will be extinct, the spanning of the great plains by railroads having made the destruction of the vast herds easy to the hunter for their 'robes'. There was a time when the first Pacific railroad was being constructed that buffalo meat was plentiful enough in markets to materially interfere with the sale of beef and lessen the price. It has already become a rarity only to be obtained in freezing weather from remote territories in the northwest."

American Meat Cooking for Restaurants & Hotels (1901)

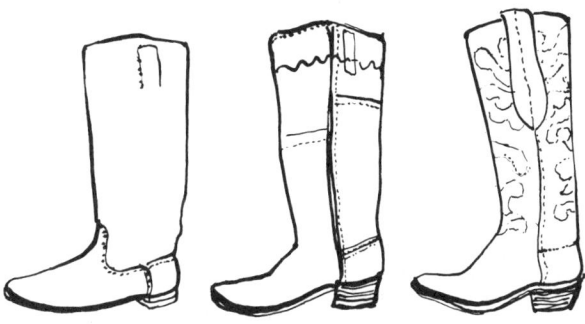

ROAST GOOSE

Make a dressing of 2 oz. onion, 1 oz. green sage chopped fine, a coffee cup of bread crumbs, a little pepper, and salt; do not quite fill the goose, but leave room to swell. The yolk of 2 eggs can be added to the dressing, if desired. Roast 2 hours or less, and serve with gravy and applesauce.

Jennie June's Cookbook (1878)

Memories of delicious goose and dressing at Christmas are recalled by Grace Voorhees Moutrey (Mrs. Curtis E.). "When the family moved to Oklahoma City in 1904, my dad wanted to buy a house at 5th and Broadway. My mother said, 'Don't take me out in the country.' Consequently, my dad bought a house at 831 West Grand Ave., which was the promenade street at that time. My mother, Ilo Voorhees, was a very genteel and kind person — also an excellent cook."

POULTRY

Farm Style

STEWED CHICKEN

In the evening when you close the chicken house door for the night, lift a nice fat hen or big young rooster off the roost and shut it up in a small house about like a dog house, so you can catch it and dress it early in the morning. Otherwise you may have to run it down!

When scalded and the feathers picked off, then washed, cover the fowl with water with a medium onion, salt and pepper and boil until tender. A little parsley from the garden, fresh or dried, was good.

Cook Dumplings on top when chicken is done.

Grace Smith (Mrs. Myles F.)
Oklahoma City

"I might add that the chicken house was closed every night to keep out skunks and coyotes!"

CHICKEN DUMPLINGS

2 cups sifted flour
2 heaping tsp. baking
  powder

Salt
Milk to wet but must
  'not be soft

Drop on top of stewed chicken (in boiling broth). Cover and cook 15 minutes. DO NOT LIFT THE LID UNTIL DONE.

> Marta Frost Reynolds (Mrs. A.D.)
> Oklahoma City

Stepping down from the westbound train at Dixon, Missouri shortly after the Civil War, Judge Lilly's daughter was assisted by a handsome young man who had recently arrived from Canada named Thomas Phelps. Following a proper courtship, he married Alice Lilly, later bringing her to O.T. Her name has been passed through several generations — granddaughter, Alice Phelps Frost, and great-granddaughter, Marta Alice Reynolds.

Eula Lindsey's

EGG NOODLES OR DUMPLIN'S

2 eggs
½ cup shortening
About 3 cups flour

½ cup milk
Salt

Work flour into above ingredients until stiff — using about 3 cups. Either roll and cut into strips for egg noodles or drop by teaspoon into hot broth for dumplin's. Cook about 30 minutes.

> Elva Lindsey Jacobson (Mrs. F. Conover)
> Oklahoma City

"This recipe was used by early Mormon pioneers. When my father tried to elope by horse and buggy with Mother, who was only 15, Grandmother Woodson chased them down the road and caught them a block away. She made them wait a year until my mother was 16."

Iva Hartley Davies'

NOODLES

Mix 4 cups of flour and 2 tsp. of salt together in mixing bowl. Make a "well" in the flour and break into this 2 eggs. Add 1 T. of water. Mix all this together until dough is stiff. Then roll out very thin. Roll up like a jelly roll and cut in ¼" or ½" strips. Spread strips out to dry. When dry, cook until tender in boiling chicken or beef broth.

Kay Davies Oliver (Mrs. Gates)
Oklahoma City

This was served on special Sundays with a baked hen. When dough was boiled fresh (without drying), some folks, especially Southerners, called it dumplings, others Chicken Pot Pie ...

Grandmother Brillhart's

CHICKEN POT PIE

Boil a 3 lb. chicken in 2 qts. water and 1 tsp. salt, cook till tender. Take chicken out when tender and save the broth.

While chicken is cooking, take: 2 eggs, 4 T. water, ¼ tsp. salt, 1¼ cup flour. Beat eggs, add water, salt and mix in flour a little at a time till very stiff dough, turn out on a floured board and knead, adding flour so it won't stick to the board. Roll out as thin as paper or as thin as you can. Cut in 1 inch pieces.

Have the broth boiling, drop a few pieces in the broth at a time so they won't stick together. Let boil for 10 min. or till the pieces aren't soggy.

Edna Lauer
Lone Wolf

Mrs. Lauer, who lives in the beautifully preserved family homestead house, recalls that this was an every-day dish the children loved. Her grandmother was the daughter of a Swiss father and a French mother who had immigrated in 1835. Regina Schumacher, born in Ohio, married there, and struck out with her young husband, J. W. Brillhart, for Oklahoma ... living first near Okarche. When the Kiowa country opened in 1901, they were among the 160,000 who registered for the land lottery and received their claim by a drawing. This was the last great land opening in Oklahoma ... very different from the Run of '89!

CHICKEN PIE

Select a nice fat hen, cut it up, stew until tender. Cool and cut the chicken in small pieces after you remove the bones and gristle. Make a white sauce (see Chicken Croquettes) and add some of the broth and slice a potato wafer-thin in the pie. Cover with crust and bake until brown. Make gravy with remaining broth. Crust:

⅔ cup of shortening	just enough water to
½ tsp. salt	make it stick
1½ cups flour	together (2-3 T.)

Pearl Ogden Pemberton (Mrs. George T.)
Oklahoma City 1889er

According to Mrs. Pemberton, who came in 1889 with her parents, this is one of her oldest recipes, "There was only lard in the early days, and this chicken pie was made with lard in 1889 and until shortening came out."

SOUTHERN FRIED CHICKEN

Wash and pat dry chicken pieces. Season with salt and pepper. Shake chicken in a brown paper bag with one cup flour til well coated, one or two pieces at a time. Shake off surplus flour and place in very hot (but not smoking) grease in heavy skillet. Brown on both sides, then turn heat down and cook about 20 minutes, taking care not to burn.

Cream Gravy — Remove chicken to platter and cover to keep warm. Drain most of the grease, leaving the brown particles in skillet. Add 2 T. flour and 1 tsp. salt, stir til browned. Over low heat gradually add enough milk until gravy is rich caramel color, stirring constantly. Let gravy simmer to thicken. More milk may be added if too thin, but do not attempt to add flour.

Some like to soak chicken a couple of hours in cold milk before flouring.

Linda Kennedy Rosser (Mrs. Ronald E.)
Edmond

Many who came to Oklahoma from the Deep South still felt the effects of the "War Between the States" and cherished traditional Southern recipes from happier days.

CHICKEN CROQUETTES

2 T. butter	¼ tsp. celery salt
¼ cup flour	1 tsp. lemon juice
1 cup milk	few drops of onion juice
1¾ cup diced chicken	1 tsp. chopped parsley
salt and pepper	egg and crumbs

Make white sauce with butter, milk and flour and add rest of ingredients. Cool, shape, dip in flour, then egg, then in fine crumbs (I let bread dry completely and roll with rolling pin). Fry in deep fat.

Mrs. John R. Brown
Shawnee

Grandmother White's

ROAST TURKEY

Select a plump turkey, and when it has been carefully prepared, picked, singed, drawn, washed, wiped and trussed — season inside with pepper and salt, and stuff with any dressing preferred; sew up the opening with strong, not coarse, thread. Put the fowl into a baking pan with two or three ounces of butter and roast in a hot oven until well done, basting frequently. Do not forget that the basting is an important part of the process of baking all kinds of meats, especially that of fowls; if this is neglected the meat will be dry and hard, instead of tender and juicy. Allow at least five hours for baking a large turkey, and keep the oven hot from the moment the fowl is put into it until it comes out brown, tender and toothsome.

New Process Cookbook (1896)

It was a very long train ride from Enfield, Illinois to Norman, O.T. in 1898 with two young children, but Mrs. R. C. White was to join her husband in the Oklahoma Territory. Among her possessions was this cookbook with which she would establish a home.

Mother Hogue's

SIMPLE CORN BREAD DRESSING

Bake and cool 1 pan each of corn bread and biscuits. Crumble in mixing bowl. Add broth or juice from chicken or turkey until moist, add several eggs, red peppers, salt and sage to taste. Bake with fowl.

Mary Evelyn Hogue (Mrs. M.S.)
Kingston, Tennessee

The simplicity of this old recipe of Mrs. Hogue's mother-in-law, Sarah Snell Hogue, makes it very appealing. She always tasted the uncooked dressing (raw egg and all) to be certain the seasoning was right.

CORN BREAD DRESSING FOR TURKEY

CORN BREAD FOR DRESSING:

1 cup flour	1 cup milk
1 cup corn meal	2 beaten eggs
3 tsp. baking powder	3 T. cooking oil
1 tsp. salt	1½ T. poultry seasoning

Beat well and bake in greased pan at 425° for 15 minutes. Cook neck and giblets in pot of water til meat falls off neck.

DRESSING:

Corn bread (approx. 3 cups)	½ to 1 cup stock
3 cup dried white bread crumbs	2 eggs beaten well
½ cup celery chopped	salt & pepper to taste
½ cup onion chopped	Poultry seasoning to taste
Stock from neck and giblets	

Crumble corn bread. Saute celery and onions. Toss together with white bread crumbs. Moisten with stock til moist but not mushy. Beat eggs til foamy and toss into mixture. Add salt & pepper to taste and ample poultry seasoning. Put in shallow baking dish making top rough for nice browning. Bake 1 hour 350° . Sprinkle turkey drippings over dressing.

Dorothy Gossett Kennedy (Mrs. E. Lee)
Oklahoma City

OYSTER DRESSING

(Variation)

Mary Lee Ervin's great-grandmother Cullens prepared almost identical dressing except that she added chopped dill pickle and at the last, 1 pint of fresh oysters and juice (or canned Louisiana oysters), mixing very gently. Mrs. Ervin suggests cutting back on stock if the dressing is stuffed in the bird. "This recipe improves, like wine, with age and can be enjoyed warmed up for quite a time after the feast day."

Dorothy's

TURKEY GIBLET GRAVY

Drippings from baked turkey   Cooked giblets
4 T. flour   2 hard boiled eggs
¼ cup water

Cook giblets and neck from turkey in water. Use stock for dressing. Save giblets for gravy. Additional chicken livers may be cooked separately for extra chunky gravy.

Make a thin paste of flour and water, and pour slowly into warm drippings from turkey. Cook til well mixed and thick (if more flour is needed add it to water first, then to gravy to prevent lumps). Add chopped giblets and chopped hard boiled egg.

> Dorothy Gossett Kennedy (Mrs. E. Lee)
> Oklahoma City

Mrs. Overholser's

CHESTNUT DRESSING FOR TURKEY

Boil a quart of chestnuts with the hulls on. When done, crack and skin off the brown peelings, mash thoroughly, salt, pepper and season with melted butter. Fill the turkey and sew up.

Caloric Cookbook (1907)

Huge Thanksgiving turkeys were delivered by Henry Overholser himself, "fastidiously dressed as was his habit, his brown eyes snapping," to those closely associated with him at the Overholser Opera House. "No fowl ever tasted quite as delicious since ... those days when 'Uncle Henry' (as he was fondly called) proudly produced the perfect turkey for the Thanksgiving spread." (From the Overholser scrapbook)

FISH
&
SEAFOOD

CATFISH AND HUSH PUPPIES

Fresh catfish out of clear water were skinned and fileted, dipped into cornmeal, then a mixture of milk and egg, then back into cornmeal before frying in deep fat, and served with Hush Puppies.

HUSH PUPPIES:

2 cups corn meal
1 tsp. baking powder
2 T. sugar (optional)
3½ cups boiling water

¼ cup butter
1 tsp. salt
1 finely chopped onion
   (optional)

Combine dry ingredients, add slowly to boiling water, stirring briskly. When smooth remove from heat and add butter. Stir in and cool. Form into finger-shaped rolls and fry in hot fat til golden brown.

Linda Kennedy Rosser (Mrs. Ronald E.)
Edmond

Rivers and streams in the Oklahoma Country ran clear and clean, which increased the desirability for settlement. Norman and Oklahoma Station were especially appealing because of their nearness to the South and North Canadian Rivers, while Guthrie had both Cottonwood Creek and the Cimarron River.

Mrs. Pemberton's

SALMON CROQUETTES

2 cups canned salmon	¼ tsp. paprika
¼ tsp. salt	1 egg
1 tea cup rolled	dash of black pepper
cracker crumbs	

Form balls and fry in shortening. I grate a little onion in mine.

Pearl Ogden Pemberton (Mrs. George T.)
Oklahoma City

Being an 89er, Pearl Pemberton enjoys recalling the early days of Oklahoma City, including colorful memories of the "button lady," who would linger near the saloons on every corner along Main Street, with a purse around her neck made of carpet covered with buttons ... for a nickel she would sew buttons on the men's clothes.

Mrs. Henry Overholser's

COD FISH BALLS

Shred one cup of cod fish. Pare and cut into cubes one pint of potatoes. Put potatoes and cod fish in kettle together, cover with boiling water, removing to Caloric for three hours. Drain well, mash and beat until very light. Add two teaspoons of butter, one egg well beaten, one-fourth saltspoon of pepper, more salt if needed. Drop by tablespoonfuls in hot fat.

1907 Caloric Cookbook

In frying, use the same amount of COTTOLENE as you would for lard, but care must be exercised in heating. Always put it on in a cold vessel — COTTOLENE heats without sputtering or smoking, and quicker than lard. Never allow it to smoke, as it is then burning. For croquettes, fishballs, oysters, etc., drop a small piece of bread in the hot fat to test. (From Capital City Cookbook, 1898, Guthrie O.T.)

Eliza Root Reynold's

FRIED FISH

Cleanse them thoroughly, dry them well, dip them in flour, or first in the beaten yolk of eggs, and then in grated bread crumbs; fry in lard or beef drippings, or equal parts of lard and butter. Butter alone takes out the sweetness and gives a bad color. Turn on both sides and cook a rich yellow brown. Fried parsley, grated horseradish, or slices of lemon are used as garnish. The fat fried from salt pork is good to fry fish in. Some fish can be dipped in Indian meal instead of flour if preferred. Trout and perch should not be dipped in Indian meal.

Earline Jones Reynolds (Mrs. Allie P.)
Oklahoma City

Eliza Reynolds and her husband, Richard, lived on Creek Indian land Southeast of Muskogee. Their son, David C. Reynolds, now 87, attended the Chilocco Indian School between 1904 and 1907 and became well-known as the evangelist, "Chief Gallopin' Horse".

Grandmother's

FRIED FROG LEGS

Clean, salt and dip frog legs into flour. (Large hind legs are best but front legs and backs of frogs can also be eaten). Fry in hot fat like fried chicken until brown on all sides. Keep covered with heavy iron lid while cooking so legs won't "hop" out.

Robin Freeman Woods (Mrs. Pendleton)
Oklahoma City

Mrs. Walbright's

FRIED OYSTERS

Lay on cloth to drain, dip in seasoned cracker crumbs, then in eggs; repeat 3 times, fry in hot lard.

1900 Stroud Cookbook

G. Y. Walbright, Editor and co-owner of the Stroud Messenger, placed an ad in the Presbyterian Cookbook of 1900: "The Stroud Messenger aims to collect and properly 'dish up' palatable news, doesn't nauseate its many intelligent readers with stale or uninteresting nothings, and it doesn't indulge in offensive personalties . . . our lady readers have passed flattering compliments on the true inwardness of the Messenger, and ordered the paper sent to their friends in the states."

ANGELS ON HORSEBACK

Cut bacon in wafer-like slices and in each slice, wrap an oyster and pin up the edges with a wood skewer. When as many as are desired are wrapped, dip them in a batter of cracker dust, egg and milk and fry them in boiling lard.

Raymond F. Long
Oklahoma City

PIGS IN A BLANKET

(Variation)

Roll a good sized oyster in a very thin strip of bacon and fasten with a small skewer; toothpicks are very good to use. Fry in boiling hot lard until done. This simpler recipe was found in the February 24, 1900 edition of the Daily Times Journal on the Ladies' Page.

Oklahoma Historical Society

An early oyster supper given at the First Baptist Church in Oklahoma City netted $200.00, and in 1899 the Chesapeake Fish and Oyster Depot advertised a wide assortment of fish, including white fish, trout and pike.

Birdie Paul's

GEFILTE FISH

2 lbs. red snapper	shaved almonds
1½ slices white bread	3 stalks of celery
soaked in water and	parsley and ¼ onion,
squeezed out	salt, cinnamon
2 eggs, beaten light	1 T. butter

Filet fish, put bones in kettle and cook. Grind fish and make small balls. Put back in skins and stew with vegetables, covered for 1 hour. Sauce: strain juice, add thickening, 3 egg yolks, beaten light. Pour cooled juice into eggs and strain. Cool in ice box until sauce is jellied.

Eleanor Paul Jacobson
Oklahoma City

"My mother was in the Run from Shawnee. She and my father were Rabbi Blatt's first couple to be married by him and my father, Gus Paul, was a City Attorney here in 1904." This very old recipe is traditional for Passover.

Mrs. Roy Hoffman's

DEVILED OYSTERS

½ lb. butter	2 qts. oysters
1 cup bread crumbs	1 egg
Minced parsley, onion	Worcestershire sauce
and red peppers	Salt
4 sweet pickles	Pepper
1 green pepper	Paprika

Cut all ingredients fine except oysters. Cook all together 10 minutes making the right consistency with oyster liquid. Fill oyster shells with mixture, letting stand several hours. Sprinkle with bread crumbs fried in butter. Bake 40 minutes.

5 O'Clock Tea Club Cookbook
Oklahoma City

Mrs. Hoffman's husband established the Guthrie Leader newspaper before statehood. He had fought with Teddy Roosevelt as a Rough Rider in the Spanish-American War, and later became the first General of the Oklahoma National Guard.

Clarence L. Henley, Esq.'s

SHRIMP WIGGLE

"When 8 or 10 or 12 were asked to a chafing dish supper the early part of the evening was spent in conversation or at cards. About 10:30 the hostess tied on a fetching lace-trimmed chafing dish apron to prepare the one hot dish of the feast. Several popular bachelors about town were excellent cooks and when asked to do so took a hand in the measuring and stirring, among them E. K. Gaylord and Clarence L. Henley, who created a social sensation with 'Shrimp Wiggle', a combination of shrimp and peas served on toast."

Overholser Mansion Scrapbook
Oklahoma City

Chafing dishes were reportedly used in colonial times but reached the pinnacle of popularity in the 1890's. In Oklahoma City the Chafing Dish Club was organized as an exclusive ladies' club around 1900. The Overholser clipping attested to the popularity of chafing dish suppers ... other social events enjoyed by the younger set were dances and tallyho rides.

MEATS

SIGNS

Walker & McCarty

CRESCENT MEAT MARKET

REAL ESTATE BROKERS
Bargains on City Lots & Farm Lands in
OKLAHOMA TER. AND STATES

BEAN
Soup
10¢

DOUGLASS & CLARK
LUNCH ROOM AND GROC
ELITE BAKERY

© Judy M. Samter '78

1889 Sign Shop, Guthrie

John Sinopoulo's
DOLMADES

1½ lb. ground lamb
1 small ground onion

1 small can mashed tomatoes
1 cup raw rice

Season and mix with salt, pepper, ½ tsp. each of ground cinnamon and ground cloves, and a little chopped mint. Place small amount in slightly wilted cabbage leaves or grape leaves and wrap. Place in kettle on rack, cover with boiling water and simmer til rice is done. Beat 2 egg whites stiff, add yolks and beat, add juice of lemon gradually, pour over dolmades when serving.

Pat Sinopoulo Gambulos (Mrs. Byron)
Oklahoma City

"The Sinopoulo brothers immigrated to U.S. as boys and began life in this country in St. Louis, Missouri. At their first jobs in a candy store, (in which they became part owners), they were introduced to candy making and all types of culinary art by their partner and his wife — a lovable Italian couple. Mr. John prepared many traditional Greek dishes, among which the above was tremendously popular with friends and family. The first joint statehood meeting composed of delegates from both territories was held in June, 1905, at Delmar Garden in Oklahoma City, owned by the Sinopoulos."

Mrs. Sexauer's
HAMBURGH STEAK

Three pounds hamburgh, two eggs, two rolled crackers, one cup milk; mix well turn into a greased pan and bake one hour.

Capital City Cookbook
Guthrie, O.T., 1898

Still standing in Guthrie are many beautiful buildings and homes designed by the Belgian architect, Joseph Foucart, who came to the Territory shortly after the Run of '89 and strongly influenced the fine structures being built in the capital during the 1890's.

Western Style

BEEFSTEAK AND GRAVY

A piece of roundsteak with bone and marrow in — about 1½ lb. cut about ¼" thick. Flour, salt, black pepper, whole sweet milk. Place steak on a wooden cutting or bread board, pound thoroughly on both sides with a meat tenderizing mallet. (I've read that chuck wagon cooks used a hammer on occasion). Dredge the meat very well with flour after salting and peppering each piece — you want a good coating. In 2 cast iron 9" skillets heat 3 T. of bacon drippings (per skillet). Of course, if you have a really large skillet — one will do, with probably 4 T. of drippings or as much as needed to cover the bottom of the pan well. When the drippings are hot, but not smoking, put in steak pieces, lower heat to medium low, brown steaks well on one side, turn and brown the other side — you want a very well-done steak; so cook slowly. Remove steaks and keep warm.

For the gravy — remove all but 3 T. of drippings, scraping up the brown bits from the extra skillet to add to the gravy pan. Add 3 rounded T. of flour, slowly brown the flour, stirring and incorporating the brown bits into the mixture. When the flour is deep golden brown, stir in sweet milk gradually. Start with 2 cups, cook over low heat, stirring. As the gravy thickens, add more milk to attain the consistency you prefer. Some people like the gravy quite thick. Correct seasoning and serve with the steak and hot biscuits.

Mary Lee Martin Ervin (Mrs. John W.)
Oklahoma City

From Reba Collins, Curator of the Will Rogers Memorial at Claremore, came this excerpt by Will Rogers, one of Oklahoma's most famous "cowboys", concerning beefsteak: "You know we fry our beefsteak in thin pieces, and let me tell you something ... All this eating raw, bloody, rare meat, like they order in these big hotels, and city people like, well that's just them. That ain't old western folks. Ranch cooks and farm women fry steak thin and hard. That old raw junk goes for the high collars in cities, they are kinder cannibalistic anyhow."

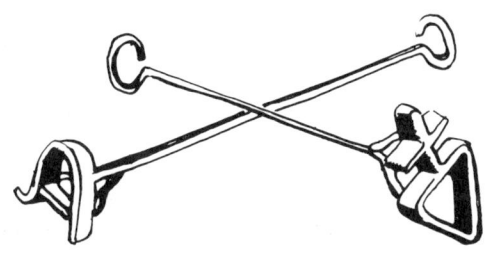

67

Anna R. Joseph's

GAHNTZE TZIMMES

3 to 4 lbs. brust
  (boneless brisket)
2 T. schmaltz (rendered
  chicken fat)
3 large carrots, cut
  in 1" rounds
½ lb. prunes, uncooked
3 large sweet potatoes,
  cut in 1" rounds

3 medium white potatoes,
  quartered
5 cups boiling water
1½ T. brown sugar
1 lemon, thinly sliced
2 T. flour

Cover prunes with water and soak several hours. Sear meat well in schmaltz in a Dutch Oven on top of stove. Transfer to a roasting pan. Place carrots, prunes, sweet potatoes, white potatoes, and lemon slices around meat. Combine brown sugar and flour and add enough water to make a thin paste. Add this paste to boiling water. Pour over the tzimmes. If necessary, add more boiling water to bring liquid to the top of tzimmes. Cover, bake 400° for one hour. Reduce heat to 325° and continue baking for 4½ hours. Uncover and bake 30 minutes longer. Enjoy, enjoy.

> Mrs. Sam Goldberg
> Wilburton

Mrs. Goldberg's father, John Joseph, started his dry goods business in Wilburton, I.T. about 1898. Traditional dishes such as this Tzimmes were served on Sabbath and Holy Days. It could be prepared the day before and cooked slowly through the night.

RARE ROAST BEEF

This is also called dish gravy or "au jus". To cook beef so that the blood gravy will flow as soon as the beef is cut is an effort of skill. It cannot be done if the beef is put into a cold oven or crowded with other meats, and must not be stabbed with a fork. Put the roast in a pan by itself and a handful of salt, a ladleful of drippings or fat set in fairly hot range for about 1½ hour.

<u>American Meat Cooking for Restaurants & Hotels</u> (1901)

There were fine hotels in the Territory in both Guthrie and Oklahoma City, such as the Threadgill Hotel, where in 1905 Major General and Mrs. S. S. Sumner had as their guest for dinner, their niece from New York. Included in festivities in her honor were Lieut. John J. Pershing and Lieut. Bowie, both stationed at Fort Reno and considered eligible young bachelors.

Elsie Burntrager's

YORKSHIRE PUDDING

1½ pts. milk   6 heaping T. flour
3 eggs   1 tsp. salt

Mix dry ingredients, stir in little milk until a thick paste and smooth. Add rest of milk and eggs, beaten together. Pour into shallow pan greased with beef drippings, or beef grease from roast. Put pan in oven under roast so drippings will drop into pudding. In case you can't drip into pudding, as soon as pudding becomes firm, pour some juice off roast into pudding and continue cooking. Roast beef should never be cooked with water and always in a hot oven for first half hour. If you can't cook roast and pudding at the same time, cook roast first and then set on top of stove and cook pudding about 30 minutes.

Helen Burntrager Rimpau
San Diego, California

Grandmother Herron's

MEAT LOAF WITH SPANISH SAUCE

Toast Bread until crisp and brown. Use one cup of ground toast to 2 cups of ground cold left-over beef roast. Add as many eggs as necessary in porportion to meat and toast. Add gravy to bind the ingredients. If no gravy is available make a white sauce. Saute' a large onion in butter and add to mixture. Shape into a loaf. Make a pie crust and wrap meat mixture, slash top of crust several times and place in shallow pan. Bake until crust is brown, about 45 minutes at 325° .

SPANISH SAUCE:

In a sauce pan saute ½ cup onions and ½ cup celery. Add 1 large can of tomatoes. Season with salt, pepper, teaspoon sugar and add hot sauce or hot peppers to your taste and add a little flour for thickening. Before removing from stove add a can of drained English Peas. Serve over sliced meat loaf.

Ruth E. Bertholf
Oklahoma City

This is an original "receipe" of Mrs. Bertholf's grandmother's, who owned and operated the cafes in the old Wollcott and Norwood Hotels of Shawnee.

MEAT LOAF

2 lbs. ground beef
1 lb. sausage
2 cups fine dry bread
crumbs
½ cup chopped onion

1 small bell pepper
1 cup milk
2 eggs, beaten
2 tsp. salt
½ tsp. pepper

Mix ingredients thoroughly. Bake 350° for 50 minutes. Spread with Glaze:

½ cup chopped dill pickles
½ cup catsup
¼ cup water

2 T. sugar
1 tsp. Worcestershire sauce

Bake another 30 minutes or until well done.

Helen Breeden
Cleveland

Christoph Chilie Parlor

MEXICAN CHILIE

4½ lbs. lean beef
(ground coarsely)
1½ lbs. suet (ground
coarsely)
14 chilie pods (Seed and
stem the pods)
1 head garlic (Peel
and grind together)

1 oz. comeno seed (ground
together fine)
½ oz. Mexican sage
¾ quart flour
1 handful salt
Water
Mexican beans

Boil the meat in a little water and salt for one hour, add the "chilie" pods and garlic, boil half-hour longer, add comenoseed and sage. Next stir in the flour, let cool and you have condensed "chilie". To serve, stir in hot water. Cook Mexican beans in separate kettle, then combine "chilie" and beans to desired thickness and serve.

Sister Mildred Christoph
Oklahoma City

"This 'receipe' is from uncle Charles Christoph and his sister Lucy, who opened a 'chilie' parlor in Ellinwood, Kansas around 1898. Around 1907 they took the recipe to Leadville, Colorado, and had a chilie parlor there for ten years. Later Charles returned to Ellinwood from the mining town and served his Mexican Chilie to the railroad hands.

Pete's Place

RAVIOLI

DOUGH:
4 cups sifted flour
½ tsp. salt

4 or 5 eggs
¼ cup tap water

Sift flour in large bowl, making a hole in the center. Add the above ingredients and work in all the flour a little at a time. Cover with a cloth and set aside.

FILLING:
3 lbs. hamburger
2 T. parsley
1 onion, chopped
1 small bell pepper,

chopped
¼ cup olive oil
1 egg
¼ cup Romano cheese

Saute the onion, pepper and parsley in olive oil, add the hamburger and sear until light brown. Cover and cook about 10 minutes. Set aside to cool. (If the meat is a little watery, add a little bread crumbs or cracker crumbs. If the filling is rough, run it through a grinder for a smoother filling.) Add a raw egg. Sprinkle with ¼ cup of Romano Cheese.

SAUCE (This is according to one's own taste; it may vary as desired): Braise small pieces of pork until brown. Add some onion, parsley and green peppers to tomato sauce. Add ¼ tsp. salt and 1 T. of Worcestershire Sauce. Simmer.

COOKING: Divide dough in half. Roll out very thin, less than 1 8". (If it is too thick it will be doughy.) Take a cutter about 3" in diameter and cut out the dough. Add about 1 T. of filling which has been pressed together to ½ of the circle. Fold the other half over and press edges together with a fork. Repeat until all dough and filling is used. Cook in 6 to 8 quarts of boiling beef stock about 10 minutes. (When the Ravioli floats, it is a pretty good sign it is done.) After it has been cooked, simmer in the sauce over a low fire before serving. Serves 6 to 8.

Bill Prichard
Krebs

Bill's grandfather, Pete Peggire, arrived in Oklahoma in 1903 from a small city near Salerno, Italy with other Italians coming to work the coal mines of Indian Territory. Pete's Place, the restaurant which Pete opened at Krebs in 1927, is still famous for this and other traditional Italian dishes.

Clara Schilling Frost's

KONIGSBERGER KLOPS

(German Style Meat Balls)

1 lb. ground round	1 medium onion
½ lb. ground veal	

Soak 3 slices of bread in ½ cup milk; mix 1 egg, salt and pepper and bread with meat — form into balls. Bring 2 qts. water to boil, add 2 T. vinegar, 1 tsp. mixed spices. Put in meat balls and cook 15 min. with 1 small bay leaf. Blend 4 T. flour with 4 T. butter in a pan. Add slowly 4 cups broth in with meat balls and cook 10 minutes, 2 T. capers in also. Drain meat balls and pour sauce over, put in cooking dish and bake 30 minutes 370° . Serve with mashed potatoes, green beans and rye bread.

Marta Frost Reynolds (Mrs. A.D.)
Oklahoma City

Charles G. Frost, a German immigrant, made the Run of '89 at the age of 45. He went back to visit his best friend and fell for his daughter, Clara Schilling, who came from Germany at 17 and they married in Kansas. His picture is at the Historical Society in Oklahoma City.

Bearman's

CORNED BEEF

Cut the beef in small pieces, leaving out the larger bones. Pack in a six gal. jar, with a weight on top. Pour over the beef boiling hot brine made as follows: 2 gal of water, 3 lb. of salt, 1 oz saltpeter, 1 lb. sugar and 2 large spoon of soda.

Kathy Bearman (Mrs. Charles H.)
Oklahoma City

One 89er recalled using corned beef that first year: "Some of my ventures in cooking were rather amusing to say the least. Canned goods were very primitive in those days, compared with present articles. I smile when I recall the result of my attempt to make cream gravy from a can of condensed milk and canned corned beef, which sticky sweet mess did not go down very well with the family.

"As time went on, we were able to obtain better food supplies, but the necessity of inventing something out of almost nothing was pretty good training and I can still cook a good meal out of things wasted by many cooks."

CORNED BEEF HASH

Take the clear pieces of cold corned beef, removing all gristle and bone. Chop fine, add twice the quantity of cold chopped potatoes. Moisten with some of the water the beef was cooked in, grease the spider with the fat that rises when cold. Warm well through. It may be moistened with milk, if preferred. Or, after the meat and potatoes are mixed together, it may be formed into flat cakes, and both sides browned on a flat griddle greased with butter or drippings.

Mrs. Owens' Cookbook (1884)

"Mother's favorite cookbook contains many interesting articles and recipes," says Mrs. V. C. Rosenstahl, whose mother, Mrs. Charles M. Doughman, lived in Parsons, Kansas.

Gold Miner's

CORNISH PASTIES

Make dough tougher than pie dough ... strong enough to stand up to a hearty filling. Roll out separate pastries about the size of dinner plates, thicker than for pie. In the center, heap small pieces of raw round steak, onion and potato. Put on a tiny dab of butter and sprinkle salt and pepper sparingly. Roll carefully to close all possible openings. Watch that no sharp piece of potato pierces the crust. Pinch down the closing area, which will be quite thick. Make a few small holes in the top with a fork. The pasty may be lying on its side or may have the closed area on the top. Bake one or more in the same pan, barely touching at 325° for ¾ hour.

Doris N. Taylor
Oklahoma City

"About one hundred years ago, Amador City, California, was a gold mining town. The miners were mostly men from Cornwall, England, called 'Cousin Jacks,' who worked twelve-hour shifts. At noon, the elementary school children were given two hours for lunch so the Cornish youngsters could go home, get their fathers' lunches, take them to the mines, eat their own lunches, and get to afternoon classes on time. My father, born in 1879, told me that any non-Cornish child would give anything in his lunch pail for a corner off the Cornish pasties brought by the sons and daughters of the miners. Dad's mother, born in 1849, had learned to walk under a covered wagon on the trek to the California gold areas in 1850. She learned to make the pasties from the Cornish women, taught her four daughters, who taught their ten daughters, who in turn taught their daughters and daughters-in-law. In 1902, my parents pioneered to Spencer, O.T. from California."

73

MOUNTAIN OYSTERS

"One of the cowmen brought a mess of mountain oysters. I knew they were just telling me bunk. Oysters grew in the ocean and not on a mountain.

"I noticed how Mamma cringed when she picked them up, dipped them in a beaten egg then rolled them in cracker crumbs before she put them into a skillet of hot grease. They looked too slimy for me. I didn't eat one."

Vera Holding
Norman

Cattlemen on the range considered these a delicacy when they became available after the castration of young bulls to convert them into steers for better beef. E. Lee Kennedy recalls that on the ranch when he was growing up, they would throw the mountain oysters on the fire used for heating the branding irons. When the two jobs were finished, they'd be scooped out of the coals, salted, and eaten.

Mrs. Mike Goldberg's
PICKLED TONGUE

For 3-4 lb. fresh beef tongue, take 1 level T. saltpeter, 1 T. salt, ½ tsp. black pepper, several cloves garlic (sliced), pinch alum, one-eighth tsp. sugar. Mix together. Rub well into tongue. Place tongue into stoneware crock; add 2 T. pickling spice. Cover completely with water. Cover meat with a weight (inverted plate). Let stand one or two weeks in a very cold place, turning tongue several times. When ready to boil, wash in scalding water, then boil until tender.

Harriet Goldberg Carson (Mrs. Joel)
Oklahoma City

"Grandfather Goldberg came to Hartshorne, I.T. in 1898 and set up a dry goods business. Mike and Sarah's house backed up to the store, and on Holy Days Jewish settlers from all around would gather in Hartshorne and sleep in their store, there being no synagogue."

Grandmother McCain's
RICE & LIVER LOAF

Cook 1 cup rice; fry 1 lb. liver til done. Grind liver. Cook 1 cup celery, ¼ cup parsley, salt, onion in liver drippings. When vegetables are done, put rice in pan with them and stir. Mix with liver and put in baking dish. Pour tomatoes over top and bake 30 minutes.

Mrs. William O. Green
Edmond

At 91 years of age, Mittie McCain Wright recalls much about the years prior to Oklahoma Statehood and is proud to be one of the hardy survivors eighty-nine years later. This recipe of her mother's was given by her daughter, Mrs. Green.

Traditional Jewish

CHOPPED LIVER

1 lb. liver — beef,
  calf, chicken or mix
2 or 3 hard boiled eggs
1 onion

2 or 3 T. fat, oil,
  margarine or rendered
  chicken fat

Place liver under broiler for about 10 minutes. Remove and cool. Remove skin and veins. Grind with eggs. I grate mine on a simple old fashion grater. Chop onion and saute lightly in fat. Combine all and add salt and pepper. If too dry, add 3 or 4 T. of beef or chicken soup.

Adeline Byers Fagin (Mrs. Max)
Oklahoma City

As a teenager, Mrs. Fagin's father, Ben Byers, arrived in America and within two years made tracks into Indian Territory with a wagonload of picture frames. Gradually his trade grew to include all sorts of necessities for the pioneer housewife: pots, pans, dishes, material, sewing supplies. Lehigh, Indian Territory, was expanding as the coal mines developed and by 1892, Ben was able to open a general merchandise store.

Lois Braidwood Freeman's

TAMALE PIE

Add 1 tsp. salt in 5 cups boiling water in heavy saucepan. Slowly add 2 cups corn meal and cook to mush, stirring constantly — at least 15 minutes. Then pour mush into 9 x 13 or larger cake pan. Pack it into bottom and against sides of pan. Let sit until meat mixture is ready.

In skillet melt about 3 T. shortening or bacon drippings. Fry 1 onion chopped finely (and 2 thin slices of garlic if desired) slowly so it does not burn. Add 1 lb. coarse ground beef and ½ lb. coarse ground pork. Stir frequently, letting meat brown. Then pour in 1 to 2 cups cooked or canned tomatoes, 2 T. chili powder, salt and pepper to taste. Let simmer about 15 minutes until it thickens some. Remove the garlic pieces completely. Pour meat mixture over the cornmeal crust and bake at 350° for 1½ hours.

Robin Freeman Woods (Mrs. Pendleton)
Oklahoma City

"While living in Cherryvale, Oklahoma around 1900, Ellen Marsden Braidwood adopted some southwestern recipes from Mexican and Indian women she knew. All her life she kept swapping and sharing recipes with all kinds of people."

TEXAS TOMALLIAS

1 cup cold boiled meat chopped fine; 2 onions, 2 tomatoes, 2 potatoes chopped all fine together. Season well with salt, black pepper and "chillies" or cayenne pepper; make a quart of corn meal mush, rather thin, adding 1 T. lard. When done, put a large spoon full of the mush into a corn husk, spread the meat on, then roll and tie.

1900 Stroud Cookbook

Mrs. Wixson's husband was manager of Long-Bell Lumber Company in Stroud in 1900. Among the diverse influences on Oklahoma cooking was the Mexican culture brought from Texas.

Mary Ellen Bearman's

CURED MEAT

To 1 gal water take 1½ lb salt, ½ lb sugar, ½ oz saltpetre, ½ oz potash. In this ratio the pickle can be increased to any quantity. Let these be boiled together, and thoroughly skimmed. Then throw it into a tub to cool, after which pour over beef or pork. The meat must be well covered with the brine, and should not be put down for at least two days after killing. Some omit boiling the pickle.

Kathy Bearman (Mrs. Charles H.)
Oklahoma City

"Grandmother Bearman's recipes are transcribed just as she wrote them in her account book prior to 1896 ... they were the first settlers in Johnson City, Stanton County, Kansas, just north of 'No-Man's Land' (as the Oklahoma Panhandle was originally called)."

Mrs. C. H. Haynes'

COUNTRY BEEF SAUSAGE

5 pounds lean ground
  beef and suet
1 T. plus 1 tsp. crushed
  red pepper

½ tsp. cayenne pepper
3 T. crushed sage
1 T. salt

Mix all ingredients thoroughly. Let mixture set at room temperature over night until spices are well blended.

Mrs. K. G. Calvin
Hugo

Well-diggers were crucial in the establishment of new areas, so C. H. Haynes' services were in great demand when he came before statehood. He was well known for his "water witching" ability, a means of determining underground water sources with a rod.

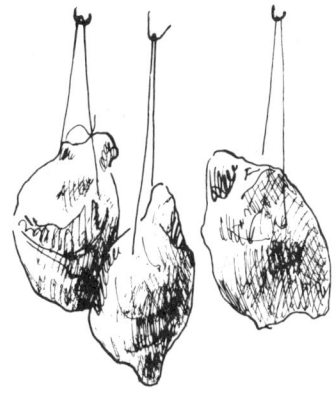

Mrs. Baker Harwell's

PORK SAUSAGE

For 40 lbs. of meat take: 1 pint salt, ½ cup black pepper, ½ cup brown sugar, ½ tsp. salt peter, 1 tsp. cayenne pepper (or 2 tsp. chili) and ½ cup sage.

Mary Harwell McBryde (Mrs. B.)
Oklahoma City

"The sausage was fried in patties and laid down in crocks or jars in the fat that resulted from the frying. Stored in a cool place and 'fished' out when needed and warmed, they were very close to the original freshly fried sausage. This is written in Mother's hand in an old cookbook."

PORK SAUSAGE

Grind up the hams and shoulders to make 4 lbs. of pork.

1 T. red pods of peppers chopped fine	1 tsp. sage (fine ground)
¾ T. salt	½ tsp. Cayenne pepper
	½ tsp. black pepper

Mix all of this together thoroughly. Fry one pattie to taste. More seasoning may be added if a spicier sausage is desired.

Mrs. J. C. Hudman
Oklahoma City

Mary Ellen Bearman's

CURED HAM

To each 20 lb fresh meat, make a mixture of ¼ lb brown sugar, 1 dessert spoon of ground saltpetre. Rub this well by the hand into the meat. Then with coarse salt, cover with ½ inch salt the bottom of barrel, put in hams and cover with ½ inch salt and so on until barrel is full. Hams should remain in barrel 4 weeks, then take out and rub thoroughly with pure black pepper. After two days hang up and smoke 8 weeks.

Kathy Bearman (Mrs. Charles H.)
Oklahoma City

"When Grandmother Bearman wrote this in the late 1800's she noted, 'This receipt is fifty years old and is the best.' For a number of years, Mary Ellen and Henry's place in Kansas was a way-stop for freighters (the driving wagons which hauled all manner of supplies south through the panhandle from the end of the railroad line in Syracuse, Kansas). Her cured hams and other good food were doubtlessly enjoyed by them."

FRIED HAM AND RED-EYE GRAVY

Fry thick slices of ham in a heavy skillet, remove to a warm platter. Leave scrapings in skillet. Stir in as much coffee as gravy needed. Mother always put cream in the coffee, but some people used it black (don't add sugar). This was a good way to use up left-over coffee. Stir well over the fire, scraping the particles up from the skillet. It's a thin gravy ... delicious over biscuits. The "red eyes" are formed by little islands of fat left from the ham floating in the gravy.

Mary Lee Martin Ervin (Mrs. John W.)
Oklahoma City

The great humorist cowboy from Oklahoma, Will Rogers, once wrote about fried ham, (quote furnished by Reba Collins, Curator of Will Rogers Memorial, Claremore), "We always had such good things to eat at my sister's in Chelsea ... fried ham; they cure their own ... Tom McSpadden, my brother-in-law, he is the prize ham-curer of any I ever saw. Smokes 'em with the old hickory log fire, then salts 'em away for all this time. Then the cooking of all this has got a lot to do with it ... Sallie fixes it all up. Then the cream gravy. Why, not to be raised on gravy would be like never going swimming in the creek ... Ham gravy is just about the last word in gravy."

Mrs. George Chase Lewis'

HAM

Soak ham overnight, next morning put into kettle enough cold water to cover. Add 1 pint vinegar, 1½ pound sugar, 1 dozen cloves. Let simmer 3 hours; place into pan skin side up. Bake 2 hours. When done remove skin. Make dressing:

1 egg, well beaten	2 T. sugar
½ tsp. celery seed	1 T. dry mustard

Spread over top of ham, sprinkle with fine bread crumbs, let brown. Remove and serve hot.

Junior League Cookbook
Oklahoma City, 1929

Ham travelled well and as one 89er recalled, "Gathering food to last for a long journey such as molasses, dried fruit, salt meat, and ground meal, my parents, with the forethought of pioneers, had stocked the 'grub wagon' well. We had ham, bread and coffee, and tremendous appetites." This recipe for cooking cured hams was already three generations old when it was included in the Jr. League book.

Mormon Style

BAKED HAM WITH RAISIN SAUCE

1 ham	2 T. sugar
2 T. sugar	1 T. corn starch
2 cups water	1 tsp. dry mustard
1 cup raisins	½ cup water
2 T. butter	¼ tsp. Worcestershire sauce
¼ tsp. salt	¼ cup drippings from ham
1/8 tsp. onion salt	

Place ham fat side up on rack in shallow pan. Do not cover or add water. Bake in 325° oven about 25 minutes per pound for those needing cooking, for precooked, bake about 15 minutes per pound. Serve with Raisin Sauce.

To prepare Raisin Sauce, carmelize 2 tablespoons sugar to a light brown stage. Add the 2 cups water and raisins. Stir in butter, salt, onion salt, the second 2 tablespoons of sugar and simmer 10 minutes. Mix cornstarch, dry mustard with ½ cup water and bring to boil. Boil 30 seconds. Add Worcestershire sauce and drippings from ham.

Dona McLain
Oklahoma City

The Oklahoma Conference of the Church of Jesus Christ of Latter Day Saints (Mormon) was organized in 1899 with Elder Lawrence Blackett as President. The Conference was comprised of The Indian Territory and the Chickasaw Nation in I.T. Notes from December 1, 1899 record 15 missionaries and included an account of a rainstorm with water 5 feet deep and a cyclone in Oklahoma City which destroyed 30 homes.

PICKLED PORK

Put a layer of meat in the bottom of a jar, packing salt and small bits of meat in all the crevices. Put in another layer of meat, filling up in the same way until jar is filled. Make a brine that will bear an egg. Pour on gradually until jar is filled. Put in a cool place. In the spring if brine looks bloody drain and make brine again (to bear an egg) and pour over.

Dorothy Hensley Keys (Mrs. Mott)
Oklahoma City

This pickling would be done in the fall when the slaughter took place after the first frost, and would sit all winter, providing meat for spring and summer.

Camp Fire

BACON

"Mrs. Anna Laskey, a blushing bride at the time of the run, dismounted from a covered wagon near the city. It was the end of her honeymoon journey from northern Iowa.

Her story of the struggle and the victory of the pioneer folk is typical of the story a thousand or more women might tell.

"Our first supper was prepared and served with pioneer equipment — two forked sticks and a crossbar upon which hung a pot and a kettle. Heaps of dry sticks ablaze soon had them bubbling.

The skillet on its bed of coals soon had the heavenly perfume of fried bacon mingled with the aroma of camp coffee to make more wolfish the appetities of the healthy, happy, hopeful, honeymooning Oklahoma homesteaders, on that eventful evening of April 22, 1889.

Tincups, pans and kettles washed and grub-box made neat, we watched the twinkling stars as the man in the moon looked down and seemed to say: "You have reached your goal; you are welcome here; make it 'Home, Sweet Home'," and finally, tired and happy, we sought rest in our wagon-box bed."

Oklahoma — The Beautiful Land
Reminiscences of the Eighty-Niners

Olga Wykert King's

SMOKED PORK CHOPS & BLACK-EYED PEAS

Put cooked black-eyed peas in bottom of baking dish. On top, lay smoked pork chops which have been spread on 1 side with prepared mustard. Add 1 tsp. vinegar for each pork chop. Bake 350° for 1 hour.

Patsy Eskridge King (Mrs. Arthur E., Jr.)
Oklahoma City

Being an '89er at 14, Art King (Patsy King's father-in-law) reached manhood during the earliest days of Oklahoma City. Mr. King was proud to have owned one of the first automobiles in the city and claimed to have been the first to hit a pedestrian as he rounded Stiles Circle. However, he maintained that the collision did more damage to the car than the man, who simply got up and walked away.

Mrs. C. H. Haynes'

BAKED PORK ROAST

Use a 6 pound pork roast with rind attached. Boil pork in water with a small amount of salt and green pod peppers. Length of boiling time is approximately 2 hours.

When done remove from water. Slice into serving pieces, about 1 inch thick, leaving rind attached. Place pork in layers into a large baking dish. Sprinkle with black pepper, salt and a small amount of cornmeal. Bake at 350° about 1 hour.

Mrs. K. G. Calvin
Hugo

Mrs. Haynes came to Oklahoma with her first husband, Reverend Samuel Harper, around the time of statehood.

Susie Etter Warram's

HEAD CHEESE

(Souse Meat)

We raised our own hogs and once a year at hog-killing time, just after the first freeze of early winter, my brother and I helped prepare the Head Cheese by gathering wood for the fire while our father split the hog head open and removed the brains (which later would be fried and eaten with eggs for breakfast). Two iron washpots were placed over the fire, and it was our job to keep the pot boiling till the meat fell off the bones.

On an outdoor work table, Mama would clean the bones, grind the meat in a sausage mill, and put it in big dish pans, cover it with cheese cloth, douse with vinegar, and chill until the natural gelatin from the pig made the mixture solid. We loved to slice and eat it with vinegar. The supply lasted all winter in the smoke house. The skin would be cooked crisp to make Cracklins, which were delicious added to cornbread.

James H. Warram
Oklahoma City

"My mother came with her parents, the Etters, to the Cherokee Nation, Sequoyah District, Indian Territory in the mid 1880's. She was always proud that her birthday in 1879 was the same as the great Will Rogers."

Grandmother's

HOG CHEESE

(Head Cheese)

4½ pounds ground pig head and feet	3 red peppers
	1 onion chopped fine
2 T. sage	1 T. black pepper
1 T. salt	1 cup vinegar

Use fine blade of food chopper to grind pepper and onions. Use coarse blade to grind cooked head and pigs feet. Mix all ingredients. Add as much of the pig feet gelatine as needed to press mixture into a bowl or loaf pan. Chill thoroughly. Slice to serve (like a lunch meat).

Mrs. K. G. Calvin
Hugo

Mary's

PENNSYLVANIA DUTCH POT PIE

2 T. butter	1 egg with 3 T. milk
1 cup flour	"beat up", then
½ tsp. baking powder	add to flour and make
	into ball (like pie
	dough)

Roll out on floured board to keep from sticking, like pie crust, "as thin or thinner," into round sheet. Let set 1 hour or more. Cut into 3 inch squares.

Boil pork (approx. 1 lb. country style ribs or chops) with enough liquid to end up with 1 quart (a must). Begin with 1½ to 2 qts. Leave fat on the pork for flavor. Add salt and pepper and 1 T. chopped onion. After cooked, remove meat — bone, remove fat.

Assembling: Use heavy iron pot or dutch oven (4 qt.). 1 medium potato, very thinly sliced. Put all the meat in bottom of pot with broth, next a layer of dough squares, then a layer of potatoes, then dough, potatoes, etc. til finished.

May have to add moisture while cooking, should be moist but not soupy. Cover and cook 20 minutes in medium oven. Stir to keep from sticking. (May also be made with chicken.)

Mary Parker (Mrs. Monroe)
Oklahoma City

Mrs. Vaught's

STUFFED GREEN PEPPERS

Cut off stem end of green peppers and remove seeds. Cook in plain water for about five minutes. Drain water and allow peppers to cool slightly. Fill each with mixture of ground cooked ham, chopped fresh tomatoes, a few bread crumbs and enough water to keep moist. Place in shallow pan in small amount of water. Cook for about 30 minutes at 350° .

Ruth Vaught Thompson (Mrs. Wayman J.)
Oklahoma City

Butcher shops opened in almost every town as the town was settled. Mrs. W. J. Pettee, joining her husband at Oklahoma Station less than a month after the Run, found a two-room shack ready for housekeeping on West Main Street, "Oh, yes, I had screen doors on my little home. One day when sitting there with a friend, a tall man with a great ten-gallon hat and boots to his knees, burst in; and before we could get our breath and ask him what he wanted, he said, 'Beg your pardon, but seeing the screen door, I took this place for a butcher shop.' "

83

Clara S. Frost's

GERMAN CABBAGE ROLLS

1 large head cabbage	2 eggs
1½ lb. ground round	2 potatoes
½ lb. lean ground pork	1 large sliced onion
½ cup raw rice	2-8 oz. cans tomato sauce
1 small onion (grated)	1 # 2½ size tomatoes
1 tsp. salt	Juice from 2 lemons
½ tsp. pepper	2 T. brown sugar

Remove 12 large leaves from cabbage. Boil in water to make them wilt so they will roll easily. (Boil 10 minutes, cool and leaves come off.) Heat over. Combine meat, rice, grated onion, egg, and 1 tsp. salt, ½ tsp. pepper. Drain cabbage leaves and put good full T. of meat mixture on top, 1 slice of potato and 1 slice of onion; roll up and fasten with toothpick. Line dutch oven or roasting pan with cabbage leaves, arrange layer of rolls seam down. Combine tomato sauce, tomatoes, salt and pepper, brown sugar and bring to boil and pour over rolls. Bake covered 1 hour, remove cover and bake another 45 minutes at 275° .

Marta Frost Reynolds (Mrs. A. D.)
Oklahoma City

Early Oil Well

84

ACCOMPANIMENTS

C.M. Bassford Store, Beement, Dewey County

VEGETABLES

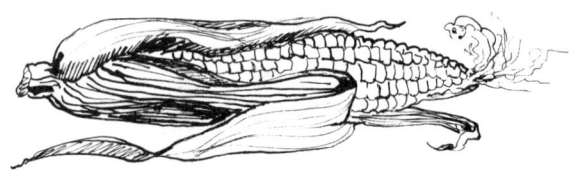

CREAMED DRIED SWEET CORN

Boil fresh young roasting ears of corn 20 minutes and cool. With a sharp knife cut the grains off, commencing at the thick end. Scrape the tiny hearts of the grains out too but keep them separate and use them without drying. Now spread the cut off corn on a white sheet and put on top of the west porch roof where it will get the most hot sun. Crawl up the ladder and rake the corn around so it will dry on all sides.

At night before you go to bed, put 2 cups dried corn to soak in about 4 cups of water. In the morning, put the corn on to boil until it is tender. Pour off excess or all water, add sweet milk and thicken with flour and last add a big tablespoon heaping of fresh churned butter.

Mrs. Myles F. Smith
Oklahoma City

Mother's

GREEN CORN CAKES

One pint of grated sweet corn, one pint of sweet milk or a part sweet cream would be better, and three well beaten eggs. Stir all together, beating hard. Season with a little white pepper, salt and two tablespoonfuls melted butter, stirring it well in and adding a little flour to make the ingredients adhere together, being careful not to have them too thick. Bake one on the griddle first to test the batter, that it may be of the right consistency, and well seasoned before baking to serve. If preferred, fry in hot drippings or lard.

New Process Cookbook (1894)

These corn fritters are delicious served with maple syrup. Sorghum molasses was often used as a substitute for syrup in the early days.

CORN PUDDING

2 cup Corn (cut from cob or 1 can)	1 tsp. Salt
2 cup Milk	2 T. Butter
2 T. Flour (mix with a little cold milk)	2 T. Sugar
	1 egg, beaten
	Dash of Nutmeg

Mix flour, salt, sugar and beaten egg. Add to corn and mix thoroughly. Add hot milk. Pour into 1 qt. Baking Pan. Dot with Butter and sprinkle lightly with nutmeg. Set in pan of hot water and bake till custard is set. About an hour at 325° .

Mrs. Eunice R. Lieurance
Burlington

This recipe has been handed from mother to daughter for about 150 years: from my mother, Anna Martin; from hers, Nannie Williams; from the Hunt family plantation in Kentucky.

Grandmother Hayne's

LYE HOMINY

Pick over shelled corn. For each qt. of shelled yellow or white field corn, dissolve 2 T. lye in 1 gallon boiling water carefully. Use an iron kettle or enameled container. Do not use tin, copper, zinc or aluminum. Add corn. Boil 35 min. or until hulls loosen. Rinse corn through several changes of hot water to remove lye, then cover with cold water. Rub to remove hulls and black tips. Let stand in fresh water 3 or 4 hours. Change water several times. Drain. Cover with boiling salted water (1 tsp. to each qt. water). Boil until almost tender.

Mrs. K. G. Calvin
Hugo

Mrs. J. A. Meinecke's

FRIED GREEN TOMATOES

Select round, smooth, firm green tomatoes. Just before turning, slice thin and soak for at least 1 hour in salt water, dip in flour and fry a deep brown in hot lard.

1900 Stroud Cookbook

Mr. Meinecke was proprietor of the Missouri House in Stroud, which advertised in 1900: "Board $3.00 per week; Board and Lodging $3.50 per week; Meals 20¢."

Mrs. Hayne's

FRIED GREEN TOMATOES

6 medium green tomatoes	Salt & Pepper
1 cup corn meal	Oil for frying

Wash tomatoes and cut out the stems. Slice about ¼ inch thick. Sprinkle with salt and pepper. Coat with corn meal and cook in heated fat in skillet. Brown both sides as you keep turning tomatoes in the skillet. If desired, you may scald tomatoes with boiling water to peel before slicing.

Mrs. K. G. Calvin
Hugo

When the garden produced bumper crops of tomatoes, pioneers looked for innovative ways to prepare them.

DANDELIONS

About a peck of dandelion leaves will be required for a pint when cooked. Look each leaf over carefully and after washing well in several waters, lay them in cold water for twenty minutes. Put over to cook in an abundance of boiling water; put in a tablespoonful of salt and cook from thirty to forty minutes. They will require a longer time if the leaves are not tender. When done put into a colander, drain and press out all the water; return to the stove in a saucepan; season with a little pepper and a teaspoonful of butter. Cut through with a sharp knife and mix thoroughly. Put in a hot dish and garnish, if liked, with slices of cold hard boiled eggs. Serve with vinegar. Some prefer to boil a small piece of fat salt pork, well washed, with the dandelions, putting it in when the water is changed. Dandelions make very nice greens and are considered very wholesome, but can rarely be obtained outside of rural districts. They certainly should be as marketable as spinach.

New Process Cookbook (1894)

This old cookbook is treasured by its owner, Mrs. E. W. Patterson, because it belonged to her grandmother, who settled in Norman before 1901.

Mrs. Frost's

DAMPF KRAUT

(Steamed Cabbage)

Take one "15¢" head of red cabbage. Wash and cut up fine. Cook 2 slices of bacon, chop up. Take about 6 T. grease. Place all together in covered stew pan and let sweat 15 minutes over slow fire (no water). Watch carefully. Quarter 1 apple, chop 1 onion fine, add ¼ tsp. salt, ¼ tsp. pepper, 2-3 T. sugar, ½ cup vinegar, and ½ cup water. Mix well and cover. Cook 30 minutes. Add more water and cook 2 hours until cooked down. Add ½ glass of red wine ½ hour before done. If too much water, take off lid.

Marta Frost Reynolds (Mrs. A.D.)
Oklahoma City

This traditional German dish of Marta's grandmother Frost has always been popular with the family, and in Bim-Bom's later years she dictated her recipe to Marta.

Cherokee

INDIAN JACK

Chop:
1 cup green peppers
1 cup sweet onion (large flat onion are sweetest)
1 cup fresh tomatoes, peeled
Add:
pinch of sugar (¼ tsp. to preserve "fresh" taste to vegetables)
1 tsp. salt
fresh ground pepper (black coarse grind)
Marinate in:
½ cup vinegar
½ cup cold water

At least 3 hours before serving to top hot fresh green beans, hot fried okra or as a summer salad. Keeps well covered in refrigerator for two to three days.

Martha Jo Russell Sturm (Mrs. George)
Oklahoma City

This recipe has been handed down through many generations of Mrs. Sturm's family as a proud reminder of their Cherokee Indian heritage.

FRIED OKRA

1½ to 2 pounds small okra
1 cup cornmeal

1 cup bacon fat

Slice okra in round "buttons"; coat well with cornmeal. Fry in hot fat in skillet til brown and crispy. Drain before serving.

Dorothy Gossett Kennedy (Mrs. E. Lee)
Oklahoma City

In the country families ate many fresh vegetables during garden season, but in the cities, according to early produce wholesaler, K. W. Dawson, "It wasn't easy selling fresh vegetables at first — meat and potatoes were a meal in those days. Dawson had to sell more than that, and his business initiative came to the front in an education campaign: 'Eat More Vegetables.' Doctors took up the cry and that helped."

New England

BAKED BEANS

1 quart of white beans
1 tsp. of soda
¼ lb. salt pork
4 T. of beef fat

or butter
molasses, 2 T. to ½
cup, or none
1 tsp. of mustard

Wash and soak the beans in cold water over night. Pour off remaining water. Put the beans into the kettle, cover with cold water, add the soda, and cook gently until the beans are slightly softened ... the soda aids the softening. Pour off the water again, and put the beans into a covered bean pot. Mix the molasses and mustard with a pint of water, and pour this over the beans, adding more water if the beans are not covered. Place the pork or other fat upon the beans, and cover the pot. If fat other than pork is used, salt must be added to the beans. The beans should bake slowly, from 6 to 8 hours, and even longer in a very slow oven.

Carol Wray (Mrs. James)
Watonga

"A dish known in old days in New England, baked to perfection in the old brick oven. Baked beans seem difficult of digestion for some people. The mustard is supposed to be helpful, and adds something to the flavor. If the molasses is omitted, or but a small amount used, and if butter takes the place of pork or suet, the beans seem more digestible. In different parts of New England the dish is varied. Some people prefer rather dry baked beans, others wish them moist and very sweet."

Country Style

FRESH GREEN BEANS

Snap and wash 2 quarts of fresh green beans from the garden. Scrub 2 lbs. small new potatoes with jackets. Drain all but water that clings. Heat heavy pot and render 5 thick slices bacon (8 or 9 thin slices), until most fat is out but meat is not crisp ... remove bacon and leave fat. Add green beans (pan still uncovered). Stir beans often the first 10 minutes till well blanched (losing some bright green color). This is almost like frying them on medium heat. Sprinkle with salt — Place scrubbed new potatoes on top of beans. Add ⅔ cup boiling water. Place on tight cover. Cook about 45 minutes, stirring only once during cooking.

Mary Miles Clanton
Oklahoma City

As a very young girl in Okfuskee County, one of Mary's chores was to work in the garden, learning to plant corn, "pol" green beans and "grabble" (dig) potatoes. She began cooking at the age of 10 giving some promise of the home economist she became.

Grandmother Haynes'

BLACK EYED PEAS

2 cups dried blackeyed peas	¼ tsp. crushed red pepper
6½ cups water	1½ T. fat
Dry salt meat (salt pork)	1 T. flour

Pick over dry peas, removing broken peas and other trash. Wash well and soak over night in 2 cups of water. Wash the salt meat and cook almost done. Add the soaked peas and water. Cook until done without stirring. Add pepper. Melt 1½ T. fat in skillet. Brown 1 T. flour. Add ½ cup water and stir smooth. Add to peas about 15 minutes before cooking is complete. If soaked over night, peas will not burst or mash up.

Mrs. K. G. Calvin
Hugo

Black-eyed peas were imported to America very early from Nigeria and were a staple in the Southern states. They eventually became a tradition with the white people, especially on New Years Day for "good luck".

RAGOUT OF TURNIPS

Peel as many small turnips as will fill a dish; put them into a stew pan with some butter and a little sugar, set them over a hot stove, shake them about, and turn them till they are a good brown; pour in a half a pint of rich high seasoned gravy; stew the turnips till tender, and serve them with the gravy poured over them.

James Neill Northe
Oklahoma City

Those first winters in the Oklahoma Territory folks who lived in the country stored vegetables by burying them in a hole covered with straw and dirt ... a stalk of a cabbage would be left sticking up as a marker. Mrs. Ed McCarrel, an '89er who has spent all but two of her 91 years in Oklahoma, recalls this process of storage for cabbage, sweet potatoes, and other hardy vegetables.

CARROT RING

2 cups mashed cooked carrots
1 T. salt
¼ T. pepper and paprika

1 T. finely grated onion
3 eggs
1 cup milk

Beat eggs slightly and add seasoning and milk; Mix with carrot pulp; Pour into a well greased ring mold; Place mold in pan with 1" hot water; Bake in 350° oven for 35 minutes. Nice extra to fill center with buttered lima beans.

Lucyl Shirk
Oklahoma City

"I have no idea how old this recipe might be, but 75 years wouldn't be too old I'm sure. Mrs. Vaught always made this at Thanksgiving time and sent it to friends for their Thanksgiving dinner."

CANDIED SWEET POTATOES

Cut boiled, peeled sweet potatoes into lengthwise slices. Place in earthen baking dish. Baste with butter and sprinkle generously with sugar (white or brown as you wish). Add a little water and bake until sugar and butter have candied and potatoes are golden brown.

Robin Freeman Woods (Mrs. Pendleton)
Oklahoma City

Anna Essary's

BUCKAROO BEANS

1 lb. dried beans	2 cloves garlic, sliced
6 cups water	1 bay leaf, whole
1 medium onion	½ lb. salt pork or ham

Boil beans in water 2 minutes and remove from heat, adding ¼ tsp. soda. Let stand 1 hour. Add remaining ingredients. Boil til beans are tender — add 2 cups tomatoes, ½ cup chopped green pepper, 2 tsp. chili powder, 3 T. brown sugar, 1 tsp. dry mustard, ¼ tsp. oregano, salt to taste. Cook til beans are finished.

Louise Schoenleber
Bethany

Beans were a necessity not only for the cowhand on long trail rides, but for settlers too. On the main street in almost any town of the Territory, a familiar sight was "the Beanery", where beans were dished up for 10¢ per bowl.

Mama's

RED BEANS

Soak dry pinto beans in water over night after picking out any stones. Add a large chopped onion, some salt pork, and chili powder. Taste as it cooks, adding more chili powder to taste. When beans are done, add a can of tomatoes if wanted. Best when cooked all day over a wood stove.

Erma Cox
Oklahoma City

This traditional Afro-American dish was normally served with cornbread and buttermilk when Erma was growing up. Her mother, Alice Ross, now 103, came to Oklahoma from Birmingham, Alabama.

CERNA KUBA

(Mushroom & Barley Casserole)

2 cups of pearl barley, wash in cold water 3 times until water shows clear. Cook barley until almost done, set aside. Chop 1 cup of raw mushrooms, saute slowly in butter or lard until about half done, set aside. Then mince small piece of parsley, ⅔ tsp. pepper, 1 tsp. marjoram, 1 clove of garlic mashed with 1½ tsp. salt until real fine. Mix all ingredients together, put in a greased pan and bake 1½ hours at 350° . Dry mushrooms can be used. Put to soak in cold water until soft. Also drained, canned mushrooms can be used. Traditionally served on Christmas Eve.

Mrs. Anna Stejskal Smrcka (Mrs. Ralph)
Yukon

In 1901 two Czech organizations jointly built a building where their families could go to have a good time. Wedding dances, anniversaries, parties, and family reunions have been held there, and the tradition has been kept through the years when it was known as Bohemian Hall, after World War II as Czech Hall, and now as Yukon Czech Hall, where Saturday night activities feature waltzes, polkas, and folk dancing.

Mrs. Issac Loewenstein's

NOODLE KUGEL

2 full cup noodles	2 pats of butter
1 cup raisins	½ cup sugar
2 eggs	1 tsp. baking powder
2 level tsp. cinnamon	

Boil noodles thoroughly, then strain and rinse in cold water. Mix all together and put into greased baking dish. Top with a light sprinkling of sugar and cinnamon. Bake in 350° oven until golden brown, 30 minutes. I use a bundt pan, looks pretty and slices nicely. This is a semi-sweet side dish good to serve with broiled or baked chicken and roasts.

Mrs. Morris Loewenstein
Oklahoma City

Issac Loewenstein came here two weeks after the run, bought land at what was later 111 W. Grand Ave, and lived in a tent where the Colcord Building now stands until he could get his home and business buildings built. Mrs. Johanna Loewenstein came with their 18 month old child, Morris, when everything was ready. Their home was in back of their meat market and their slaughter house was south and east of the main part of the settlement. In later years a theatre was built on that land, which Issac and Morris ran for many years.

MACARONI AND CHEESE

2 cups cooked Macaroni	2 cups (½ pound) grated
1 egg	mild cheddar cheese
1 cup milk	1 to 1½ T. butter

Grease 1½ quart baking dish with most of the butter. Beat the egg right in the pan. Add 1/8 tsp. salt. Add milk to pan, a dash of pepper if desired. Blend. Spread 1 cup macaroni in pan, then ½ of the cheese over it. Repeat for second layer. (May be done in one layer for large pan) The milk mixture should barely cover the macaroni — only ends of the macaroni showing, please! If there isn't enough milk mixture, add a little. The cheese should be on top. Dot with remaining butter. Cook at 400° for 10 minutes, then lower oven to 350° . Cook 15-20 minutes more til knife stuck in center doesn't show liquid but cheese is bubbly, not brown. Do not cook til dry. It's delicious juicy.

Elizabeth Gaither (Mrs. J.W.)
Norman

"My mother got this recipe from her mother ... she just made it 'by eye'. It's a good meat substitute, but we always had it right along with fried chicken or roast."

PANNED POTATOES

Put a lump of butter, enough to fry, in a baking pan, pare and slice Irish potatoes as for frying, put in pan, sprinkle with salt and pepper, and cover with rich milk and cook in oven until potatoes are tender and milk is all absorbed.

Viola Gulick Krob
Aline

Pearl E. Pemberton, one of the few living '89ers, recalls that, "My father was out planting vegetables one Sunday morning, and a man went by and told him it was the Lord's day. My father said God hadn't found Oklahoma and He wouldn't know it was here until he raised some beans and Irish potatoes."

Anna Joseph's

POTATO LATKES

(Pancakes)

Six potatoes	1 heaping tsp. salt
1 **egg**, beaten	1 small onion, grated
½ cup bread crumbs	(optional)
or matzo meal	

Peel potatoes and grate them finely. Drain well and add egg, and bread **crumbs**, then salt and onion. Mix well. Drop by spoonfuls into hot fat, **flattening** slightly. Turn and brown. Serve hot with sour cream or with **applesauce**, as a accompaniment to pot roast. Variation:

POTATO KUGEL
(Pudding)

Add ½ tsp. baking powder and 3 T. melted butter to same mixture, put **in greased** baking dish, and bake in moderate oven.

Harriet Goldberg Carson (Mrs. Joel)
Oklahoma City

Latkes are traditionally served on the first night of Chanukah, usually for a family dinner. Mrs. Carson's grandfather, John Joseph, began his career in Indian Territory as a peddlar, and as his business thrived and his customers increased he opened a dry goods store in Wilburton around 1898.

POTATO CAKES (1900)

2 cups leftover mashed potatoes	2-4 T. flour
2 whole eggs beaten well	salt & pepper to taste

Add eggs to potatoes and beat by hand until light and fluffy. Add flour **gradually** until potato mixture stands in peaks. Drop by tablespoon and **fry until** golden brown. Serve hot.

Mrs. Fanchon S. Huddleson
Oklahoma City

This recipe was given to Mrs. Huddleson many years ago by an Indian neighbor in Hominy, Oklahoma.

96

VEGETABLE TIME TABLE

Potatoes, boiled, 30 minutes
Potatoes, baked, 45 minutes
Sweet Potatoes, boiled, 50 minutes
Sweet Potatoes, baked, 60 minutes
Squash, boiled, 25 minutes
Green peas, boiled, 20-40 minutes
Shelled Beans, boiled, 60 minutes
String Beans, boiled, 1-2 hours
Green Corn, 30-60 minutes
Asparagus, 15-30 minutes
Spinach, 1-2 hours

Tomatoes, Canned, 30 minutes
Cabbage, 45 minutes to 2 hours
Cauliflower, 1-2 hours
Dandelions, 2-3 hours
Green Beets, 1 hour
Onions, 1-2 hours
Beets, 1-2 hours
Turnips, white, 45-60 minutes
Turnips, yellow, 1-1½ hours
Parsnips, 1-2 hours
Carrots, 1-2 hours

Mrs. Earnest Taylor
Thomas

"This was taken from Great grandmother Greene's cookbook entitled 'To The Cupboard', published by the Society of Christian Church Workers, Barry, Illinois, 1896."

SALADS

Amanda's

HOT SLAW

Cabbage chopped fine; 1 egg, beat in a pint cup, add piece of butter the size of a walnut, 1 tablespoon flour, ½ cup cream, fill cup up with best cider vinegar.

Have iron skillet real hot, pour in and stir constantly till thick, then pour over cabbage which has been salted and sugared.

Dorothy Hensley Keys (Mrs. Mott)
Oklahoma City

TURNIP SLAW

Take raw turnips, peel and chop or grate as you would cabbage. Sprinkle with sugar and let stand a while, then cover with your favorite cabbage slaw dressing.

Dorothy Hensley Keys (Mrs. Mott)
Oklahoma City

Mrs. Keys' father, Travis Hensley, prominent in state journalism, was one of the founders of the Oklahoma Press Association, served in both houses of the Oklahoma State Legislature, and served as Mayor of El Reno.

Alice Gordon's

CUCUMBER SALAD

12 ripe cucumbers   6 green peppers
12 white onions

Cut cucumbers size of dice, chop onions and peppers fine. Sprinkle with cup of fine salt. Mix well together and hang up to drain 24 hours. Then add ¼ lb white mustard seed, 1 gill [½ cup] celery seed. Pack in jars and cover with vinegar. Make them airtight and they will be ready for use in 6 weeks.

Kathy Bearman (Mrs. Charles H.)
Oklahoma City

"Mary Ellen (Crawford) Bearman pioneered with her husband from Ohio to southwestern Kansas in the mid 1880's, before any land in the Indian Territories opened for settlement and brought this recipe with her."

R. D. Miller's

WILTED LETTUCE

Cook 2 slices of bacon in skillet til crisp. Remove bacon and add to hot grease, sugar and vinegar to taste. Pour over lettuce, toss and serve immediately. The bacon may be crumbled and added to the salad.

Dr. Jene Miller
Edmond

"My father, R. D. Miller, came to Hollis, Oklahoma, in 1909 and practiced law there for 50 years."

1870

COLE SLAW

1½ lb. chopped cabbage	1 cup whipping cream
1 tsp. salt	⅓ cup vinegar
⅔ cup sugar	

Mix well and let stand in ice box before serving.

Florence Baxter
Oklahoma City

This recipe from the Brookville Hotel in Brookville, Kansas, is over 100 years old.

Mrs. Soward's

DANDELION SALAD

In the Spring one takes to salads as a duck takes to water. Nature provides them in the early dandelion, in the sweet dock, and in the common parsley, though many people have not yet learned that even this pertinacious weed has its use.

In America, lettuce and celery are the bases of most salads, just as the crisp chicory, which does not thrive well in our climate, is in France. Spinach is perennial, and so is cabbage; and potatoes and onions are always at call.

There is a difference, however, between "greens," boiled and dressed, and the true salads. Try dandelions, for instance, and the difference you will soon discover.

Instead of boiling the dandelions, which must be young and fresh, you should pick the leaves over, carefully removing any withered stems of blighted sprigs; wash thoroughly in several waters, and place on newspapers to absorb all the moisture. Then chop pretty fine, place in a bowl, and turn over either German or French Dressing.

Anita Ellis (Mrs. Marvin)
Guthrie

This was taken from a newspaper clipping from The National Tribune, May 10, 1894, found in the cookbook of the late Mrs. Thomas E. Soward, Guthrie pioneer.

Mary Emily Hensley's

PIMIENTO SALAD

½ package gelatine (2
  envelopes Knox's gelatine)
½ cup sugar
½ cup cold water on
  gelatine
½ cup vinegar

1 cup boiling water
1 teaspoon salt
Juice of 1 lemon
2 cups celery (chopped)
3 pimientos (chopped)
1 cup pecans (chopped)

Dissolve gelatine in ½ cup of cold water. Add the 1 cup boiling water, sugar, vinegar, lemon juice and salt. Put in ice box until syrupy, then add the celery, pimientos and pecans.

Dorothy Hensley Keys (Mrs. Mott)
Oklahoma City

In 1934, Travis F. Hensley was elected to the Oklahoma Hall of Fame and in 1978, to the Journalism Hall of Fame. Among his publications were the El Reno Democrat (1892), Hensley's Magazine (1903), and the People's Press.

Ellen Gulick's

CHEESE SALAD

Three hard-boiled eggs, 1 cup grated cheese mixed with the egg. Add alternately butter and vinegar till the consistency of whipped cream. Salt and pepper to taste; serve on lettuce leaves.

Viola Gulick Krob
Aline

Mrs. H. Ebright's

POTATO SALAD WITH NUTS

Cook the potatoes til tender. When cold, cut in dice shape, and mix with them a finely chopped onion and 10 cents worth of English walnuts. Make a dressing as follows: the yolks of 2 eggs beaten thoroughly, 1 level tsp. salt, 1 tsp. of pepper, 2 of sugar, 2 of prepared mustard, 1 T. butter. Stir in the mixture 4 T. best vinegar. Put the dressing into a bowl set in hot water over the stove and stir til it thickens.

1900 Stroud Cookbook

Mr. Ebright was co-owner of the The Stroud Messenger, whose ad in the cookbook promoted "The Latest Styles Ladies Visiting Cards Kept in stock and Printed."

Grandmother Paralee's

POTATO SALAD

5 lbs. Irish potatoes
6 eggs (boiled and chopped)
4 T. vinegar
3 cups mayonnaise made
with lemon
1½ cups diced, fresh green
peppers

½ cup (4 oz.) pimiento
peppers
1 cup onions
Paprika — sweet, Hungarian

Cook the peeled, coarsely cut potatoes in boiling, salted water until tender — about 30 minutes. Drain and mash while hot, add the vinegar and mix well. When cooled, add the remaining ingredients except paprika and one egg and pepper garnish. Place in ice box for 24 hours or so. Stir and taste — more mayonnaise and vinegar and salt may be needed — if so, add. The salad should be full-bodied, stiffish — do not add too much mayonnaise. Place in serving bowl, dust paprika over the top and garnish.

Mary Lee Martin Ervin (Mrs. John W.)
Oklahoma City

"My mother cut one hard-boiled white into 4 sections, leaving the yolk whole and made a "flower" yolk for the center and the 4 white sections as petals with strips of green pepper for stem and leaves. This was part of the traditional picnic fare with fried chicken, deviled eggs, bread and butter sandwiches, iced tea and lemonade."

1901

CHICKEN SALAD

(For forty guests)

Four chickens, same quantity of celery. Salad Dressing: Twelve eggs, four tablespoons melted butter, four tablespoons pure olive oil, three tablespoons mustard, two teaspoons salt, one teacup vinegar, one pint cream. Beat yolks, add butter and oil slowly, then the mustard mixed smooth in a little hot water, then the beaten whites, then the vinger and salt. Put on stove and cook until thick as custard. One hour before serving mix chicken and celery, add cream to dressing and pour over the chicken.

Miss Salad and Her Trousseau (1901)

When the Daily Times Journal of March, 1900, wrote up the Black Cat Party given by "Mesdames George Gerson and B. B. Pollack", the menu consisted of chicken salad, lettuce, olives, potato chips, nut sandwiches, fruit frappe, assorted cakes and fruits.

BANANA AND ORANGE SALAD

Slice bananas and oranges, the orange very thin, in the proportion of one orange to three or four bananas. Arrange on lettuce leaves, add dressing.

SALAD DRESSING: Beat three eggs until very stiff, add one cup of sweet cream, one-half teaspoon of salt. Mix thoroughly. Add one-half a cup sharp vinegar, one-half tablespoonful of mustard, one-half a cup of melted butter, dessert spoonful of sugar. Beat again. Set the bowl in kettle of hot water until the dressing thickens. Mix the mustard in a little vinegar so as to avoid lumps.

Miss Salad and Her Trousseau (1901)

One of the Territories' earliest produce wholesalers was K. W. Dawson. From Reminiscences of the '89ers: "Oklahoma City's first carload of bananas was shipped here from Galveston in 1895. Bananas might as well have come from Mars. Nobody knew anything about them. The produce house had no place to keep them. They were green. No one knew how to ripen them. The bananas were put in the basement of the Herskowitz Building. Dawson and his partner got busy. They talked bananas to the merchants, people on the street, every place, but couldn't get rid of them. Dawson ate so many he has not cared for bananas since. Still they had bananas — and they had to be sold. A spieler was hired in a last desperate attempt. The spieler and the bananas were put in a stand at Main and Robinson. The spieler started yelling at everybody walking or riding: "All right, folks, step right up now and get your bananas. The big yellow delicacy of the tropics. Something new and different. Here's your chance, folks, at ten cents a bunch; try these lucious bananas." The thing caught on. Bananas went like wildfire. The whole town started eating bananas — and has been ever since."

Mrs. R. R. Carlin's

LOBSTER SALAD

One can of lobster, one cup cabbage chopped fine, one cup bread crumbs, four hard boiled eggs, chopped fine, two teaspoonsful prepared mustard, little salt, pepper and vinegar. Use pickles chopped fine if wanted.

Capital City Cookbook
Guthrie, O.T., 1898

As many '89er wives did, Mrs. Carlin waited until her husband had proved up his claim and there was some semblance of civilization in the new town before she joined him a month after the Run. R. R. Carlin was one of the very first Insurance and Real Estate men in Guthrie.

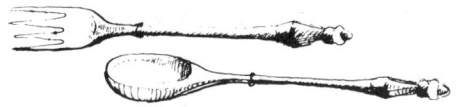

Mrs. O. D. Halsell's

OYSTER SALAD

Drain the liquor from a quart of fresh oysters; put them in hot vinegar enough to cover them and place over the fire. Let them remain until plump but not cooked, then drop them immediately in cold water. Drain. Mix with them two pickled cucumbers cut fine, also a quart of celery cut in small dice. Season with salt and pepper. Mix all well together, then pour over the whole a mayonnaise dressing. Garnish with celery tips and bits of pimiento.

Capital City Cookbook
Guthrie, O.T., 1898

The Guthrie Daily Leader, in operation since shortly after the Run of 1889, was the only Democratic Daily in the Territory prior to 1900. The Capital City Cookbook of 1898, was found recently in the '89er room of the Leader offices. It includes an interesting range of ingredients available at that early date ... with Guthrie's proximity to the center of the state, several railroads crossed here, facilitating shipments of fine foods, fresh fish, and produce.

Grandmother Braidwood's

WALDORF SALAD

1 cup diced apple	1 cup chopped celery
½ cup diced pears	1 cup chopped walnuts
½ cup diced bananas	Mayonnaise to moisten well

Pare and dice fresh apples, pears, and bananas; dip in lemon juice to prevent darkening. Toss with mayonnaise. Just before serving add chopped celery and walnuts, tossing again and adding more mayonnaise as needed. Serve on crisp lettuce leaf.

Robin Freeman Woods (Mrs. Pendleton)
Oklahoma City

"Grandmother added more or less of a salad ingredient depending on what she had. She also left out the bananas entirely if the salad was prepared very long ahead because they tend to darken. Often additional diced apples substituted for pears which were not always available. This was one of Grandmother Braidwood's favorites. She had attended cooking school as a young lady and knew all the 'chef's' secrets. Her cooking was truly cosmopolitan."

MAYONNAISE DRESSING

Have the oil, two yolks of eggs, and a bowl ice cold. Put the yolks in the bowl, stir two minutes, then add by degrees three-quarters cupful oil, a few drops at a time while stirring with a small wooden spoon; when the oil is half used up, add one teaspoonful salt, stir two minutes, then continue and use the remaining oil: when the sauce becomes too thick add a little vinegar, about one tablespoonful in all; add last half teaspoonful English mustard and half pint of whipped cream. The Mayonnaise may be used plain without the whipped cream.

<u>Miss Salad and Her Trousseau</u> (1901)

"To make a perfect salad there should be a spend-thrift for oil, a miser for vinegar, a wise man for salt, and a madcap to stir the ingredients up and mix them well together." — Spanish Proverb.

Mrs. O. D. Halsell's

SALAD DRESSING

Six tablespoons vinegar, two tablespoons butter, three tablespoons milk, one teaspoon salt, two teaspoons mustard, one teaspoon sugar, two eggs and a pinch black pepper. Heat vinegar and butter, beat eggs, mix mustard, salt, sugar and pepper to vinegar and butter. Then add eggs slowly cooking till a thick custard. (Make in double boiler.)

<u>Capital City Cookbook</u>
Guthrie, O.T., 1898

The Williamson-Halsell Frazer Company Wholesale Grocers, of Guthrie and Oklahoma City, imported teas and cigars and handled "a full line of fancy groceries such as Heinz's Fancy Pickles and Campbell's Jams and Preserves in Tins." "Houses" in both cities had Telephone No. 10.

CHEESE & EGGS

Butter Churn

Grandmother White's
EGG GRUEL

Beat the "yelk" of one egg with one tablespoonful of sugar; pour one teacupful of boiling water on it, add the white of an egg beaten to a froth, with any seasoning or spice desired. To be taken warm.

New Process Cookbook (1896)

Mrs. E. W. Patterson inherited this old book from her grandmother, whose husband was Superintendent of schools in Waurika many years ago. Like some other early printed sources this book called yolk "yelk".

Laura Ambrose Long's

SCRAMBLED EGGS AND DUMPLINGS

Cut up left-over dumplings into small pieces and put into hot skillet lightly greased with bacon grease. Beat up enough eggs in a bowl to have at least one per person and one extra for the pot. Pour the beaten eggs over the cut-up dumplings and scramble together. Serve for family supper.

DUMPLINGS:

¾ cup sifted flour	1 egg
2 tsp. baking powder	⅓ cup milk
½ tsp. salt	

Sift the flour, baking powder, and salt together. Beat the egg and add the milk. Then mix all together just until moist through. Drop the dumpling batter by spoonfuls in hot boiling water or stock. Cover tightly to hold in steam and boil gently for 15 minutes without opening the pot. The dumplings should be light and fluffy. Serve at once.

Laura Ambrose Long (Mrs. Raymond F.)
Oklahoma City

"Father Ambrose insisted on dumplings almost every day, and dumplings served in sauerkraut (cooked separately and then served in the sauerkraut) were his favorites. Then dumplings were also served with almost any vegetable and meat combination such as a stew."

105

Mrs. Edgar S. Vaught's

CHEESE SOUFFLE

Make white sauce composed of 1 T. Butter, 1 heaping T. Flour, and 1 cup milk. Cook until stiff and remove from fire. While still hot add 1 cup grated cheese. Separate 3 eggs. Beat yolks well and add to white sauce. Beat egg whites stiff and fold into white sauce. Pour into greased casserole and bake at 350° about 20 minutes. One cup of ground or cubed cooked ham may be added.

Ruth Vaught Thompson (Mrs. Wayman J.)
Oklahoma City

The Daisy butter churns in 1 quart, 2 quarts, or gallon size, simplified home butter-making with a screw-on lid supporting an iron handle and gears, which turned wooden paddles in the glass jar.

Addie Hensley's

COTTAGE CHEESE

1 quart or more sour milk. Put in a warm place and leave til the whey separates from the curd. Pour into a bag, hang and let it drain until all of the whey has dripped from it. Turn it out and mash with a fork until very fine, add a little milk or cream and salt to taste. I like a little black pepper sprinkled over the top. I use a 1 pound cotton sugar sack well washed, to make my cottage cheese in and I hang it on the clothes line.

Dorothy Hensley Keys (Mrs. Mott)
Oklahoma City

Claude Eugene Hensley was the son of pioneer editor and publisher, Travis Franklin Hensley, and together they published the "People's Press" in El Reno. In 1899, Claude Hensley published the first trade publication in Oklahoma, "The Oklahoma Grocer".

Mrs. S. P. Marks'

WELSH RAREBIT

Put a half ounce butter in a frying pan. When hot, gradually add 4 ounces of mild American cheese. Whisk it thoroughly until melted. Beat together a half pint of cream and 2 eggs, whisk into the cheese, add a little salt, and pour over thin slices of crisp toast, and serve.

1900 Stroud Cookbook

Notice that American cheese was available here in 1900.

SCRAMBLED EGGS WITH SWEETBREADS

4 eggs
½ tsp. salt
Pepper
2 T. butter

½ cup milk
1 sweetbread, parboiled
and cut in dice

Beat eggs slightly, using a silver fork, add salt, pepper, milk and sweetbreads. Cook same as scrambled eggs.

5 O'Clock Tea Club Cookbook
Oklahoma City

Judge R. M. Rainey was prominent in Oklahoma politics and was one of the participants in transferring the State Seal to Oklahoma City from Guthrie in 1910, three years after statehood.

Mother's

CHEESE PUDDING

Cut crusts from sliced bread, then each slice into four pieces. Dip each slice into melted butter (about 3 sticks for a large flat baking dish). Put a layer of bread, cover with thick layer of sharp grated cheese, then another layer of bread, then cheese. Beat 6 eggs, add 3 cups milk, salt, red pepper, Worcestershire sauce and pour over cheese. Bake ½ hour or longer, until firm.

Mary Baker Rumsey (Mrs. Joseph F.)
Oklahoma City

This recipe was brought from Texas when the Baker family moved to Oklahoma City in the teens. Mrs. Rumsey should be considered a modern pioneer because of her leadership in organizing and serving as the first president, in 1927, of the Junior League of Oklahoma City, an organization which has had much impact on the development of volunteerism in the community.

Helen Pettee Fugitt's

RICTUM-DITY

1 cup grated cheese	1 tsp. salt
1 can tomatoes	2 T. butter
1 green pepper chopped	2 eggs
½ onion grated	Dash red pepper

Mix tomatoes, cheese, onion and chopped pepper. Melt butter in chafing dish, add mixture, and when heated add eggs well beaten and seasonings. Cook until eggs are of creamy consistency, stirring all the time. Serve hot.

Junior League Cookbook
Oklahoma City, 1929

W. J. Pettee, Helen's father, brought enough merchandise with him to establish the first retail hardware store in Oklahoma City on the day of the Run, April 22, 1889. It operated for over 65 years in the same location. For many years "hardware" referred to a wide range of products including fine china, and Pettee's carried many items made exclusively for their store.

DEVILED EGGS

Boil eggs 30 minutes, drop in cold water, so as to shell easily. Cut in halves, take out yolks, mix with salt, pepper, pickles (cut in bits) and vinegar, not too soft. Fill whites. A little dry mustard adds flavor.

Billye Gaines
Holdenville

From the 1890 cookbook of Ann Byrd's grandmother Gose are tips for making hens lay in the winter: "Keep them warm; keep corn constantly by them, but do not feed it to them. Feed them with meat scraps when lard or tallow has been tried, or fresh meat. Some chop green peppers finely, or mix Cayenne pepper with corn meal to feed them. Let them have a frequent taste of green food, a little gravel and lime, or clamshells."

CAKES

Mineral Wells Park Pavilion, Guthrie

CHOCOLATE ROLL

6 T. sifted flour	4 egg yolks well beaten
½ tsp. baking powder	1 tsp. vanilla
¼ tsp. salt	2 ounces unsweetened chocolate,
¾ cup sifted sugar	melted & cooled
4 egg whites stiffly beaten	

Sift flour once, measure, add baking powder and salt and sift 3 times. Fold sugar into stiffly beaten egg whites, a small amount at a time. Add egg yolks and vanilla. Fold in flour gradually then beat in chocolate gently but thoroughly. Pour into pan 10x15 inches, lined with grease paper and bake in hot over 400° 13 minutes or til done. Quickly cut off crisp edges of cake. Turn from pan at once onto cloth covered with powered sugar. Remove paper. Spread 7 minute frosting over cake and roll carefully. Wrap in cloth til cool. Cover with chocolate coating made by adding 1 tsp. melted butter to 1 ounce unsweetened chocolate melted.

SOFT CHOCOLATE ICING:

4 ounces unsweetened choc.	1 Cup sugar
cut in pieces	2 T. butter
1¼ cups milk	1 tsp. vanilla
4 T. flour	

Add chocolate to milk in double boiler and heat ... when melted beat with egg beater til blended. Sift flour with sugar. Add a small amount of chocolate mixture, stirring til smooth. Return to double boiler and cook till thickened. Add butter & vanilla. Cool and spread on cake.

Pearl Ogden Pemberton (Mrs. George T.)
Oklahoma City

When Mrs. Pemberton, an 89er, married in 1904, she recalls that eggs were 5¢ a dozen. For many years the Pembertons were in the wholesale grocery business in Oklahoma City.

JAM CAKE

Cream 1½ cup sugar and ¾ cup butter. Add 1 cup (seedless & skinless) blackberry jam and 4 egg yolks. Add dry ingredients, alternately, 3 cup flour, 1 tsp. cinnamon, with 1 cup buttermilk and 1 tsp. soda, 1 cup pecans, chopped. Lastly add 4 beaten egg whites. Fold in carefully.

Bake 350° for 25-30 minutes in four oiled and floured pans (8" round).

Before layers cool, spoon the following over each layer stacking them as you go: 1½ cup sugar and 1½ cup milk. Cook until it begins to thicken and take from heat and add 1 well beaten whole egg. After the 4 layer cake completely cools, this may be iced, but it is not necessary.

Laura Rennie Hamilton (Mrs. William A.)
Anadarko

"This Jam Cake is always served at the Christmas dinners of the descendants of Mr. & Mrs. Albert Rennie, Sr. ... this has been a tradition as long as I can remember. The cake can be made long before Christmas day and kept in a cool place. This cake travels well."

Laura Matthews was born at Buffalo, Missouri, July 27, 1873 and moved to Muskogee, Indian Territory at the age of 16 ... served as an apprentice teacher. Her father, A. D. Matthews, an attorney, helped organize the first U.S. Court at Muskogee, under Judge Shackleford ... when a Federal Court was established in Ardmore, her father was appointed as Judge of the U.S. Court, and she served as Deputy Court Clerk.

BLACKBERRY CAKE

1 cupful of brown sugar	1 tsp. cinnamon
1½ cupful of flour	1 tsp. allspice
¾ cup butter	1 tsp. nutmeg
3 eggs	1 cupful blackberry jam
1 tsp. sugar	1 level tsp. soda

Cream butter, brown sugar. Add eggs, then remaining dry ingredients and jam. Bake in layers.

Mrs. Herbert D. Coulter
Meno

Many recipes for Blackberry Cake or Jam Cake have been handed down with a number of variations. Notice that this one calls for brown sugar and no nuts. Some called for raisins and nuts. This recipe was in Ellen Staton's cookbook pre-dating 1870.

Grandmother Villines'

JELLY ROLL

Take one cupful of white sugar, ½ teacupful of sweet milk, two eggs, one cupful of flour, two teaspoonfuls of cream of tartar, ¼ tsp. saleratus (soda), and such flavoring as you like, a pinch of salt. This will make two cakes in a square tin. Have the oven ready, put the cakes in and while they are baking, get a cloth and the jelly ready on the table. As soon as they are baked, take them out and turn them one at a time on the cloth, spread quickly with jelly or marmalade and roll up tightly in the cloth and lay them where they will cool. Handle them carefully or they might fall. Cut with a sharp knife in slices.

Christine McKown Boren (Mrs. Lyle H.)
Oklahoma City

The jelly used in the jelly roll was usually home-made from plums off their own trees. The Thomas F. Villines family settled in Maud, Oklahoma in 1909. They had six girls and one son and ran a large general mercantile store there for 40 years. Alice Villines McKown, the third daughter, was Mrs. Boren's mother and grandmother of David L. Boren, Governor of the State of Oklahoma.

Ada Goodwin Doty's

BLUE RIBBON GINGERBREAD

1 cup molasses
½ cup sugar
½ cup shortening
1 cup boiling water
2 tsp. soda
2 eggs
2 cups flour

¼ tsp. salt
½ tsp. cloves
½ tsp. allspice
½ tsp. cinnamon
½ tsp. nutmeg
½ tsp. ginger

Cream shortening. Add sugar with spices and salt. Add molasses and blend well. Dissolve soda in boiling water and add to sugar mixture. Add the flour and blend. Add last the two well beaten eggs. The batter will be thin like waffle batter. Bake in 350° oven.

Mrs. Naomi Doty Matheny
Oklahoma City

Ada Bell Goodwin came from Missouri with her family about the turn of the century, met Olin Doty in Fort Cobb, and they married in 1903. She often entered baked goods in early day State Fairs, and her gingerbread won blue ribbons three times early in the 1900's. The family still enjoys it and pride themselves that it was a three-time winner.

Great-Great Grandmother Burgess'
COLONIAL GINGERBREAD

½ cup 'shorting'
2 T. grated orange rind
(1 orange)
½ cup brown sugar
(packed tightly)
3 eggs
2¾ cups flour
1 tsp. soda
½ tsp. salt

2 tsp. ginger
1 tsp. cinnamon
1 tsp. mace
1 tsp. nutmeg
1 cup molasses or sorghum
½ cup strained orange
(or juice of 1 orange)
¼ cup brandy, flavoring
fruit juice or coffee.

Cream 'shorting' and orange rind together; add brown sugar and cream thoroughly. Blend in well-beaten eggs. Beat rapidly until batter becomes smooth. Sift the flour before measuring; then sift flour, soda, salt, and spices together and add to the creamed mixture alternately with molasses, juice and flavoring. Pour into a well greased floured oblong pan. Bake at moderate oven 350° for 30 to 35 minutes. Served topped with whipped cream.

Una Lee Voigt
Yukon

"Sarah 'Sally' Roberts Burgess, born in Virginia in 1787, pioneered to Kentucky, where her husband had a sorghum mill, thence to Kansas in 1855. Many of the family 'receipes' from Virginia were brought with her and handed down to succeeding generations.
This 'receipe' is just as written by my grandmother, Nancy Ann Burgess, born 1855, who gave it to my Aunt Zena Dail Brown in Piper, Kansas ... Aunt Z gave it to me on my wedding day Aug. 26, 1922."

My Mother's
GINGERBREAD

1 cup molasses
1 cup sugar
1 cup shortening
1 cup sour milk
Flour to make a good batter

2 eggs
2 tsp. soda
2 tsp. ginger
1 tsp. cinnamon

Bake and test with toothpick; if it comes out clean and shrinks from side of pan, gingerbread is done.

Effie Bacher
Kildare

"Mother was born in 1861. She was a wonderful cook as well as a precious mother. I'm now an elderly lady ... I'll be 87 years young, February 28th (1978). I've used this 'receipt' so much ... had seven children and we loved gingerbread."

HOT WATER GINGERBREAD

1 cup sugar
1 cup molasses
½ cup shortening
1 tsp. ginger
1 cup boiling water

1 egg
1 tsp. salt
3 cups flour
1 tsp. soda

Mix well all ingredients except soda and water. Dissolve soda in water and pour over other mixture. Bake in moderate oven about 30 minutes.

Nina Rudd
Hennessey

Mrs. Rudd's father, James A. Shackelford, made the Run into the Unassigned Lands on April 22, 1889 and was the first to build a log cabin with a wooden floor, an accomplishment of which he was justly proud ... it was in this cabin Mrs. Rudd was born 8 months after the Run, December 12, 1889. The Shackleford claim was located in 31-17-5 in Kingfisher County, and the land still belongs to the family.

Mrs. Pemberton's

SPICE CAKE

⅔ Cup butter
1¼ Cups sugar
3 eggs
⅓ cup molasses
½ tsp. soda
2½ tsp. baking powder

2½ cups cake flour
1 tsp. cinnamon
¼ tsp. cloves
⅔ cup milk
½ tsp. salt
½ cup milk

Cream butter and sugar til light. Add eggs and molasses. Sift dry ingredients together and add alternately with ⅔ cup milk. After mixing, add additional ½ cup milk. Bake in two layers in medium oven.

Pearl Ogden Pemberton (Mrs. George T.)
Oklahoma City

During those first few months following the April 22nd settlement of "Oklahoma Station", Mrs. Pemberton was too young to remember how stores and businesses sprung up in tents and crude buildings, but records show that in 8 months, 10 bakeries, 34 groceries, 15 meat markets, and 37 restaurants had opened ... restaurants were a necessity because many men had come without their wives and families in order to stake claims and establish farms or businesses before sending for loved ones.

Grandmother Bruns'

INEXPENSIVE CAKE

One cup of black molasses, one-half cup of brown sugar, one-half cup of butter, one cup of hot water, one dessert-spoon (tsp.) soda, 2 cups of flour, one dessert spoon of spices, using ginger or not, to your taste. This may be used for pudding, or by adding fruit makes a nice fruit cake. Bake in a quick oven.

Mary Mitchell Miles (Mrs. W. Howard)
Oklahoma City

Elzada Emeline Bruns came to Indian Territory as a young woman in 1880, from Illinois ... she died in 1953 at 98 years of age.

Quail

MARBLE CAKE

Use basic 1-2-3-4 cake:
1 cup butter
2 cups sugar
3 cups flour

4 eggs
3 tsp. baking powder
1 cup milk
1 tsp. vanilla

Cream butter and sugar. Add eggs. Sift dry ingredients and add alternately with milk, mixing lightly. Add vanilla flavor. Remove ⅓ of batter. To it, add mixture of:

3 T. sifted cocoa
1 tsp. allspice
2 tsp. cinnamon

1 tsp. nutmeg
pinch each of cloves & mace

Into well greased tube pan place half the white mixture, then the dark and finally the white. Swirl gently with knife. Bake slowly in medium oven approximately 1 hour.

Dorothy G. Kennedy (Mrs. E. Lee)
Oklahoma City

Every pioneer woman carried the 1-2-3-4 recipe in her head because of the simple pattern of ingredients. Marble Cake held high favor with former generations for Thanksgivings, and was very successful with this cake as the basis.

Ida Elizabeth Olbert Hanan's

POTATO CAKE

2 cups sugar	2 tsp. baking powder
½ cup cocoa	pinch of salt
¾ cup shortening	1 cup mashed potatoes
4 eggs	1 cup nuts (walnuts or pecans)
2 cups flour	

Cream shortening and sugar with cocoa. Add eggs, then dry ingredients with mashed potatoes. Bake 45 minutes at 350° in 10x13 cake pan. Frost with brown sugar frosting and top with walnuts.

Daleen Hanan (Mrs. Rob)
Edmond

This was the traditional holiday cake for many families. Mrs. Hanan always made a small "test cake" so she could tell if more liquid should be added. Her father-in-law, Oscar P. Hanan, made the Run and staked a claim 15 miles north of Enid near Hillsdale ... still in the family. When the Hanans came to the U.S. from Ireland they dropped the "O" which had previously made their name O'Hanan.

Mother's

POTATO CAKE

1 Cup mashed potatoes (hot)	2 tsp. Baking powder
½ Cup grated chocolate	4 eggs separated
1 Cup pecans	1 tsp. cinnamon
2 Cups sugar	1 tsp. cloves
½ cup shortening	1 tsp. nutmeg
½ Cup milk	1 tsp. vanilla
2 Cups flour	

Mix first three ingredients. In separate bowl mix batter, add potato mixture. Last add beaten egg whites. Bake in tube pan 350° for 1 hour.

Mary Evelyn Hogue (Mrs. Marvin Snell)
Kingston, Tennessee

There are many variations of Potato Cake, and this old recipe handed down from Carrie Lovell Reeves to her daughter uses spices. Mrs. Reeves made this cake often after her marriage at Pauls Valley in 1905.

CLABBER CAKE

½ pound butter
2 cups sugar, cream with
the butter.
2 eggs beaten, add to the above
2 cups clabber, add to the above
and stir well.

3½ cups cake flour
⅔ T. soda
3/8 tsp. cocoa

Mix and put into a buttered and floured cake pan. Bake in 350 degree oven.

Dorothy Hensley Keys (Mrs. Mott)
Oklahoma City

Ann Bush Wheeler and her husband, William Nelson Wheeler, brought their family to Canadian County in 1889. They established a cattle ranch in Okfuskee County, from which cattle was driven to Wichita and Sapulpa for the eastern markets.

Aunt Annie Sturgeon's

MAHOGANY CAKE

1½ cups sugar
⅔ cup butter
1½ cups milk
1 tsp. vanilla
2 scant cups flour

⅔ cups sugar
½ cup cocoa
1 tsp. soda
3 eggs

Cream 1½ cup sugar and butter, add well beaten eggs. Take one-half the milk, add to the cocoa and ⅔ cup sugar, cook until consistency of custard. Cool and add to the butter, sugar, and eggs. Then add the other half of milk with a tsp. of soda dissolved in it, and lastly add the flour and vanilla, and beat. Bake 350° for 35 minutes in layers.

Mrs. L. W. Clark
El Reno

"This recipe was taken out of one of my dear, old, Aunt Annie Sturgeon's (Mrs. Johnie) cookbooks ... it won 67 first prizes at the 1903 World's Fair. Aunt Annie made the Run to Oklahoma and settled on a farm east of Kingfisher. This cake was a family favorite."

Two Tookahs'

CHOCOLATE CAKE

1 cup butter
1½ cups granulated sugar
2 eggs
2 cups sifted cake flour
1 cup buttermilk

1 tsp. soda
2 T. vinegar
4 T. cocoa or 2 sq.
   melted chocolate
2 tsp. vanilla

Cream butter and sugar together. Add one egg at a time. Beat well. If cocoa is used sift it in with flour and add alternately a little at a time with buttermilk. If melted chocolate is used, add cool mixed with vanilla. Dissolve soda in vinegar and add last while still foaming. Pour into two square, greased and lined in bottom with waxed paper cake pans. Test after 40 minutes. Bake up to 1 hour in 350° oven. Test with broom straw directly in the middle until it comes out perfectly dry. Let both pans cool for 20-30 minutes before inverting pans on cake rack and attempting to remove cakes. Ice with following chocolate icing and this cake ripens as does a pound cake, but keep covered tightly at all times.

SPECIAL ICING:

2½ cups powdered sugar
2 level T. cocoa
3 T. butter

3 T. half & half
   (original calls for "thick" cream)
1½ tsp. vanilla

Cream butter in bowl; add the sugar and cocoa mixture which has been sifted together along with cream that has had the vanilla added to it. Beat well and ice double layer cake immediately.

Manon Turner Bagg Atkins (Mrs. Robert L.)
Oklahoma City

Tookah Butler, born 1862, third child of Edward Butler (Ga-na-che-ti) full blood Cherokee-Creek, and Scotch-Irish wife Elizabeth Belle Reeder Butler, was given her Indian name of Tookah, meaning "bright eyes", and "clear sight and far vision" by her young soldier father while on Civil War army leave, seeing her for the first time. Her childhood was spent in historic North Fork Town, Creek Nation where her father's store and their home were both located on the famed Texas Road, which brought great activity here. Now most of this historic area is under Lake Eufaula. On Sept. 6, 1883, Tookah Butler and Clarence William Turner married and established a home in Muskogee where numerous outstanding Oklahomans were entertained such as Charles N. Haskell, 1st Governor of Oklahoma and William H. Murray. Tookah's 1st daughter, born 1885, was named Tookah Jr. .... this recipe was named for both Tookah Butler Turner and Tookah Turner Bagg.

Mrs. Clarence Mills'

BROWN STONE FRONT CAKE

¾ cup butter or Crisco
5 eggs
2½ cups sugar
1 cup buttermilk

1 tsp. soda
1 tsp. vanilla
¾ cup cocoa
2 cups flour, sifted

Beat eggs together with sugar and butter. Put soda into milk and stir and add cocoa. Beat together. Add this to other mixture and then add flour. Bake. Ice with Caramel Frosting.

Junior League Cookbook
Oklahoma City, 1929

Cake walks were popular features at charity circuses at the time of statehood, as well as dances and "box parties" (box suppers).

Great-Grandmother Overholser's

DEVIL'S FOOD CAKE

½ pound butter
2 cups sugar
2 whole eggs
1 level tsp. soda
1 tsp. vanilla

½ cup buttermilk
2 cups flour
4 squares bitter chocolate
1 cup boiling water

Cream butter, sugar, and eggs. Mix soda with buttermilk. Mix alternately with flour. Add chocolate melted in water, then vanilla. Bake at 350° for 30 minutes.

Sue Overholser Hagan (Mrs. Jerry)
Oklahoma City

"This is the moistest Devil's Food I've ever eaten and extremely rich in taste ... usually only ½ a recipe was made in a single layer and iced with chocolate. My great-grandfather, Levi Overholser, came shortly after the Run to Oklahoma City, where his brother Henry Overholser had established himself as a developer and entrepeneur."

Aunt Ellon Staton's

DEVIL'S FOOD CAKE

½ custard cup of sweet milk
⅔ cup of white sugar
"yelk" of 1 egg
½ cup of grated chocolate
Boil this till thick
1 cup of sugar

½ cup of butter
½ cup of sweet milk
2 eggs beaten separately
2 cups of flour
1 tsp. of soda

Mrs. Herbert D. Coulter
Meno

Aunt Ellon died in Kansas in 1870, and her cookbook of treasured recipes was brought to Oklahoma prior to statehood. This recipe, hand-written in the book, gives no specific instructions for mixing. This was very common in old books as it was assumed that everyone knew how to mix a cake properly. Yolk was sometimes called "yelk."

Martin DeBois'

MARSHMALLOW CAKE

Whites of eight eggs, two and one-half cups sugar, one cup butter, one cup sweet milk, two teaspoons of Royal baking powder, four cups of flour or enough to make a stiff dough. Mix well and add eggs last.

ICING

Two cups sugar to boil and as it boils add three five cent boxes of marshmallows, have the whites of three eggs beaten stiff and when the marshmallows have dissolved beat it to the whites of the eggs.

Capital City Cookbook
Guthrie, O.T., 1898

When Guthrie families of 1898 took picnics to Mineral Wells Park, Mama took a favorite cake to top off the meal. Large groups would gather in the arched, white-washed wood pavilion, which stands as a reminder of quieter times, and is still popular for reunions ... here throngs came to celebrate Statehood Day on November 16, 1907.

120

MINNEHAHA CAKE

One and a half cups granulated sugar, half cup butter stirred to a cream, whites of six eggs, or three whole eggs, two teaspoons cream of tartar stirred in two heaping cups of sifted flour, one teaspoon soda in half cup of sweet milk; bake in three layers. For filling, take a tea cup sugar and a little water boiled together until it is brittle, 242° , when dropped in cold water; remove from stove and stir quickly into a well beaten white of an egg; add a cup of stoned raisins chopped fine, or a cup of chopped hickory nuts and place between layers and over the top. A universal favorite.

Mrs. R. W. Treeman
Perry

"My grandmother, Mrs. E. W. Herrick, put all that good raisin-filled frosting between the layers and frosted the top and sides with plain white boiled frosting — beautiful and delicious. This recipe is in her cookbook on a much-used looking page and is said to be over 150 years old. She charmed all of us children with this cake. My parents brought me to Perry (part of the Cherokee Strip) in 1893 when I was a baby and where I have lived ever since."

POUND CAKE

½ lb. real butter, beaten fluffy
5 large eggs added to butter one at a time — Beat real good
1¾ cup sugar, added to eggs 1 T. at a time
2 cups sifted flour
1 tsp. vanilla or rum flavoring

Grease and flour tube cake pan. Bake 55 or 60 minutes in a 325° oven. Let cool in pan.

Faye Miller (Mrs. Alvin)
Norman

Having made the Run of '89, August Miller saved his money until he could afford to open his own shoe shop in 1892, said to be the first in Norman. His son, Alvin, worked in the Pioneer Shoe Shop from the time he was a boy until his retirement in 1977.

BURNT SUGAR CAKE

1½ cups sugar	2 T. caramelized sugar
½ cup butter	2½ cups flour
2 eggs	2 tsp. baking powder
1 cup water or milk	1 tsp. vanilla

Cream butter and add sugar gradually. Add yolks and cream. Put burnt sugar in 2 T. boiling water, add vanilla. Add 2 cups flour and milk alternately, beating thoroughly. Sift baking powder with ½ cup flour. Beat egg whites stiff and fold into mixture with flour and baking powder. Combine all. Bake 1 hour.

Light caramelized sugar: put sugar in a smooth granite sauce pan (or heavy skillet). Place over hot part of range and stir constantly until melted and color of maple sugar. Care must be taken to prevent sugar from adhering to side of pan or spoon. Continue until syrup is quite brown and a whitish smoke appears.

Betty Daugherty Newell (Mrs. Jack)
San Diego, California

MATZOS CAKE

5 egg yolks	½ wineglass Liquor
1 cup sugar	1 tsp. cinnamon
½ cup matzos meal	½ cup nut meats
1 tsp. baking powder	½ tsp. cloves
5 egg whites beaten stiff	½ tsp. allspice

Beat together egg yolks and sugar. Sift meal 12 times. Add remaining ingredients. Bake slowly. They had no thermostats then so they inserted straws into the center, and when the straw came out clean, the cake was done.

Eleanor Jacobson
Oklahoma City

"*This cake was usually baked for Passover. Today we use potato flour, so there is no need to sift 12 times. My Aunt, Mrs. Hasgall, came to Oklahoma City in the early days from Chicago. Her husband, Sol, was a well known insurance salesman here.*"

Mrs. Sturgeon's

WHITE CAKE

1½ cups sugar	½ cup butter
2½ cups flour	4 egg whites unbeaten
3 tsp. baking powder	½ tsp. salt
1 cup cool water	½ tsp. lemon or vanilla extract

Cream butter and sugar. Sift flour once and measure. Add alternately until you have used half of the water and flour. Beat batter 3 minutes, put baking powder and salt in the remainder of flour and add water alternately, then add extract, add stiffly beaten egg whites last. Bake in three layers 30 minutes at 350° .

Mrs. L. W. Clark
El Reno

This cake won 32 First Prizes, including the World's Fair of 1903. In an 1898 Territorial cookbook was this ad: "SOUDERS 10 cent Lemon and 15 cent Vanilla Extracts are guaranteed fully equal to many other brands at double the price."

Anna's

WHITE CAKE

¾ Cup butter	3 Cup flour
1 and ¾ Cup sugar	4 tsp. baking powder
1 Cup ice water	8 egg whites
1 tsp. lemon flavoring	

Cream butter and sugar. Sift four 5 times before measuring. Mix baking powder with flour. Add a small amount of water and then flour alternately to butter mixture, until you get all flour and water used, then add lemon flavoring. Last fold in beaten egg whites. Use 3 9-inch cake pans and cook in hot oven 375° for 25 minutes.

ANNA'S WHITE ICING:

2 C. sugar
1 C. water
1 tsp. vinegar

Stir til dissolved and cook to soft boil; use half of this and pour on 3 egg whites beaten stiff with ¼ tsp. cream of tartar. Return syrup to stove and cook til hard boil and add to mixture. Continue beating egg white mixture on first step and second step. Add 3 T. sifted powered sugar and 1 tsp. vanilla. Top with cocoanut if desired.

Mary Lelia Kidd Holmes (Mrs. W. M.)
Norman

This cake was always served for Sunday dinner by Anna, the family cook for many years. The E. B. Johnson family, Mrs. Holmes' grandparents, were early pioneers.

Papa's

ANGEL FOOD CAKE

(White Sponge)

Whites of 9 large or 10 small eggs	1 T. lemon juice
1 cup sifted, granulated sugar	1 tsp. vanilla extract
1 cup sifted flour	A pinch of salt

Have everything in readiness, materials, pan, and oven. Add salt to the whites of the eggs and beat with the wire spoon egg beater until light and frothy, then continuing the beating, introduce the lemon juice. Beat until the whites will stand right up stiff enough to be cut, then dipping down at the side and coming up through the center of the mass with the wire beater, gradually fold in the sugar, the flavoring, and lastly the flour. As soon as there is no dry flour visible, even though there may be a lumpy appearance, pour into the cake pan and place in an oven which will not brown within 20 or 30 minutes. Bake for nearly or quite 50 minutes or until light brown all over, then remove from the oven and allow the cake to cool in the inverted tin. When cold cut out and place in a closed receptacle.

Edna M. Couch
Norman

"My father, Eugene Couch, learned to make this cake when he attended cooking school prior to 1900 and taught it to Mother. It was his favorite cake, and I was so pleased when I learned to make it as a girl, and he said it was just as good as Mama's. We called it angel food cake, and it was served at many of the family reunions which began at the family homestead in 1907 (with Great-grandmother Couch in attendance at 79 years of age)."

Annie Wilkerson Canton's

WHITE CAKE

1½ cups sugar	3 level tsp. of baking powder
½ cup of butter	1 tsp. vanilla
3 cups flour	1 cup milk or water
4 eggs (whites only)	

Sift flour with baking powder 2 or 3 times before measuring. Cream butter and sugar together, gradually add milk or water. Slowly add flour, and vanilla and fold in beaten egg whites. Pour in a greased cake pan.
LEMON FILLING:
⅔ cup sugar
1 egg
lump of butter the size of a walnut
1 lemon, grate rind and take juice
Mix all together and boil slowly over water, stirring constantly until thick.

Dorothy Hensley Keys (Mrs. Mott)
Oklahoma City

Frank M. Canton was a Deputy US Marshall in Pawnee, Oklahoma in 1894 and in 1907 he was appointed Adjutant General by Governor Haskell. Mrs. Canton worked for many years at the Oklahoma State Historical Society.

The Widow Jupe's

BLITZKUCHEN

1 cup sugar	1½ cups flour
⅓ cup butter	2 eggs
½ cup milk	2 T. baking powder

Cream butter, add sugar, and unbeaten eggs. Beat well. Sift flour and baking powder together and add alternately with milk. Put in greased cake tin and top with the following: 2 T. sugar mixed with ¼ tsp. cinnamon — sprinkle over batter and add ¾ cup coarsely chopped unblanched almonds. Bake 30 minutes at 350° .

Judy Mideke Samter (Mrs. Pat)
Oklahoma City

Before statehood "the Widow Jupe" (Kate Schmitz Jupe) and five children left Dalhart, Texas, to join other members of the family in Oklahoma City. Young Willie, the eldest son, delivered groceries on his bicycle for a tiny grocery at 3rd. and Harvey. Later he was hired by the Crescent Grocery and Meat Market to deliver for them in a "sharp" two-horse wagon with umbrella.

SCRIPTURE CAKE

½ cup butter	Judges 5:25
2 cups sugar	Jeremiah 6:20
2 cups flour	I Kings 4:22
2½ T. baking powder	
6 egg whites	Isaiah 10:14
½ tsp. almond extract	Genesis 43:11
Milk to make stiff batter	Hebrews 5:12

Lastly, follow King Solomon's advice for making good boys, and you will have a good cake. — Proverbs 23:14

FILLING:

3 egg whites	Job 6:6
1 large cup sugar	Jeremiah 6:20
Water to cover sugar	Genesis 24:17

Boil until it threads, pour slowly over the beaten whites, and add a large cup of hickory nut meats. — Genesis 43:11.

Veta C. Minderman
Oklahoma City

An 89er recalled that, "the church was a social center. The Ladies' Aid was organized almost as soon as the church. The socials were attended by everybody gladly, for the men enjoyed the home-cooked food; and the women seemed to be doing the things they had been doing back in the states.

Every time a new building was finished, or rather had a floor and walls, the women gave a church social in it, and sold cake and ice cream for 15 cents."

The Mitchell Family

GUMDROP CAKE

1 pound of gumdrops (big ones are better) cut into pieces. (Don't chop or grind. Omit black ones for lighter cake).	½ tsp. cloves ½ pound white raisins (dark will do)
½ cup sugar	½ tsp. soda dissolved
½ cup butter	in 1 T. hot water
1 egg	½ tsp. salt
¾ cup sweetened applesauce	1 tsp. baking powder
½ tsp. cinnamon	2 cups flour

Cream butter, add sugar and mix. Add 1 cup flour, seasoning, egg, soda. Sift 1 cup flour over fruit and gumdrops. Add to cream mixture. Bake 1 hour at 350° . When cake is done, turn out of pan and cover while hot with favorite preserves.

Wanda Mitchell
Collinsville

This gumdrop cake recipe has been handed down through the Bill Mitchell family for many years. The exact origin is not known. It is made by the present family members each Christmas as it is colorful and is used on other festive occasions.

Mrs. Lena B. Williams'

BANANA NUT CAKE

Cream together
  1½ cups sugar
  2 eggs
Add
  4 T. Buttermilk
  3 mashed bananas
  1 tsp. vanilla

Stir in
  ½ cup butter
  2 cups flour
  1 tsp. soda
  ½ cup Pecans

Cook 325° (till done)

1. ICING:
3 eggs well beaten
½ can evaporated milk
½ cup nuts

1½ cups sugar
1½ cups cocoanut
1 tsp. vanilla

Cook until medium thick. May add 1 cup of pineapple in place of cocoanut. Add 2 mashed bananas as soon as removed from the fire. Stir well.

2. PLAIN ICING:
2 cup sugar
1 cup milk

(Flavoring butter)

Mrs. Fanny Toon
Oklahoma City

"This cake is a very good keeper especially when the No. 1 icing is used. If made 2 or 3 days ahead of time it will mellow. My mother baked this cake the year round but we especially remember it during Thanksgiving and Christmas Holidays. The cake was usually tucked in the bottom of the safe (or cabinet) until dinner was ready — but we always knew it was there! Mother was born in Indian Territory and would be 89 years old if she were still living."

FRESH APPLE CAKE

2 cups white sugar
1¼ cups cooking oil
2 large eggs
1 tsp. salt
1 tsp. vanilla

2½ cups flour
1 tsp. soda
3 cups chopped fresh apples
   (Rome or Jonathan)
1 cup nuts

Mix oil, sugar, salt, vanilla and eggs. Beat 2 minutes. Add flour and soda (will be *very* stiff and firm batter). Add nuts and apples. (Batter will immediately become less firm.) Pour into greased, floured tube pan. Bake 325° oven for 60-70 minutes.

Duane R. Weinert
Oklahoma City

In 1893, the Broadway Fruit House of Oklahoma City advertised that they were "dealer in all kinds foreign and domestic fruits green, dried, and canned, also nuts, vegetables, butter, eggs, and feed of all kinds. Have always on hand fresh popcorn and peanuts, figs, dates, candies, tobacco, and cigars. 17 Broadway."

Sarah S. Goldberg's

APPLESAUCE CAKE

One big kitchen spoon shortening
   (½ cup)
One cup sugar-heaping
2 eggs, well beaten
pinch salt
1½ cups applesauce, sweetened
1 cup raisins (pour boiling water
   over and drain)

2 cups flour
1 tsp. soda
½ or 1 cup nuts
½ tsp. cloves
1 tsp. nutmeg
1 tsp. cinnamon

Cream shortening and sugar well. Add eggs. Sift flour, salt, cloves, nutmeg, cinnamon three times. In a large bowl stir the applesauce and soda. Sauce will turn black and foam up. Stir real well. Now alternately add flour and sauce to creamed mixture. Stir well. Add nuts and raisins. Bake in a 350° oven for at least 1 hour.

Mrs. Sam Goldberg
Wilburton

"My mother-in-law, Mrs. Mike Goldberg, always made this for family gatherings and signalled a party. This never-fail recipe has been handed down to three generations and if followed makes a delicious, moist cake that keeps indefinitely."

Malvina Melrose Lytle's

APPLESAUCE CAKE

3 cups sugar
½ cups pure butter
3 large eggs
5¼ cups sifted flour
3 cups seasoned hot
  applesauce (made from
  fresh apples, sweetened
  with sugar and flavored
  with cinnamon)

1½ cups seedless raisins
1½ cups pecans (or walnuts)
3 tsp. soda
About ¼ tsp. salt
2¼ tsp. ground cloves
3 tsp. cinnamon

Cream butter and sugar together until fluffy. Add eggs one at a time and continue to beat. Reserve about 2 tablespoons of flour and dredge nuts and raisins with this. Then sift remaining dry ingredients together. Alternate flour mixture and hot applesauce, adding flour first and last. Add nuts and raisins dredged in flour. Bake for about 50 minutes in a moderately warm oven 350° until the cake rises and is firm to the touch.

It doesn't need an icing, but it may be iced if you prefer. Serve it like a fruit cake. If protected, it will keep for weeks."

Marianne Harris (Mrs. Roy C.)
Oklahoma City

"This recipe has been in the Lytle family for over 100 years. Grandmother Lytle brought it with her on the covered wagon when they made the Run, coming from Tawanda, Kansas. Grandmother used to keep the cakes for weeks in her piesafe ... she always made it from fresh applesauce, preferred winesap apples, sweetened and flavored with cinnamon. She used mostly ingredients that came from her own farm; the apples, of course, came from their own orchards ... the pecans from their trees."

"Mrs. Fort Cobb's"

QUICK CARAMEL ICING

2 cups brown sugar
6 T. cream
4 T. butter
1 cup powdered sugar (approximate)

1 tsp. vanilla
Few drops almond
  extract

Stir over low heat until sugar is dissolved. As soon as it starts to boil, remove from heat and stir in powdered sugar (enough to thicken). Add vanilla and almond and beat until smooth. Spread on cake and stack layers.

Eva Doty
Oklahoma City

This icing was always used on Applesauce Cake by Ethel Doty Davidson, Eva's sister, who filed her own claim at Fort Cobb in 1902. During her long and active life there, she became affectionately known as "Mrs. Fort Cobb" until her death in 1975 at the age of 96.

Emily Hancock Dobbs'

RAISIN CAKE

1 Cup raisins	½ tsp. salt
2 Cups water	¼ tsp. nutmeg, allspice
Boil together til 1 cup	& cinnamon (each)
juice is left	2 Cups flour
Drain off juice, keep, and	2 T. shortening
let stand til cool	1 tsp. soda

Sift dry ingredients, add raisin juice, and mix thoroughly. Add raisins and bake in greased 10" inch iron skillet for 45 minutes at 350° .

Mrs. Ova S. Hull
Oklahoma City

Cake skillets were never washed with soap. In fact they were usually just wiped clean, but if washing was necessary, only hot water was used and the skillet was allowed to dry in the oven. Originally, Mrs. Hull's grandmother made this "everyday" cake in a Dutch oven in a wood stove of her log cabin.

EGGLESS, MILKLESS,

BUTTERLESS, RAISIN CAKE

Boil together for three minutes:	When cold add a pinch of salt
1 cup water	1 tsp. soda dissolved in a
1 cup brown sugar	little warm water
⅓ cup lard	2 cups flour sifted
2 cups of seeded raisins	½ tsp. baking powder
1 tsp. cinnamon	
½ tsp. cloves	
¼ tsp. nutmeg	

Bake in slow oven.

Raymond F. Long
Oklahoma City

This recipe came with Mr. Long's mother many years ago from Iowa. A notice on the back of the hand written recipe states: "Notice: Please do not give this recipe away, but sell for 10¢ per copy; proceeds to be given to some church or charity."

PRUNE CAKE

2 cups sugar
½ cup shortening
3 eggs
  Add one at a time and beat
1½ cups cooked prunes
  Remove the seeds
1 tsp. cinnamon
1 tsp. allspice
1 tsp. cloves

1 tsp. nutmeg
½ tsp. salt
1 tsp. soda dissolved in 3 T.
  of hot water
1 cup prune juice
  Alternate with flour
2½ cups sifted flour
1 cup nut meats added last

Bake in loaf pan or a wax paper lined angel food cake pan for 1 hour at 375° .

Instead of prunes, watermelon preserves in their syrup and ½ cup of red maraschino cherries may be added.

Opal Matthews
Collinsville

This cake is made by the C.C. Matthews family in place of fruit cake. It keeps very well and stays moist. It is good without icing.

ALASKA MINCEMEAT CAKE

2 Cups water
1 and ¾ cups sugar

¾ cup shortening
9 ounces dry mincemeat

Break mincemeat into small pieces, put in large pan with other ingredients, bring to a rolling boil, boiling 3 minutes. Let cool.

3 Cups flour
2 tsp. soda
1 tsp. salt

Mix with mincemeat mixture. Bake in tube pan, greased and floured. Bake 375° for 60 to 70 minutes.
  optional:
½ cup nuts
1 cup candied fruit

Mrs. Lois O'Mealia
Thackerville

This recipe is said to be over 100 years old.

Big Mammy's
FRUIT CAKE

3 pounds flour	½ pound orange peel
1 pound sweet butter	1 dozen eggs
1 pound brown sugar	1 T. allspice
3 pounds raisins	1 T. cloves
2 pounds currants	2 T. cinnamon
1 pound cherries	2 T. nutmeg
1 pound figs	1 cup wine
1 pound citron	1 cup brandy
1 pound dates	1 cup molasses
1 pound candied pineapple	1 tsp. soda
2 pounds pecans	3 tsp. Baking powder

Soak spices in hot molasses 30 minutes, 1 tsp. soda dissolved in a little warm water. Add baking powder to flour.

Prepare fruit, mix in large pan. Cream butter and sugar, add beaten eggs and dry ingredients alternately with molasses, wine, and brandy.

Pour over diced fruit. Save small amount of flour to dredge fruit before mixing. Steam 3½ to 4 hours and dry out in oven 10 to 15 minutes. To steam place water in bottom of pan and set cake pan in it. Makes three big cakes.

Mary Evelyn Hogue (Mrs. Marvin Snell)
Kingston, Tennessee

"Ala Williams was born in 1861, moved to Davis I. T. with her husband, Dr. H. P. Lovell about 1893 from Arkansas. She made this cake every year, using a dishpan for mixing. After Big Mammy died, Mother, my sister, and I made it every year on the Sunday after Thanksgiving, then wrapped it in cloth and poured wine over it. It is rich, waxy, and dark ... very good. Big Mammy was a great cook and loved to read cookbooks."

Grandma Dobbs'
DATE CAKE

Put 1 tsp. soda on one cup chopped dates. Pour 1 cup boiling water over this — cool — add 1 cup sugar, 2 T. shortening, 1 beaten egg, 2 Cups flour, and 1 tsp. baking powder — Mix well. Add 1 cup chopped nuts (Grandma used black walnuts which we kids cracked and picked meat out with horse shoe nails).

Bake in 10 inch Iron skillet 350° 40-45 minutes.

Mrs. Ova S. Hull
Oklahoma City

"Grandma in all her life never used anything for heat except wood. She knew exactly how hot to get the oven from 'feel' and all cooking instructions she gave me were 'a pinch' and a 'handful', a 'double handful'."

FRUIT CAKE

2 cups pecans	6 eggs
1½ lb. candied fruits	¼ cup brandy flavoring
(¾ lb. pineapple, ¾ lb. cherries)	4 cups sifted flour
1 lb. seedless white grapes	1 tsp. salt
½ lb. soft butter	1 tsp. nutmeg
1 lb. sugar (2½ cups)	1½ tsp. cinnamon

Line pans with foil. Use two 9x5x3" loaf pans or a 10x4 tube pan. Mix butter, eggs, sugar, flavoring in mixer.

Sift remaining ingredients, then mix with butter, egg mixture. Work into batter with your hands the nuts and fruits. Bake the tube 3 hours, the loaf 2 hours at 275°. One half hour before done, brush with honey or white sugar.

Kay Oliver (Mrs. Gates)
Oklahoma City

This recipe has been updated. Rosa Thompson was born at Stella, Indian Territory in 1879 ... she made these fruit cakes every year for Christmas until she died in 1966.

PORK FRUIT CAKE

1 lb fat salt pork put through meat grinder	1 tsp. cinnamon; cloves and nutmeg to taste
1½ cups boiling water	1 lb. currants, raisins, citron
2 cups sugar	and peel (orange and lemon)
1 cup molasses	chopped fine
1 tsp. soda	Flour to make very stiff.
1 tsp. salt	

Bake in slow oven in a large pan and it will keep moist for months.

Mary Harwell McBryde (Mrs. B.)
Oklahoma City

Mrs. Baker Harwell came to Texhoma, Texas County, Oklahoma in 1904, homesteading as a single person ... she taught school for several years when schools were financed by subscription rather than taxes.

Martha W. King's

KENTUCKY FRUIT CAKES

2 Cups butter	2 lbs. seedless raisins
8 eggs	1 lb. almonds
8 Cups flour	½ lb. English walnuts
1 T. baking powder	½ lb. citron
4 Cups sugar	1 lb. dates
1 Cup dark molasses	½ lb. candied cherries
2 Cups sour milk	½ lb. each of candied
2 T. ground cloves	orange & lemon peel
1 T. soda (in sour milk)	

Bake 4 hours.

I use 1 cup of any kind of wine and add two more cups of flour. Use this two cups of flour to flour the fruit well, flouring the fruits and nuts prevents them from sinking to bottom of cake. Raisins must be washed and dried, all fruits cut in strips. This recipe makes four cakes. Liquor poured over it after cool keeps it moist.

Mrs. Tom B. Wilson
Oklahoma City

In October of 1891, a small group organized a women's club called "Philomathea, Lovers of Learning," a club of "earnest, intellectual women who combined charity work with their culture". In 1898, the Philomathea Club sold fruit cakes to finance the first public library in Oklahoma City, forerunner of the Oklahoma County Libraries.

Martha F. Vandivier Webster's

FRUIT CAKE

Butter Pans and Make Batter:	3 tsp. vanilla
4 eggs	2 cups sugar
1 cup butter	4 cups flour
1 cup milk	4 tsp. baking powder

Cut up: 3 lbs. raisins, 1 lb. citron, 1 lb. figs, ½ lb. pecans

Add: 1 T. allspice, 2 T. cinnamon, 1 tsp. nutmeg, 1 tsp. mace and 1 cup peach pickle juice.

Mix all fruit and spices, pour batter over fruit and mix well. Bake these at 325° with a pan of water in the oven.

Martha J. Birchum (Mrs. J. W., Jr.)
Chickasha

"Fruit cake was made by my grandmother Webster around the first of November, wrapped in cloths soaked with whiskey or wine and placed in tin boxes."

Mary Drennan Wyatt's

KENTUCKY PORK CAKE

2 lbs. fat salt pork
  (no lean)
Grind and pour two cups hot, strong
  coffee over the pork. Stir.
Add:
  6 Cups dark brown sugar
  2 Cups molasses
  2 Cups sour milk to which
  2 T. soda has been added.
Sift 12 Cups flour.
  Use 2 cups to dust
  3 pounds raisins
  2 pounds currants
  1 pound black walnut meats
  1 pound hickory nut meats
  2 pounds candied citron,
    orange peel, lemon peel
  2 pounds candied cherries

To remaining flour add:
  2 T. cinnamon
  2 T. ground cloves
  2 T. nutmeg

Sift into first mixture. Add 2 T. vanilla and fruit.
Bake as fruit cake.

> Mildred Macahan Eckhard (Mrs. Herschel A.)
> Oklahoma City

Mildred Macahan Eckhard's great-great uncle was a doctor and agent for the Osage tribe around 1880 at the Osage Agency (now Pawhuska) ... Mrs. Eckhard's mother, Beatrice Wyatt Johnson, was born there in 1883. This recipe was Beatrice's grandmother's (Mary Drennan Wyatt, a daughter of the American Revolution).

Grandmother's

NEVER FAIL ICING

Beat white of one egg stiff.
Boil 1 cup sugar and 3 tablespoonfuls of water until it makes a soft ball in cold water. Pour into the egg, beat all the time. Have 12 marshmallows cut up fine and beat them into the egg syrup. Beat all lumps out.

> Mrs. E. W. Patterson
> Oklahoma City

This recipe was handwritten in the front of Mrs. Patterson's grandmother's 1896 cookbook with the notation "Icing that never fails, Hazel's".

Virginia

FRUIT CAKE

3 eggs
2 cups sugar
1 tsp. salt
2 tsp. cocoa
2 tsp. cinnamon
½ tsp. cloves
1 cup sorghum
½ cup jelly or preserves
4 tsps. baking powder

1 cup sour milk
1 tsp. soda
¾ cup butter
4 cups flour
2 pounds raisins
2 pounds dates
2 pounds mixed fruit or peel
1 cup flour for rolling fruit.

Mix all ingredients and stir in fruit last. Bake in slow oven 275° one and half to two hours. This recipe makes five cakes, using loaf pans approx. 5x9x3½ inches.

Lucille & Lorene Stevenson
Oklahoma City

"This recipe came to my Mother from her Grandmother, Diana Ludwick Payne, whose early home was on a plantation near Richmond, Virginia. I have heard mother tell that when she was a child, in Illinois, her Grandmother sent a Fruit Cake to Mother's family each Christmas, and one Christmas the cake was temporarily lost in shipment and did not reach them until in the spring ... it was just as good as she remembered the Fruit Cakes of other years."

First business building in Okla City

PIES

1898 Street Fair, Okla. City

VINEGAR PIE

4 T. flour
1 cup sugar
1 cup boiling water
1 egg, beaten

1 tsp. lemon extract
1 tsp. nutmeg
3 T. cider vinegar

Mix flour, sugar and boiling water. Cook five minutes, stirring all the time. Add well beaten egg. Cook two minutes longer. Stir in remaining ingredients. Pour into pre-baked pie shell.

Ina Carver Voss (Mrs. Leslie M.)
Oklahoma City

Vinegar Pie was a favorite of many pioneer families, including the J. G. Smiths, who made the Run of '89 when Lava Smith (now Mrs. Ed McCarrel) was two years old. She recalls that during those first few years they lived in a succession of homes on their claim east of Edmond: first a dugout, then a tent was added, next a log house, and when she was eight they moved into a fine two-room pine board house.

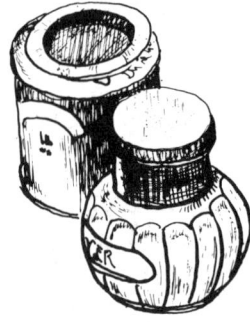

Irene Martin's
VINEGAR PIE

Unbaked pie crust
  (9 inch pan)
3 eggs
1½ cups sugar
4 T. cider vinegar

Dash of salt
Big pinch of
  Cinnamon
1½ T. butter

Beat eggs slightly and add sugar, vinegar, salt and cinnamon. Mix thoroughly. Pour into unbaked pie crust. Dot butter on top (I melt it and stir it in). Bake in a 300° oven 40 minutes until light brown and crusty on top.

Edna M. Couch
Norman

There is much variation in recipes for Vinegar Pie, the principal thing in common being the presence of apple cider vinegar. Mrs. Martin's family liked this pie which was baked in the oven in the pie shell. They always made it on the Fourth of July.

CHESS PIE

2 cups sugar	4 eggs, lightly beaten
1 T. corn meal	½ cup melted butter
1 T. vinegar	½ tsp. vanilla

Combine sugar and meal. Add remaining ingredients in order. Beat well. Pour into a 9-inch unbaked pie shell. Bake 375° for 15 minutes. Lower oven to 300° and bake 35-40 minutes until done or golden brown. Cook til knife inserted comes out clean.

Frances Massey Miller (Mrs. Richard G.)
Oklahoma City

"A favorite pie of 89er days, one that required the simple ingredients most early settlers had in the larder." Mrs. Miller's father, G. E. "Jack" Massey was 10 years old when his father made the Run of '89 into Oklahoma Station, returning to Texas for his young son two weeks later. The industrious boy purchased a barrel of cider at Gainesville, Texas, which he sold along with apple pies and papers in front of a tent across from the Santa Fe Depot. Water was so scarce (there being only two wells and the North Canadian River), it was sold for "two bits a bucket".

Grandmother Maddux's

CHESS PIE

3 egg yolks beaten well	1 tsp. lemon extract
1 cup sugar	3 T. milk
1/8 tsp. salt	

To well beaten egg yolks, gradually add sugar and flour, beating well. Add salt, lemon extract, and milk and mix well. Put in unbaked pastry shell. Bake at 350° for 15 minutes or till pastry is brown. For meringue, beat 3 egg whites till it stands in peaks. Add 3 T. sugar gradually and mix gently. Put on top of the filling in peaks, sealing around the edge. Brown the meringue in a 250° oven. Then turn off heat and open oven door to cool pie in the oven to keep meringue from falling.

Mrs. J. C. Hudman
Oklahoma City

"In 1905, when I was 9 years old, my grandmother, Mrs. Benjamin Clinton Maddux, taught me to make Chess Pie when I visited her in Uvalde, Texas."

Unbaked

BUTTERMILK PIE

2 cups buttermilk
2 T. flour

Yolks of 2 eggs
Juice of ½ lemon

Boil in double boiler. Pour into baked pie crust. Whip whites of eggs, put on top and brown a little.

Billye Gaines
Holdenville

The wood range had almost completely replaced the open hearth for cooking by the time Oklahoma was settled.

Baked

BUTTERMILK PIE

1½ cups sugar
¼ cup flour
3 eggs

½ cup melted butter
1 tsp. vanilla
¾ cup buttermilk

Mix all ingredients together and pour into unbaked pie shell. Bake in oven until set and well browned on top at about 325° .

Vera Mae Tyler
Oklahoma City

There were many versions of Buttermilk Pie, some baked in the oven, some not. Mrs. Ed McCarrel's father staked his claim 7 miles east of Edmond. She remembers her mother making Buttermilk Pie when fruit was unavailable. In the spring and summer they would go down to the creeks and pick elderberries, "little tiny berries that were so sweet we had to add some vinegar to cut the sweetness."

Annie Houghland Henthorn's

POOR MAN'S PIE

PIE CRUST:

1 cup corn meal	1 cup lard
1 cup white flour	6 T. cold water
1 pinch salt	Mix lightly, roll out
2 pinches of white sugar	and put in pie pan.

PIE MIX:

2 cups whole milk (cream not skimmed off)	1 egg, beaten
	½ cup white sugar
	1 T. white flour

Mix well all together. Pour in pie shell. Grate nutmeg over top and bake till solid. For special or Sunday a few pieces of fruit can be added to mix just as you put it in the oven.

Nita Lemon
Oklahoma City

"Temperature of oven — Build a good fire in a wood range cook stove. When wood has burned down and a nice bed of coals are made, place 2-3 pieces of regular 'oven' wood on coals. Test — by opening the oven door just enough to slip your hand inside, count to 5: if too hot, then it is right to bake. If oven gets too hot, you can cool the oven by lifting one or two lids slightly for a few minutes."

Anna McDaniel's

BEAN PIE

(Another Poor Man's Pie)

2 cups mashed white or pink beans	Pinch of salt
	Banana or other extract as desired
2 eggs, well beaten	
½ cup sugar	

Bake in rich crust until set.

Wilma Elizabeth McDaniel
Tulare, California

"The uninitiated had no idea of its humble contents, and one did not have to be too precise in measurements. My parents, Benjamin Fletcher McDaniel and Anna Finster, were married in Indian Territory. I still recall the ingenious ways that my mother substituted for scarce fruit in Creek County. She made pies from vinegar, sheep sorrel, green grapes, sweet potatoes, Irish potatoes, green tomatoes, buttermilk, squash, pecans, molasses and carrots."

SHOOFLY PIE

¾ cup flour	½ tsp. soda
½ cup light brown sugar (packed)	⅓ cup boiling water
½ tsp. cinnamon	⅓ cup light molasses
½ tsp. nutmeg	3 cups of canned apples
¼ cup butter	Pastry for 9-inch pie

Mix flour, sugar and spices; cut in butter until mixture is crumbly. Dissolve soda in boiling water; add molasses and apples. Arrange alternate layers of the sugar-butter mixture and apple mixture in a 9-inch pastry-lined pie pan, ending with the crumbly mixture. Bake 375° - 400° about 40 minutes or until browned. Serve warm — plain or with ice cream.

Washington Jones
Oklahoma City

"Dollie and Ashford T. Miner and 13 children came to Oklahoma from Bear Strop, Texas in 1903, where he had been a deputy sheriff. Wanting to set up a family business, he started a tannery in Weleetka."

Mrs. Braidwood's

EGG CUSTARD PIE

Line 9 inch pie tin with your best pastry. Crimp edges up high around edge of tin so filling won't run over.

1 cup sugar	2 eggs beaten until
2½ cups milk	creamy
2 scant T. melted	pinch of salt
butter	½ tsp. nutmeg

Place sugar in mixing pan. Pour milk over sugar and stir to dissolve. Add pinch of salt, ½ tsp. nutmeg, and melted butter. Stir well. Beat eggs until creamy and fold into mixture. Do not beat — fold gently. Pour into the pastry-lined tin. Sprinkle a little more nutmeg over the top. Bake 10 minutes in moderately hot oven 350° and then turn oven down to slow 300° and bake 30-40 minutes more until knife blade comes clean when stuck into custard. Allow to cool in tin.

Robin Freeman Woods (Mrs. Pendleton)
Oklahoma City

"I remember that Grandmother Braidwood turned her old oven off and left the pie in without opening the door because she couldn't count on the temperature gauge. Earlier cooks probably let the fire die out gradually in wood stoves."

Mrs. G. A. Nichols'

EGGNOG PIE

1¼ cups milk	1 T. cold water
1 cup sugar	1 T. gelatin
3 egg yolks	½ tsp. nutmeg
2 whole eggs	2 T. whiskey
1½ T. flour	

Scald milk. Beat egg yolks and whole eggs well, add sugar and flour. Pour in hot milk. Cook until thick, add gelatine, which has been softened in cold water. Remove from fire. Add stiffly beaten whites of 2 eggs and flavoring. Pour in baked pie shell. Set in ice box to cool. When ready to serve, top with whipped cream and thin shavings of chocolate.

5 O'Clock Tea Club Cookbook
Oklahoma City

Dr. G. A. Nichols practiced dentistry in Oklahoma City prior to statehood, at about which time he took up residential development in the present Heritage Hills and later in Crown Heights, Lincoln Terrace, and Nichols Hills.

Granny's

GRAHAM CRACKER PIE

½ cup butter	1 pinch salt
1 cup sugar	24 crushed graham
2 beaten eggs	crackers
1 cup milk	2 tsp. baking powder
1 tsp. vanilla	½ cup pecans

Add in order given –- Bake in 9-inch pan about 45 minutes at 350° . While baking cook 1 cup crushed pineapple with 1 cup sugar — be careful not to burn this mixture. Pour over hot cake. Serve with whipped cream if desired. (I have added maraschino cherries to the pineapple mixture for color, and it is delicious.)

Mary Mitchell Miles (Mrs. W. Howard)
Oklahoma City

"This pie is really more like a cake and was served at all holiday festivities as long as I can remember. It was in Granny's book of favorite recipes dated 1888. She came to Indian Territory from Illinois about 1880 at the age of 25, and lived in Oklahoma the rest of her 98 years."

LEMON MERINGUE PIE

½ cup cake flour
1¼ cups sugar
Dash of salt
1½ cups water
3 egg yolks, slightly

beaten
½ cup lemon juice
1 tsp. grated lemon
rind

Combine flour, sugar and salt in top of double boiler, add water and egg yolk, mixing thoroughly. Place over hot water and cook 10 minutes stirring constantly. Remove from double boiler; add lemon juice and lemon rind. Cool. Pour into baked pie shell. Use 5 egg whites for meringue. Makes 9 inch pie.

Carrie Abernathy Mothershead (Mrs. George L.)
Oklahoma City

Carrie Howell was attending the University of Arkansas, where her father, General Julius F. Howell, was a professor of history, when she met and fell in love with a young attorney, George C. Abernathy. This was at the turn of the century when it was not so common for a young lady to receive a University education.

LEMON CUSTARD PIE

Juice of 1 lemon
Some grated rind
   (if desired)
2 rounding T. flour
⅔ cup sugar
Yolks of three eggs

1 T. butter (slightly
   rounding)
1 cup sweet milk
Use the 3 egg whites
   for meringue

Cook until thick and put into baked pie shell and top with meringue.

Eva B. Doty
Oklahoma City

Nancy Jane Aiken's family moved from Aiken, South Carolina to Illinois establishing the town of Aiken, Illinois. Nancy Jane married Rev. Hiram A. Doty. They came to Kingfisher in 1891. The claim they filed turned out to be on Indian land, so they bought a claim about 6 miles from Kingfisher. This recipe was used in 1900 but is much older, possibly 150 to 200 years old.

LEMON SPONGE PIE

Beat 2 egg yolks slightly, add ¼ cup sugar and ¼ tsp. salt; mix well. Add 1 cup cold water and the juice of 1 lemon. Cook in double boiler stirring until thick enough to coat spoon. Dissolve 1 package lemon jello in 1 cup boiling water. Add custard mixture and grated rind of the lemon; cool. When it begins to thicken, fold in 1 stiffly beaten egg white. Pour in baked pastry shell; chill until firm. Cover top with thin layer of whipped cream; sprinkle with rolled corn flakes or grated macaroon crumbs.

Mrs. Gerald B. Bremseth
Oklahoma City

"There was a note on this recipe of my Grandmothers', an '89er, that the approximate cost was $.32." Jell-O was available as early as 1903.

Great-Grandmother's

PIONEER LEMON PIE

Mix 2 cups sugar, 1 T. flour and 1 T. corn meal together. Add 4 eggs, ¼ cup lemon juice, ¼ cup milk, ¼ cup butter and grated rind of 2 lemons that have been well mixed together. Pour into unbaked pie shell. Bake 325° oven 45 minutes or until done.

Mrs. W. C. Minton
Duncan

"This recipe has been used by four generations of my family: my great-grandmother in the mid-1800's; by grandmother in the late 1800's; my mother in the early 1900's; and passed on to me when I established a home in 1936."

Mrs. Emmerson's

JEFF DAVIS PIE

3 eggs
1½ teacups cream
1 T. flour
1½ cups sugar

½ cup butter
Add a cup of preserves
if you wish

Bake in pie crust.

1900 Stroud Cookbook

Many pioneers who had come to Oklahoma from the South still had strong emotions about the Civil War. Jeff Davis, President of the Confederacy, was one of many patriots for whom recipes were named. Mrs. Emmerson's husband was president of the Bank of Stroud.

100 Year Old

DUTCH APPLE PIE

6 cups sliced, pared tart
  red apples (6 medium)
½ cup sugar
1 tsp. ground cinnamon
1 (9 inch) unbaked pie

shell with fluted edge
1 cup sifted flour
¾ cup sugar
½ cup soft butter

Combine apples, ½ cup sugar and cinnamon in bowl, mix well. Arrange apple mixture in pie shell. Combine flour and ¾ cup sugar in bowl. Cut in butter with pastry blender or two knives until crumbly. Sprinkle crumbs over apples. Bake in 400° oven 50 minutes or until top is golden brown and apples are tender.

Aleene Eads
Welch

An iron apple or peach peeler containing numerous gears, a spring blade and a table bracket made the fruit harvest easier to prepare. One variety, dated 1885, sliced and cored the apple simultaneously with the peeling process — all with a simple series of turns of the wooden handle.

Grandmother Reynolds'

COCOANUT PIE

For three pies; one quart of milk, five eggs, one grated cocoanut. Beat the eggs and sugar together to sweeten, and stir into the milk when hot; then add the cocoanut and spice. Put it in a rich 'paste' and bake twenty minutes.

Earline Jones Reynolds (Mrs. Allie P.)
Oklahoma City

Indians of the Five Civilized Tribes of Indian Territory lived very much like their white neighbors. Eliza Root Reynolds' cookbook was published prior to 1877 and contained many sophisticated recipes.

Mary Dodd Poarch's

FRIED FRUIT PIES

Cook dried fruit in water: approx. 1 cup fruit to 2 cups water. Sweeten to taste. If too much water, thicken with cornstarch. Prepare enough biscuit dough for 16. Roll out dough and cut in 5 or 6 inch diameter circles. Place heaping T. filling in center of circle, fold in half, and pinch edges closed. Fry in hot oil til brown, turn and brown other side. Dust with powdered sugar.

Anita Poarch (Mrs. John E.)
Edmond

From mother-in-law to daughter-in-law this recipe has been handed down for three generations since 1905, when Mary Dodd Poarch gave it to Inez Jones Poarch upon her marriage. To Dry fruit (apples, peaches, or apricots): Inez Poarch used to place it on a screen frame and then put on roof of log cabin to dry. Evidently the kitchen to the cabin was a lean-to with a relatively low roof. She says it was not necessary to cover the fruit because the insects were not nearly the problem 70 years ago as they are today. The fruit was not wormy or insect infested for the most part. They never thought of spraying. Southern exposure is important so fruit receives direct rays of the sun.

Nutmeg Grater

Mother's

PEACH PIE

Place one-half of a fresh, peeled peach flat-side down in the center of an unbaked pastry shell. Encircle that peach half with other halves to pastry's edge. Dot liberally with butter. Mix 1½ cups sugar (all white or ½ dark and ½ white) with 1 tsp. cinnamon (NEVER nutmeg — that is for apples!) and 3 T. flour; stir well and sprinkle all over peach halves. Add no liquid as peaches make their own. Bake in moderate to hot oven 425°. Bake until peaches are tender and crust is golden brown.

Mary Miles Clanton
Oklahoma City

Mary's great-grandmother Rutherford left her Georgia plantation for Oklahoma in the 1880's, and several generations since have lived in Okfuskee County of Eastern Oklahoma, where peach orchards thrive even today. Art Peters, also of Oklahoma City, recalls that his Grandpa Peters, who ran a peach orchard near Edmond, always said if he couldn't have two pieces of peach pie he didn't want any!

Eliza Root Reynolds'

DRIED APPLE PIE

Wash the apples in 2 or 3 waters, and put them in to soak in rather more water then will cover them, as they absorb a great deal. After soaking an hour or two, put them into a preserving kettle with the same water and with the thin peel of 1 or 2 lemons chopped fine. Boil tender; when they rise, press them down but do not stir them. When tender add sugar and boil 15 or 20 min. longer. Dried apples soaked overnight are made tasteless and are mashed up by being stirred. When cooked stir in a little melted butter, some cinnamon, and powdered cloves. It is important that the apples be of a tart kind. Make pie as usual.

Earline Jones Reynolds (Mrs. Allie P.)
Oklahoma City

Eliza Root was born near Wagoner, I.T. to a French father and a Creek mother, Martha Root, who had come as a very young child on the Trail of Tears, between 1825 and 1830.

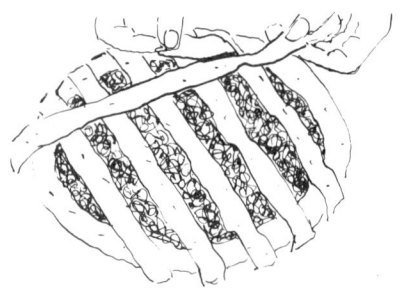

Nan Davis'

PINEAPPLE PIE

2 cups pineapple
2 T. juice
¼ tsp. salt
1/8 cup corn starch

½ cup sugar
1 T. butter
1 T. lemon juice
1 T. lemon rind

Combine all ingredients. Cook until thick, then cool. Bake until golden brown in double crust.

Osa Smith (Mrs. George A.)
Spencer

Nan Davis came to Oklahoma around the time of statehood, settled in the Guthrie area. Like other people of minority races, they saw it as a place of new opportunities.

Great-Grandmother Sturm's

PEACH FLUET

Make Pastry:	Cold milk
1 cup flour	¼ tsp. salt
2 tsp. baking powder	3 T. butter

Blend and add only enough cold milk to handle comfortably, approximately ¼ cup. This really is not a pie pastry but a rich biscuit dough. Roll to ¼ inch round and line 7 inch pie tin. Fill with fresh sliced peaches. Great-grandmother Sturm always arranged the slices in formal swirls ... it is pretty but tedious and doesn't alter taste. Sprinkle lightly with cinnamon; then sprinkle well with at least 1 cup sugar or more. Dilute ½ pint of sour cream with milk or cream to spreading consistency. Spread over top of peaches and bake at 400° approximately 30 minutes. Best served hot but also good cold. Ripeness of the peaches determines the amount of sugar needed.

Martha Jo Sturm (Mrs. George N.)
Oklahoma City

"This has been popular in the Sturm family for four generations since it was brought by Mary Hagen Sturm to the U.S. from Luxembourg in 1835."

Mrs. John Sinopoulo's

FRUIT AND CUSTARD PIE

1 cup cream	½ cup chopped pecans
3 egg yolks	¼ cup chopped dates
¾ cup sugar	¼ cup candied cherries
1 tsp. flour	¼ cup raisins

Make custard of cream, eggs, sugar, and flour, cooking. When thick add remaining ingredients (fruits put through a food chopper). Cook 5 minutes. Pour into a baked pastry shell and serve with whipped cream.

Pat Sinopoulo Gambulos (Mrs. Byron)
Oklahoma City

Mrs. Gambulos' Aunt Kay was a native of Chicago, the first woman graduate of the Chicago Arts Institute. She moved to Oklahoma City with her mother shortly after 1900 bringing many old family recipes and became a renowned hostess as the wife of John Sinopoulo, founder of Delmar Garden, and later owner of the Overholser Opera House, which he remodeled into the Orpheum. Their home, named "Sundial", was built in the style of an Italian villa they admired on their honeymoon and included 3 acres of vineyards and fruit trees.

GREEN TOMATO PIE

Pastry for 9-inch
double crust
1⅓ (1¼) lbs green
tomatoes, 5 medium
or 3½ cups sliced
¾ cups seedless raisins,
washed
1½ tsp. grated lemon
rind,
2 T. lemon juice
1 T. cider vinegar

½ tsp. salt, scant
1⅓ to 1½ cups
sugar
3 T. flour
½ tsp. cinnamon
1/8 tsp. ginger
1 T. fine dry white
bread crumbs
2 T. butter (or
margarine)

Adjust rack 5 to 6 inches above bottom of oven. Start oven 10 min. before baking; set for hot (425°). Make pastry. Wash tomatoes; remove stem & blossom ends; cut in quarters and slice VERY thin on cutting board. Put into 3-quart bowl and stir in to next five ingredients. Blend sugar with flour and spices.

Roll out ½ of pastry and line a 9-inch pie pan, fitting well into angles; trim off even with pan rim. Roll out pastry for top; cut design for generous steam vents in center. Sprinkle crumbs evenly over bottom of pastry-lined pan, then 2 T. of the sugar mixture. Fold rest of sugar mixture into tomatoes, and turn into pastry-lined pan, spreading level. Dot with butter. Moisten pastry rim all around and lay on top pastry; press down gently all around edge to seal, and trim off with scissors ½ inch BEYOND pan rim. Fold the ½ inch overhang under lower pastry, so fold is even with rim, and crimp edge with fingers or fork. Bake 15 minutes, then reduce heat to moderately slow 325° and bake 50 minutes longer. Remove to cake rack; cool 2 to 3 hours before serving.

James Neill Northe
Oklahoma City

150

PUMPKIN PIES

Take a small pumpkin, or half of a large one, stew long and slowly (Mrs. D. N. Collins, of Stroud, suggested in 1900 that the pumpkin be stewed nearly all day til smooth and dry), then strain it, after peeling, and cutting it in small pieces. Mix with this quantity of pulp, one quart of sweet milk, three eggs, and two table-spoonful of corn starch mixed first smooth with a little of the milk. Salt, sugar, and ginger must be put in to taste. A large cup of sugar is about right; one nutmeg. The ginger is indispensible to a genuine pumpkin pie. If part cream can be used the pie is much richer, as well as more delicate in flavor. Bake with an under crust only.

1877 Cookbook

In 1895 the First Territorial Pumpkin Show was held in Oklahoma City, the forerunner of the State Fair. According to legend, the owner of the massive blue-ribbon pumpkin, winner in several categories, brought great embarrassment upon himself when he accidentally bumped his pumpkin with his arm, knocking it to the ground in a thousand pieces.

Carrie Rutledge's

PUMPKIN CUSTARD PIE FILLING

1½ cups milk	3 T. flour
½ cup cream	½ tsp. salt, cinnamon,
½ cup brown sugar	ginger, allspice
½ cup white sugar	2 cups pumpkin
4 eggs	

Scald the milk. Add pumpkin, cook 15 minutes. Add to mixture 4 well beaten eggs. Pour into baked pie crust.

Carrie Rutledge
Hennessey

Mrs. Rutledge, now 93 years old, has made and sold hundreds of these pies at Thanksgiving and Christmas in Hennessey ... she has never given out the recipe before.

Kesiah Moseley Hendricks'
SWEET POTATO PIE

One pound of steamed sweet potatoes finely mashed, two cups sugar, one cup cream, one-half cup butter, three well-beaten eggs. Flavor with lemon or nutmeg. Bake in pastry shell.

Mrs. R. R. Hayes
Oklahoma City

"My grandfather, Samuel W. Moseley, came in a covered wagon in the Run of 1889 ... four teenage sons came with him. About a month later Grandmother, Mary Meyers Moseley, came on the train bringing my mother, Kesiah, 10, and Bell, 15. The family of eight lived in a tent on their claim, located 1 mile south of Star school. Grandfather had planned to build a house that summer, but with clearing land, planting crops, and working the roads in Oklahoma City for the 'fabulous' sum of $3.00 a day (for him and his span of mules), he didn't get the house even started.

Winter came and a dug-out was made for the family to withstand the cold. Sweet potatoes were plentiful and easy to store for winter use. This sweet potato pie was the dessert made for their first Christmas dinner in Oklahoma Territory."

Grandmother's
SWEET POTATO COBBLER

3 or 4 medium sweet potatoes	¾ tsp. yellow coloring
1 cup sugar	1 tsp. nutmeg
2 T. cornstarch	1 cube butter
1 T. vinegar	1 cup milk

The potatoes may be prepared two different ways — (1) Peel and cut sweet potatoes in small pieces. Cover with water and cook slowly till tender. Save the water; or (2) Scrub sweet potatoes and cover, unpeeled, with water. Cook till easily pierced with fork, and then remove peeling and cut in small pieces. Mix all other ingredients and bring to boil. Add enough of saved water to make a thin sauce, stirring constantly. Put potatoes in the sauce and bring to boil. Remove to baking dish and cover with a rich pastry. Bake at 375° till the crust is brown, approximately 40 minutes. When serving, furnish Half & Half for individual servings.

Mrs. J. C. Hudman
Oklahoma City

"The memory of my grandmother's sweet potato cobbler when I was a little girl prompted me, in 1953, from what I could remember to experiment with these ingredients until I worked out the recipe."

Nancy Jane Doty's

IRISH POTATO PIE

3 Medium sized Irish
  Potatoes
A little flour
Allspice

Teacup of sugar
Butter size of an
  egg

Pare and slice thin three medium potatoes. Boil in salt water. Prepare a crust. When done place potatoes in the pie. Sprinkle with flour, put in a teacup of sugar and the butter. Flavor with allspice. Put on a top crust and cut crosswise, about two inches. Fold back and butter the top. Then sprinkle with sugar and allspice.

Eva B. Doty
Oklahoma City

Eva Doty's father, Reverend Hiram A. Doty, Methodist District Super-intendent in Kingfisher, was also a circuit rider preacher, going by horse and buggy or spring wagon from home 2 weeks or more at a time.

Anna Cullop's

MINCEMEAT

5 bowls chopped apples
3 bowls chopped meats
1 bowl white syrup
1 bowl vinegar
1 bowl cider
1 bowl suet or butter
2 bowls raisins
5 bowls sugar
1 bowl Brandy (or leave
  it out and add more

  cider)
2 T. cinnamon
nutmeg
cloves
1 T. salt
2 T. black pepper
3 lemons grated and
  squeezed

Add all but meat and spices. Boil until raisins are tender. Pour over meat and spices and heat all through. Add Brandy after mincemeat has cooled. If suet is used scald it.

Nora Ransford
Oklahoma City

The rural peddlar and the town hardware merchant carried assorted labor-saving machines, such as mechanical apple peelers, cherry stoners, and butter churns.

153

MINCEMEAT

Vera Holding of Norman recalls memories of Thanksgiving at Fort Cobb in 1900: "Mama piled some bite-sized hunks of veal from a milk calf that had been killed by lightning into a big dishpan and slowly cooked it on the old wood stove, added a cup of vinegar, two cups molasses, chopped apples, a pound of raisins and all kinds of spices, until it was bubbling and the mixture sent out a spicy aroma which filled the tent and wafted down Main Street. Giving me a big wink, Papa reached into his hiding place behind the grocery sacks, uncorked a bottle of brandy and doused some into the dishpan of mincemeat."

Mrs. Kohler's

MINCEMEAT

"Boil lean beef and grind with fine blade also a small piece of suet raw ... grind apples or chop but use coarse blade if you grind ... scald and wash the amount of raisins and currents you think it will take ... cook by adding cider and spices ... use the amount of sugar you need. I use a little vinegar as it gives it a better taste. I used a little pineapple juice in what you had.

◯ beef	cinnamon ▱
suet ◯	cloves ▱
◯ apples	allspice ▯
▱ raisins	nutmeg ▱
⅏ currents	
⌂ cider	
⌣ sugar	

Just fix and taste until it tastes right. Cook and can. Cinnamon is the main spice, as it takes much more than other spices. I am sure you can do it. I have made some the second time.

Mrs. Kenneth D. Sutherlin
Oklahoma City

"My mother, Mrs. Ed Kohler, used this recipe most of her 91 years. She was famous for her cooking in Northeastern Oklahoma. Mincemeat was a cold weather dish at our house, made at butchering time, when the temperature had cooled enough to keep meat outside on screened porch. When I wanted the recipe she did the best she could to show me as her usual way was to use a 'pinch of this and a dash of that'. When she says, 'I have made some the second time', she means the year the recipe was written. She drew little symbols by the ingredients for fun. I thought it was clever."

154

Carnegie Library, Okla. City

PUDDINGS & DESSERTS

Grandmother's

ICE PUDDING

Boil one pint and a half of new milk with one tsp. of isinglass (gelatine). Beat five eggs and mix them with milk as you would for custards. Take a tin 'mould' with a cover, oiled not buttered, and line it with candied fruits, such as plums, green gages, etc. Then pour the custard in very gradually, so that the fruit will remain at the bottom. Put on the cover and bury the 'mould' in ice for the whole day, only turning out the pudding at the moment it is wanted.

Earline Jones Reynolds (Mrs. Allie P.)
Oklahoma City

Eliza Root Reynolds was the grandmother of Allie Reynolds, who was a renowned pitcher sometimes called "Super Chief" for the New York Yankees between 1947 and 1954.

Grandmother's

APPLE BROWN BETTY

6-8 tart apples
2 cups of browned bread crumbs
¼ cup melted butter
¾ cup brown sugar
2 T. apple cider or

lemon juice
½ tsp. cinnamon
¼ tsp. cloves
¼ tsp. nutmeg
¼ cup hot water

Combine crumbs and butter. Place ⅓ of crumb mixture in a greased dish. Peel, core, and slice apples thin and arrange ½ of slices over crumbs in dish. Mix spices and sprinkle ½ over apples in dish. Add a second layer of crumbs, apples, and spices. Sprinkle remaining crumbs on top and pour cider (or lemon juice) and hot water over all. Bake til brown and crispy in hot oven. Serve with ice cream or lemon sauce.

Frances Massey Miller (Mrs. Richard G.)
Oklahoma City

"When fall arrives the apple crop comes in, and my mind recalls that sweet, spicey aroma that floated from the kitchen of our home ... and I remember that favorite dessert, Grandmother's Apple Brown Betty."

CORNSTARCH PUDDING

2 squares unsweetened chocolate	½ tsp. vanilla
2 cups raw milk	3 T. cornstarch
¼ cup sugar	¼ tsp. salt
	¼ cup milk

Put chocolate squares with 2 cups raw milk in double boiler. Mix sugar, cornstarch, and salt well in separate bowl and add ¼ cup milk and mix. After the raw milk and chocolate is scalded add the sugar mixture cooking 15 minutes, stirring constantly until thickens and afterwards occasionally. Add vanilla and turn into a serving dish. Chill and serve with or without sugar and cream.

Streeter B. Flynn, Jr.
Oklahoma City

This recipe of Mrs. Dennis T. Flynn dates from around 1904. Mr. Flynn was Delegate to the United States Congress from Oklahoma Territory for several terms prior to 1902, and worked diligently toward "single statehood", combining Indian and Oklahoma Territories.

BANANA CREAM

FOR DESSERT, SUNDAY, JANUARY 11, 1903,

try JELL-O, prepared according to the following recipe:

BANANA CREAM.

Peel five large bananas, rub smooth with five tablespoonfuls of sugar; add one cup sweet cream beaten to a stiff froth, then one package of lemon Jell-O dissolved in one and a half cups, boiling water. Pour into molds or cups, and when cold, garnish with candied cherries and serve with thin cream.

A nice dessert for any meal, at any time. Four flavors — Lemon, Orange, Raspberry and Strawberry.

At grocers, 10 cents.

GET A PACKAGE TODAY.

Raymond F. Long
Oklahoma City

This 1903 newspaper clipping was among old recipes and books which belonged to Mr. Long's mother. It is interesting to note that Jell-O was available in Oklahoma grocery stores at this early date.

QUEEN OF PUDDINGS

2 cups stale bread crumbs   ½ cup sugar
1 qt. scalded whole milk   1 tsp. vanilla
3 eggs

Soak crumbs in milk until soft, add the beaten egg yolks mixed with the sugar, then add the vanilla. Pour into a baking dish and set in a pan of hot water. Bake in moderate oven until firm in the middle. Spread with plum or berry jelly or preserves. Make meringue of the 3 egg whites, adding ¼ tsp. cream of tarter, 6 T. sugar and a pinch of salt. Cover jelly or preserves and put back in oven and brown lightly. Serve hot or cold with cream.

Mrs. John R. Brown
Shawnee

APPLESAUCE COTTAGE PUDDING

Sift 1 cup all purpose flour with 2 tsp. baking powder, ½ tsp. salt, 1 cup sugar. Mix in 2 eggs, 1 cup applesauce and 1 tsp. vanilla. Stir in ½ cup chopped walnuts and 1 cup bran flakes. Pour into greased, floured 8 inch square pan. Bake at 350° oven for 35-40 minutes or until golden brown. Serve warm with custard sauce or whipped cream.

Aleene Eads
Welch

Dry, processed cereals were available in Oklahoma in 1900, as evidenced by the following newspaper story inviting the ladies of Oklahoma City to visit a local store where, "Miss Ethel Holland, Pillsbury's Practical Demonstrator, will serve a dish of vitos and also a dish of Pillsbury's Flaked Oats free ..."

CHRISTMAS PUDDING

Crumble stale bread rejecting the brown part of the crust. Make a layer of crumbs, then add a layer of cranberries. Cover with sugar, dot with bits of butter, alternate the layers of bread crumbs and berries until dish is filled, finishing with a layer of crumbs. Stir a beaten egg in a cup of fruit juice and pour over the top. Serve with a liquid sauce or with cream and sugar.

Viola Gulick Krob
Aline

This pudding recipe of Ellen Gulick's is over 70 years old.

PERSIMMON PUDDING

1 quart ripe native
persimmons (will make
about 1 pint pulp)
2 cups buttermilk
3 slightly beaten eggs
1 tsp. salt
⅔ cup sugar (or ½ cup
sugar and ½ cup honey)

1½ tsp. soda dissolved in
¼ cup water
2½ cups toasted bread
crumbs
½ cup oil or melted
shortening

Put persimmons through colander to remove the seeds. Add other ingredients and stir well. Pour into two greased or oiled bread pans or one pan of equal size. Pan should be at least 1½ inches deep. Bake in moderate oven about one hour or until knife comes out clean. Cool and serve with whipped cream.

Edna M. Couch
Norman

"The Gordon family of my Grandmother Cynthia Gordon Couch, brought the recipe from North Carolina about 1869. The Gordon cousins in Kansas make it using flour instead of bread crumbs. My Aunt Irene, almost 90, says my mother changed the recipe to bread crumbs. We now gather persimmons in the fall and freeze pint cartons of pulp for making pudding throughout the year."

New England

BLUEBERRY GRUNT

1 cup flour
1 cup sugar
2 tsp. baking powder
¾ cup milk

¾ stick butter
pinch of salt
4 cups blueberries

Melt butter in baking dish. Mix batter and pour on top. Add blueberries and bake 30 minutes at 375°. Serve with thick cream.

Mrs. John R. Brown
Shawnee

Sometimes this is called a "slump", as the terms slump and grunt are frequently interchanged. However, a slump usually refers to dumplings dropped onto boiling fruit, whereas a grunt is either steamed or baked. Both are New England dishes.

FLOATING ISLAND

2 slightly beaten egg yolks
¼ cup sugar
1/8 tsp. salt

2 cups milk, scalded
½ tsp. vanilla (brandy
may be used)

Combine egg yolks, sugar and salt: gradually stir in scalded milk. Cook over hot, but not boiling water until custard coats the spoon. Stir constantly. Remove and let cool before adding vanilla or other flavoring. Last of all, stiffly beat egg whites adding 6 T. of sugar to form a meringue. Then gently fold egg whites into cooled custard mixture. Chill until very cold before serving.

Manon T. B. Atkins (Mrs. Robert L.)
Oklahoma City

"The delicacy of this makes it a delicious dessert for tiny children to older generations. This also may be used as a delicious sauce over pound cake or jello."

Mrs. Dennis T. Flynn's

PRUNE WHIP

⅓ pound prunes
(about 15)
5 egg whites

½ cup sugar
½ T. lemon juice

Pick over and wash prunes and soak several hours in cold water to cover. Cook in the same water until soft. Remove stones and rub prunes through a strainer. Add sugar and cook 5 minutes or until the mixture has the consistency of marmalade. Beat egg whites until stiff and add to the cooling prune mixture. Add lemon juice and blend thoroughly. Pile total mixture on a buttered pudding dish and bake 20 minutes in a slow oven. Remove from oven and let cool. Best to serve with boiled custard.

Streeter B. Flynn, Jr.
Oklahoma City

After Dennis Flynn made the Run of '89, he was made the first Postmaster of Guthrie ... later moving to Oklahoma City. He was the founder of Oklahoma Gas and Electric Company.

INDIAN MEAL PUDDING

1½ pints milk
1 egg, beaten
2 T. melted butter
½ cup sugar

½ cup molasses
2-3 cups chopped raisins
1 tsp. each of cinnamon,
nutmeg and ginger

Take corn bread after being prepared for the meal (baked), crumble into bits, add the above and stir thoroughly and bake in a slow oven. Serve with sweetened cream or milk.

Veta C. Minderman
Oklahoma City

The Ladies Aid Society of the Methodist Episcopal Church of Forgan, Oklahoma, located in the very tip of the panhandle, published a cookbook of traditional recipes in 1921, and Veta Minderman still uses her mother's copy, which included this recipe.

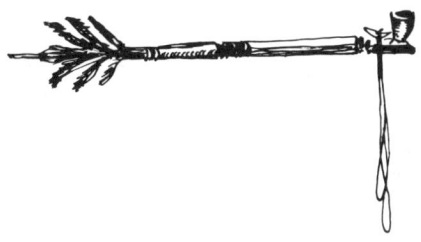

Mrs. J. E. Harris'

OLD FASHIONED BOIL CUSTARD

4 quarts milk
6 eggs, separated
1 cup sugar

3 T. flour
¼ tsp. salt
1 T. vanilla

Scald milk. Do not let boil. Mix sugar, flour, and salt; add beaten egg yolks. To this mixture add several tablespoons of the scalded milk, mix well before adding this to the scalded milk. Let this thicken, remove from heat. Beat egg whites and add stiffly beaten whites to milk. Add vanilla and cool. Serve in glasses, very good with cake.

Mrs. Ray Harris
Eufaula

"My mother-in-law came to Oklahoma from Belle Buckle, Tennessee, with her parents and settled in the Eufaula area shortly after statehood. Her grandmother served this custard on holidays with fruit cake. It was a 'must' on holidays as far back as she could remember."

Aunt Belle Coltrane's

BAKED CUSTARD

1 qt. whole milk	½ scant cup white sugar
4 whole eggs	1 tsp. vanilla
ground nutmeg	

Preheat oven to 350°. Scald milk (be careful not to scorch). Beat eggs slightly and add sugar gradually. When milk is very hot, pour some into the egg mixture and stir briskly (if it's too hot, it will cook the eggs!), then add that mixture to remaining milk. Add flavoring and pour into buttered baking dish . . . sprinkle with nutmeg and set the dish in a larger vessel and put hot water to 1 inch around dish. Bake until a silver knife inserted comes clean. Cool on rack. If baked too long or too much sugar is used, custard will get watery when cool. ('89er Pearl Pemberton adds a 5th egg.)

BREAD PUDDING:
(Variation)

Use one slice of good home-made bread about 1 inch thick. Butter one side and submerge into the uncooked custard til covered. When the bread rises, sprinkle with sugar and bake as usual.

Because there is no longer whole, rich cow's milk available, use 1 can of evaporated milk diluted as directed to make 1 quart. This is richer than grocery milk.

Freeda Mathews Skinner
Oklahoma City

John J. Coltrane hauled supplies for the Santa Fe Railroad into the Unassigned Lands prior to the Run of '89 and was familiar with the area. On April 22, Coltrane staked a claim at Norman near the South Canadian River, though he preferred the North Canadian closer to Oklahoma Station . . . a few days later he worked a trade with a fellow for land at N.E. 36 and Sooner Road (the old trail from Kansas used by Captain Couch and the Boomers). Like many young couples, the Mathews were convinced to join their relatives and ventured forth on a honeymoon trip in a covered wagon headed for "Oklahoma lands". Mrs. Skinner still has the traveler's log and trunk from her parents' trek from Kansas, sadly retraced by Mr. Mathews after his young wife died . . . he left his 2 month old baby girl to be raised by the childless Aunt Belle and Uncle John.

Mrs. M. B. Blake's

LEMON SOUFFLE

3 eggs	Rind and juice of
3 T. butter	1 lemon
4 T. flour	½ cup milk
1 cup sugar	

Cream sugar, flour, and butter together. Beat egg yolks and add, then lemon juice, rind, and milk. Beat egg whites stiff and fold in. Put in buttered casserole, bake 1 hour slowly at 300° .

Eleanor Blake Kirkpatrick (Mrs. John E.)
Oklahoma City

Following six years at Mangum in the dry goods business, Mack Bardsley Blake moved his family to Oklahoma City in 1910, where he and two cousins from Texas began the Baker-Hanna-Blake Wholesale Dry Goods Company. All were members of old Southern families who had gone to Texas following the War Between the States.

Mother's

BREAD PUDDING

1 cup bread crumbs, dry & finely pulverized	large piece of butter
	½ cup pecans
	½ cup dates
1 cup sugar	½ cup coconut
1½ cup milk	½ tsp. baking powder
2 eggs	

Soak bread crumbs in milk for a few minutes. Beat eggs and add sugar, then both to milk and crumbs. Then add dates, nuts and coconut and baking powder and melted butter. Cook in flat baking dish. Serve with hot caramel sauce or whipped cream.

Mary Baker Rumsey (Mrs. Joseph)
Oklahoma City

From November 10, 1899, Times Journal newspaper, Oklahoma City; "How to dispose of stale bread: Hide it from the children ... then the children find it and eat up every morsel of it."

BREAD PUDDING

Use stale bread broken into small pieces. Mix 1 egg and ½ cup of sugar and 2 T. of butter with milk enough to cover the bread, to make a custard. That means plenty of milk or the mixture will be too thick. Add a cup of seedless raisins and any canned fruit you may have leftover. Fruit juices are good too. Season with cinnamon, nutmeg, and vanilla. Bake in a moderate oven until browned.

Dorothy Hensley Keys (Mrs. Mott)
Oklahoma City

For 18 years Ina Gainer was the Society Editor of the Oklahoma City Times under the name of "Sallie Sooner." Her parents came to Indian Territory prior to 1889, locating at the Sac and Fox Indian Agency south of present Shawnee, where her father was connected with government work and her mother taught in the government Indian school. Later they lived in El Reno, where Ina and Addie Wheeler (Mrs. Keys' mother) were "seat mates" in school prior to statehood.

Mrs. Marsden's

BISHOP WHIPPLE PUDDING

1 cup chopped pecan meats
1 cup chopped dates
½ cup sugar
⅔ cup flour

2 eggs, whipped with sugar
1 tsp. baking powder
    sifted with flour

Mix well and steam for ½ to ¾ hour. Serve with whipped cream.

Robin Freeman Woods (Mrs. Pendleton)
Oklahoma City

"This old recipe, brought from England with the Marsdens, was in my grandmother's own handwriting on crumbling yellowed paper. No milk made the recipe more useful to pioneers who did not always have fresh milk."

Eliza Root Reynolds'

INDIAN HUCKLEBERRY PUDDING

Take a quart of boiling milk and water, stir into it Indian meal enough to make a stiff batter. Add a little salt, a small cup of suet chopped, a little molasses, and a pint of huckleberries. Boil one hour and a half in a bag, leaving room to swell. Eat with sweet liquid sauce.

Two eggs and half a teaspoonful of soda may be used instead of suet, and the batter, in that case made a little thinner. This makes a more delicate pudding.

Earline Jones Reynolds (Mrs. Allie P.)
Oklahoma City

A strong, young Scots-Irishman, Richard Marion Reynolds, came from Kentucky prior to 1884 to Indian Territory, where he cut timber, cleared the land, hauled logs with a team of oxen, and fell in love with a Creek/French girl named Eliza Root.

Mary Ann Woodhouse's

PLAIN SUET PUDDING

| 12 oz. flour | 6 oz. beef suet, chopped fine |
| ¼ tsp. salt | 1 tsp. baking powder (rounded) |

Mix dry ingredients and add enough water to make a stiff dough. Put in wet cloth shaping either long oval or round. Pin cloth loosely as it swells. Drop in boiling water to cover. Cook 2-3 hours. Slice and serve hot with syrup, honey or jam. May be sliced and reheated in covered pan or oven.

ROLY POLY PUDDING:
(Variation)

Make suet pudding dough and pat into oval shape about ¼-¾ inch thick. Spread plum jam on dough to about 1 inch from edge. Roll as a jelly roll, pinch wet edges together. Place in wet cloth like suet pudding and cook the same. Serve sliced with cream sauce without sugar. A sweet sauce would spoil taste.

Helen Rimpau
San Diego, California

"These very old recipes belonged to my grandmother, Mary Ann Woodhouse." Suet pudding was a means of using pieces of the beef unsuitable for anything else and turning it into a delicious dish to be eaten with jam, honey, syrup, or molasses.

APPLE DUMPLINGS

Make baking powder biscuit dough — not very short. Place apples, little butter and sugar inside of squares of dough, pinch together. Butter a plate and place dumplings on it. Set inside of steamer and steam for 1 hour. Serve with sauce or cream.

Raymond F. Long
Oklahoma City

Apples were plentiful in the Twin Territories because orchards were among the first plantings upon settlement, producing quick crops and providing the versatile fruit which could be used all winter by drying or storing in barrels in the cellar.

Mother Hogue's

CUSTARD SAUCE

2 cups milk (approx.)
1 or 2 eggs
1 T. butter
1 T. flour mixed in

a little water to
thicken
½ to 1 cup sugar

Cook until "sorta" thick, add a dash or two of cinnamon and nutmeg. Serve over baked apples or apple dumplings.

Mary Evelyn Hogue (Mrs. M.S.)
Kingston, Tennessee

"My husband's parents were married in Texas in 1898, and Sarah Snell Hogue made this custard sauce frequently after moving to Oklahoma."

BLACKBERRY DUMPLINGS

Place a quart of berries, sweetened on the stove and bring to a boil. Make a biscuit dough and drop small pieces in the boiling berries. Cover and let boil 15 to 20 minutes. Serve with cream.

Viola Gulick Krob
Aline

This was taken from Cappers Weekly Cookbook and was used by Mrs. Krob's mother more than 70 years ago. Wild blackberry thickets furnished plump, dark berries for anyone willing to brave the thorns.

SUET PUDDING

1 cup finely chopped and ground suet	1 tsp. soda
1 cup molasses	2 eggs
1 cup buttermilk	1 nutmeg, grated
1 cup seeded raisins, cut in half	1 tsp. salt
1 cup currants	Flour to make a heavy batter

Blend all ingredients and add flour, beginning with 2½ or 3 cups of sifted flour. Place in a greased mold or bundt pan and steam for three hours. (Either place bundt pan in steamer on top of stove, or place on a rack in a heavy turkey roaster or pan in the oven.) Serve hot with the following sauce.

LEMON SAUCE:

1 cup sugar	1 T. cornstarch
1 large T. butter	1 tsp. lemon extract
1 cup boiling water	

Blend ingredients and cook until thickened.

Marianne Harris (Mrs. Roy C.)
Oklahoma City

Suet pudding was always served in the early days by the Lytle family during the Christmas holidays. "It's an old English recipe and tastes best when served warm with a lemon sauce. We children always loved the lemon sauce, which soaks into the pudding if poured on when the pudding is still almost hot. Our grandmother was lovingly called 'Muzzie,' so we named our family pudding after her."

Old-Fashioned

CHILDREN'S APPLE PUDDING

Boil a cupful of rice until soft and drain thoroughly; place a cloth in a pudding mold and lay the rice around it in even thickness. Add a large cupful of sliced apples, a little grated lemon peel, cinnamon and sugar. Cover with rice, tie closely and steam for an hour. Serve with a simple sauce or plain cream and sugar.

Viola Gulick Krob
Aline

Eliza Reynolds'

CHERRY PUDDING

One pint of bread crumbs, one cup of sugar, four eggs, a quart milk, grated lemon rind, a little powdered cinnamon, and salt. Mix thoroughly, butter a "mould", and spread in a thick layer of the preparation, and then a layer of cherries, then another layer of bread, etc., and one of cherries, alternately until it is filled. Close tight and steam for two hours. Eat with a sweet liquid sauce. (Blackberries may be used instead of cherries.)

Earline Jones Reynolds (Mrs. Allie P.)
Oklahoma City

Many recipes in Mrs. Reynolds' cookbook had marks beside them indicating which she preferred, particularly in the pudding section. Puddings were especially popular in the early days because of their simplicity in preparation, ingredients, and serving.

In many cases, a cookbook had uses other than recipes ... Eliza Root Reynolds used hers as a family record book, entering the births of three children between 1884 and 1888: Lewis Reynolds, Martha Reynolds, and an unnamed baby.

Grandmother's

ENGLISH PLUM PUDDING

Beat 6 egg yolks and 4 whites very light and add to them a tumbler of milk; stir in gradually ¼ lb. of dry fine bread crumbs, a lb. of flour, ¾ lb. of sugar, and 1 lb. each of beef suet chopped fine, currants nicely washed and dried and stoned raisins well floured; stir well, then add two tsp. nutmeg, 1 T. mace, 1 T. of cinnamon and cloves, a wine glass of brandy, 1 tsp. salt and finally another tumbler of milk. Boiled puddings are lighter when boiled in a cloth and allowed to swell. The pudding cloth should be made of firm white material. Wring the bag out of hot water, flour the inside well and pour in the pudding mixture (which should be beaten the minute before pouring). Tie bag securely, leaving room for pudding to swell. Place in a kettle with saucer at bottom and immediately pour in enough boiling water to cover. Boil five hours keeping covered with boiling water filled up from tea kettle. Serve with favorite pudding sauce. This will keep for months. When wanted, boil one hour.

Mrs. R. W. Treeman
Perry

"This was copied exactly from my grandmother's (she grew up in England) cookbook. Always made at Christmas time, we thought the little pointed topped puddings were something special."

THREE SAUCES FOR ENGLISH PLUM PUDDING

RICH BUTTER SAUCE:

¼ cup butter (approx.)
2 T. flour, heaped up
½ cup sugar
Extra sugar needed if
    fruit juice is used
    instead of water
1 cup boiling water

(approx.) or fruit
    juice of choice
½ tsp. vanilla or other
    flavoring
½ tsp. nutmeg if
    desired

Mix sugar and flour in pan. Add lump of butter about size of an egg. Pour boiling water over all just until thick. Stir constantly. Add vanilla and nutmeg. Serve over plum pudding.

CLEAR SAUCE:

Place in dry pan and mix well 1 cup sugar and ⅓ cup flour. Add lump of butter (about 2 rounded tablespoons). Pour in 2 cups boiling water, stirring constantly. Bring to boil again and continue stirring. Remove from fire as soon as thick. Add 1 tsp. vanilla and ½ tsp. nutmeg. No other flavor or spice was ever substituted.

ENGLISH WINE SAUCE:

Beat 1 lb. sugar into 1 scant lb. butter. Grate 1 large nutmeg into creamed mixture. Stir in 2 cups favorite wine. Put on fire to warm but do not let boil. Stir constantly and serve warm over plum pudding. (My own grandmother never served this in my lifetime, since she became a tee totaler and active in temperance movement.)

Robin Freeman Woods (Mrs. Pendleton)
Oklahoma City

"These recipes came from Wiggin, England about 1880 with Ellen Marsden Braidwood's mother, Jane Robinson Marsden. Plum Pudding has been continuously in use to date as Christmas and Thanksgiving traditional dessert. The Clear Sauce is our family's favorite."

Aunt Pauline's

STRAWBERRY SHORTCAKE

3 cups flour
3 T. butter
1½ cups sour cream
   or clabber
1 egg

1 T. sugar
1 tsp. salt
1 tsp. soda dissolved
   in small amount
   of warm water

Add the soda with the beaten egg to the milk. Salt the flour, mix it well. Mix in butter smoothly and mix all, handling as little as possible. Bake in buttered and floured cake pans. Put enough dough in the pans so the cake will be thick enough to split in two layers and not be too crusty but lightly brown. With sharp knife split from side to side and butter each side while still warm. Add some slightly crushed strawberries between the layers. Put whole berries on top and serve with cream, plain or whipped. Cut the short cake in good sized squares. Don't hoard it. Better own your own cow and churn the cream.

Dorothy DeWitte Wilkinson (Mrs. Jim)
Oklahoma City

"When Pauline's parents, T.D. and Sarah Ann Tyler, came to Newkirk, Oklahoma in 1895, she brought her cook books and hand-copied 'receipts', some of which go back to 1865. T.D. (grandfather of Dorothy Wilkinson) was a farmer and Vice-President of the bank at Newkirk when he died in 1908. Pauline Townsend and husband moved to Tulsa in 1905, where she became a well-known artist, honored at Oklahoma's Semi-Centennial in 1957."

Granny Bruns'

PLUM PUDDING

Use one quart of bread crumbs, one-half cup of molasses, one-half cup of sugar, one cup of raisins, a small piece of citron, one nutmeg, one teaspoon cinnamon, one-half teaspoon cloves, three eggs, one cup of sour milk and one-half cup of suet. Steam for three hours.

Mary Mitchell Miles (Mrs. W. Howard)
Oklahoma City

"I remember my Granny drying grapes to make her own raisins."

CREAM PUFFS

For shells: a pint (2 cups) of boiling water; melt in it half a pound (1¼ cups) lard and stir, while boiling, into this three-quarters of a pound (2⅓ cups) of flour. Boil until a thick paste is formed. The best way to boil is, to set one kettle in another, or a pail in a kettle of boiling water with the ingredients in the pail, as in boiling a custard. When thick, take from the fire, add ten eggs and a little salt. Mix thoroughly, drop with a spoon on buttered tins, some distance apart. This makes 5 dozen cakes. Bake in a quick oven for 25 minutes, about as hot as for pies. When cool open carefully with a knife, and fill with mock cream made as follows:

One quart of milk, four eggs, three-quarters of a pound (1½ cups) of white sugar, five ounces (1¼ cups) of flour, extract of vanilla to taste. Make a smooth paste of the flour in some of the cold milk, put in a kettle of boiling water with all the milk; when thickened a little, add the eggs well beaten with the sugar. When creamy it is done. Take from the fire, and add a little vanilla. Do not use until cold.

This is the only 'receipt' for making cream puffs that we have used with success. But this never fails, if the directions are followed; and when done they are nice enough to set before a king.

Earline Jones Reynolds (Mrs. Allie P.)
Oklahoma City

This was taken 'as is' from Grandmother Reynolds' 1877 cookbook. The secret to light puffs is adding the flour all at once fearlessly to the boiling mixture. For richer puffs, use 1 cup butter, rather than lard or shortening, and add 4 eggs, one at a time, beating well into the mixture til waxy and smooth.

WILD GRAPE DUMPLINGS

2 cups wild ripe grapes   1 cup sugar
   (stems removed)

Cover grapes with water and boil 15 minutes. Strain and add 1 cup sugar and enough water to make 1 quart of juice. Return to fire and bring to brisk boil.

DUMPLINGS:

2 cups flour   1 tsp. salt
½ cup sugar   ¾ cup sweet milk
4 T. baking powder

Mix to a soft dough. Drop from teaspoon about the size of a small egg onto the boiling juice. Cover and simmer 15 minutes. Good hot or cold.

Mrs. Charles M. Godfrey
Cushing

Mrs. Lindsey's

PORKO AFKE

(Grape Mush)

Stem wild grapes, cook until soft, strain through a cloth, put juice on stove, sweeten as for jelly, let boil five minutes, stir in meal until you have a mush. Serve with or without milk.

1904 Tulsa Cookbook

MERINGUE

Whites of 4 eggs, 7/8 cup confectioners sugar, 2 T. lemon juice. Put whites of eggs and sugar in bowl, beat mixture until stiff enough to hold its shape, add lemon juice drop by drop, continuing the beating. It will take 30 minutes to beat mixture sufficiently stiff to hold its shape, but when baked it makes a most delicious meringue. Bake slowly for a long time til lightly browned.

Irene M. Fallon
Mountain View

This was a good way to use the whites from eggs when the yolks were used in another dish, such as a cake. They could be baked in a "dying oven", one which had been used for baking and the logs burning out ... delicious when piled high with fresh berries or other fruit and topped off with whipped cream.

Sequoyah

DAINTY DESSERTS

COOKIES

Mrs. John Sinopoulo's

GRANDMOTHER'S SOUR CREAM COOKIES

2 cups brown sugar
1 cup butter
1 cup sour cream
3 eggs
Raisins, as many as
  you like

1 tsp. soda
pinch of salt
a drop of almond flavoring is
  great or vanilla
Enough flour to make a
  very soft dough

Cream butter and sugar. Add and mix other ingredients, except flour and baking powder. Mix them in last ... amount not specified — just enough to make the dough soft. Drop on cookie tin and bake at 350° . They have a flavor unsurpassed.

Pat Sinopoulo Gambulos (Mrs. Byron)
Oklahoma City

The Sinopoulo brothers, John and Peter, were perhaps the first Greek immigrants to settle in Oklahoma City, and they became prominent in the entertainment business in the young city. Their Delmar Garden was the first amusement park and was located near the North Canadian River (close to the present Public Market) where early citizenry enjoyed boat rides on the river, lemonade and beer in the Beer Garden, and entertainment on holidays.

OLD-FASHIONED SUGAR COOKIES

(This is one of my oldest recipes)

1½ cups sugar	1 tsp. soda
1 cup butter	½ tsp. nutmeg
2 eggs	Enough flour to make soft
1 cup sour milk	dough (about 4 cups)

Cream butter and sugar, then add eggs. Mix well. Add remaining ingredients. Roll on floured board and cut with cookie cutter (handle dough as little as possible for lighter cookies). Bake in medium oven til lightly browned.

Pearl Ogden Pemberton (Mrs. George T.)
Oklahoma City

Mrs. Pemberton's father, Frank B. Ogden, made the Run of '89 in a horse-drawn buggy and after staking a claim returned to Texas to get his wife and two little daughters; one was Pearl Ogden Pemberton. Their first home was on Main Street, and as Pearl grew up so did the city which was established that day of April 22, 1889 at Oklahoma Station ... later to be called Oklahoma City.

Elzada Emeline Bruns'

PERFECT SUGAR COOKIES

Scant 1 cup butter	1 tsp. soda
Scant 1 cup sugar	3 cups flour
2 eggs	½ tsp. vanilla
½ tsp. nutmeg	

Cream butter and sugar thoroughly; add eggs one at a time; sift dry ingredients together and add to egg mixture. Chill dough thoroughly (original recipe says to put dough in a container of SNOW until cold); roll dough to about 1 8 to ¼ inch thickness and cut in desired shapes. Sprinkle with a dab of sugar before baking about 8 to 10 minutes at 350°.

Mary Mitchell Miles (Mrs. W. Howard)
Oklahoma City

"These cookies have been the first recipe given to young ladies in our family to learn to cook and bake since 1898. Granny said she added the nutmeg at some time and we used to laugh about that ... there's no telling when that was. She came to Indian Territory from Illinois in 1880 and died in 1953 at the age of 98."

Nettie Taylor Walker's

BEST TEA CAKES

2 cups flour	1 cup sugar
1 tsp. baking powder	1 egg
¼ tsp. salt	1 tsp. thick cream
¼ cup butter	1 tsp. vanilla
¼ cup lard	

Mix and sift 1½ cups of the flour, baking powder, and salt. Cream butter and lard. Beat in eggs, vanilla, and cream. Stir flour mixture into this. Mix thoroughly. Sift in remaining flour until dough is stiff enough to roll out (chilling helps). Place on a lightly floured board and roll out to desired thickness. Cut with floured cutter and place on ungreased baking pan. Brush with milk and sprinkle with sugar if desired. Bake in moderate oven 350° 6 to 8 minutes.

Lola Walker Ellis
Holdenville

"My great-grandfather's family brought this recipe from Mississippi by way of Texas and then to Oklahoma. It was already several generations old by then."

Governor David H. Boren's

GREAT-GRANDMOTHER'S COOKIES

1 cup butter fat	1 tsp. nutmeg
2 cups light brown sugar	1 cup raisins
2 eggs	½ cup chopped pecans
¼ cup sour cream	3½ cups flour
1 tsp. cinnamon	1 tsp. vanilla
1 tsp. cloves	1 tsp. soda

Cream the butter and sugar. Add the eggs and sour cream and beat for two minutes. Add the rest of the dry ingredients sifted together. Chill and spoon small bits of the dough on a greased baking sheet. Flatten down three inches apart. Bake in moderate oven 350° for 10 minutes.

Christine McKown Boren (Mrs. Lyle H.)
Oklahoma City

Governor Boren's great-grandmother, Mrs. Thomas F. Villines, came to Oklahoma shortly after statehood. Her grandchildren and great-grandchildren always found these favorite cookies in her cookie jar when they went to visit, according to Mrs. Boren.

RAISIN COOKIES

1 pound raisins	2 well-beaten eggs
1 cup water	2 tsp. soda
2 cups sugar	1 tsp. each of cinnamon,
½ cup butter or	cloves, and nutmeg
shortening	Approx. 5 cups flour

Cook raisins in water for 20 minutes. Keep the raisin water to put in dough. Cream butter and sugar. Add eggs, spices, soda, and flour along with raisin water to make a stiff dough. Drop from spoon onto oiled cookie sheet, bake in moderate oven 350° 10 to 15 minutes.

Art Morris
Oklahoma City

Mr. Morris remembers as a young boy growing up that these cookies were a staple in the home, always on hand to serve visitors ... if they could be hidden well enough from the children. They are very moist and stay that way. Mr. Morris makes them on special occasions for his fellow residents at Superbia Retirement Village.

Sally Burgess'

GINGERBREAD COOKIES

¼ cup butter or "shorting"	2 cups flour
½ cup brown sugar (pack	1 tsp. ginger
tightly)	½ tsp. cinnamon
1 egg	pinches of cloves, allspice,
¼ cup molasses	and salt
2 T. cream	grated rind of 1 orange

Mix and beat smoothly butter, sugar, egg, molasses, and cream. Add grated orange. Sift together dry ingredients; stir in batter. Drop by spoonfuls on cookie sheet or roll and cut into shapes of gingerbread boys.

Una Lee Voigt
Yukon

"Making gingerbread cookies can furnish winter-evening fun. Make a batch of your favorite dough; have it ready after the day's work is done. Cut patterns from stiff paper; use farm-life for ideas and inspiration. Everyone will enjoy cutting an amusing design representing his favorite tree, house, child, or pet. Family participation makes gingerbread joys complete. Give them for Christmas to decorate the tree. From a 200-year-old 'receipe'."

Mrs. J.J. Culbertson's
PENOCHE STICKS

1 lb. brown sugar	1½ cups flour
1 cup nuts cut small	¼ tsp. salt
4 eggs	1 tsp. baking powder

When water in double broiler is boiling, put whole eggs in upper part, beat, then add the brown sugar and let cook for 20 minutes (stirring all the time). Take off fire, add nuts, then flour that has the baking powder and salt sifted with it, and mix well. Spread in well-greased shallow pan and bake 15 minutes at 375° . Let it get cold and then cut in squares. Sprinkle with powdered sugar.

5 O'Clock Tea Club Cookbook
Oklahoma City

J.J. Culbertson was an early landowner and developer in Oklahoma City. The Oklahoma State Governor's Mansion sits on land that was part of Mr. Culbertson's extensive produce farms which furnished large amounts of fresh garden vegetables and fruits to the bustling young metropolis.

Mrs. Harry Rosenthal's
LEPKUCHEN

1¼ cups sugar	1 tsp. allspice
1 cup molasses	2 cups nuts
6 egg yolks	1 cup citron
2 whole eggs	3 cups flour
6 squares bitter chocolate	1 heaping rounded tsp. baking powder
1 tsp. cinnamon	

Sift dry ingredients and add to beaten eggs & molasses. Add melted chocolate, citron, and nuts. Spread very thin in buttered jelly roll pans. Bake at 350° for 15 minutes.
ICING:

1 box powdered sugar	½ tsp. almond extract
½ cup hot cream	

Harriette Orbach (Mrs. Robert L.)
Oklahoma City

"My grandmother came to Oklahoma City in 1898 from Louisiana, and she made this every Christmas along with pralines and other creole dishes."

Mrs. Joseph W. Back's

LEPKUCHEN

½ gallon pure sorghum
1 quart melted pure
   lard
½ cup soda
½ cup sour milk
½ cup cinnamon

½ cup nutmeg, cloves, &
   allspice mixed
some salt (about 2-3 tsp.)
2 quarts pecans
7 quarts flour, approximately

Warm the sorghum and melt the lard. Pour together and stir in spices and salt. Mix soda in sour milk and add to lard mixture stirring well, then mix in nuts and flour stirring until too stiff to stir more. Then knead the flour in with your hands. Be sure and use a large, large pan. At this point, my mother rolled and cut the cookies and baked them, but I form the dough into large round rolls, chill, then slice and bake them at 350° . They burn easily. Half a recipe is ample. We call them Leppies.

Mrs. Leo E. Bellmon
Ponca City

"These were usually made at Christmas time after the sorghum had been made from cane, the nuts had fallen, and the fall butchering of hogs supplied fresh, pure lard. (They are not as good with shortening) ... Both of my parents came from Germany and Papa made the Run at the opening of the Cherokee Strip in 1893, staked a quarter-section and proved up on his claim ... later passed to me."

Clara Frost's

LEOPOLD SCHNITTEN

(Christmas Cinnamon Bars)

½ lb. butter
1 cup flour
1 tsp. cinnamon

½ cup sugar
¼ lb. grated almonds
½ tsp. allspice

Let butter soften in warm place. Cream in sugar well. Add flour, spices, almonds. Press dough thin as possible into a buttered pan. Bake to light brown. Cut into oblong "squares". While warm spread thick with cinnamon and sugar.

Marta Frost Reynolds (Mrs. A. D.)
Oklahoma City

"Bim Bom (grandmother Frost) could not speak English when her husband brought her as a young teenage bride to Oklahoma City from Germany. She returned home for the birth of her first child, my father.

179

MOLASSES COOKIES

1 cup shortening	3 eggs
1 cup sugar	1 tsp. soda
1 cup sorghum	4 cups flour
1 tsp. ginger	

Place in saucepan the shortening, sugar, and sorghum. Cool to lukewarm and add eggs one at a time beating after each. Add dry ingredients, increasing the flour if it is not a stiff dough. Roll out and cut. (Bake in medium oven for a few minutes) This makes 5 dozen cookies and will keep very well in covered cookie jar. "Most older folks like them."

Mrs. W. A. Willms
Kingfisher

"I've been making Grandmother's cookies since I married 53 years ago." ... Many people of German descent were attracted to the beautiful farm land around Kingfisher, Crescent, and Clinton. The town of Corn (originally Korn) has an annual German festival, and the town of Loyal changed its name from Kiel during World War I as a gesture of patriotism. Much of the German heritage in food remains today.

OATMEAL COOKIES

1 cup butter	4 T. sweet milk with
1 cup white or brown	1 tsp. soda dissolved in it
sugar	1 tsp. cinnamon
2 cups flour	½ tsp. salt
2 well beaten eggs	2 cups rolled oats
1 cup raisins	1 cup chopped nuts (any kind)

Cream butter and sugar well, add milk and eggs, sift flour with salt and cinnamon three times, then add to mixture. Add oats, raisins and nuts last. Drop by spoon on greased cookie sheet and bake in moderate oven 10 to 15 minutes.

Mrs. R.K. Singleton
Oklahoma City

"This old family recipe of grandmother's won first prize in three county fairs back in the 1920's using white sugar and omitting nuts."
Some observations on Oatmeal Cookies: Mrs. L.W. Clark of El Reno holds back a little flour to dredge the raisins and nuts for easier mixing ... ¼ tsp. of freshly grated nutmeg improves the flavor ... use ½ white and ½ brown sugar ... butter is what makes a cookie crispy; if shortening is used increase the milk.

Grandma Hargrove's

OATMEAL COOKIES

1 cup sugar	2 cups dry oatmeal
1 cup shortening	1 tsp. soda
1 cup raisins (cooked)	1 tsp. baking powder
1 cup water (for raisins)	1 tsp. salt
2 eggs	1 tsp. cinnamon
2½ cups flour	1 tsp. vanilla
1 cup chopped pecans	1 tsp. nutmeg

Cook raisins in the water, and keep the liquid ... mix with all other ingredients, adding oatmeal, raisins, then nuts last. Drop from spoon onto greased cookie sheet and bake at 350° til brown.

> Cynthia Crowe Meyerson (Mrs. James E.)
> Oklahoma City

This recipe was brought from Kansas many years ago and is still popular in the family. Cooking the raisins and using the raisin water makes these cookies chewy and moist.

LADY FINGERS

Four tablespoons of powdered sugar, four eggs, three tablespoons of flour and a little grated lemon peel. Stir the sugar and "yelks" of the eggs thoroughly together; add the flour and rind of half a lemon, grated fine, being careful not to grate through into the white, bitter part; lastly add the whites of the eggs beaten stiff. Bake in lady finger tins lined with buttered paper. Sprinkle with a little powdered sugar daintily just before putting into the oven, which should not be too hot, for the lady fingers should be a delicate brown. In the absence of tins, sheets of white paper may be put in a large tin and the dough given the required shape by squeezing it through a funnel."

<u>New Process Cookbook</u> (1896)

Lady Fingers were very popular for genteel gatherings and were often served with dainty ices at socials. Most bakeries made them regularly. By June of 1889 there were already 10 bakeries in Oklahoma City. In 1904, the newspaper reported that Mrs. R.J. Edwards "at 5 o'clock served dainty ices and lady fingers after which the guests departed."

181

Traditional Czech
POPPY SEED COOKIES

1 cup butter	1 tsp. soda dissolved in
2 cups sugar	3 T. milk
2 eggs, beaten	5 T. poppy seed
Flour enough to make stiff dough	1 tsp. vanilla

Cream butter and sugar, add beaten eggs, vanilla dissolved in soda, poppy seed, and the flour. Knead the dough lightly, roll out to ½ inch thickness, cut with cookie cutter and bake at 375° for 10 minutes. These are very rich "krispy" cookies and will keep for a long time in a dry place.

Mildred Svoboda Stejskal
Yukon

Yukon is well known for its annual Czech festival each fall when the traditional foods of the people who founded the town are served, the dances and costumes of the old country displayed, and the heritage of these gentle farm people enjoyed by all who come.

Martha F. Vandiver Webster's
HOG'S EARS

1 cup flour	⅓ cup water
¼ tsp. salt	1½ cups simple syrup
Chopped Pecans	

Sift flour and salt together. Add enough water, ¼ cup or more, to make a thin stiff dough. Cut off small portions of the dough and roll out very, very thin on floured board. Repeat this operation till all dough is used — 12 times. Fold each "ear" over loosely and drop into deep hot fat, cook till light brown and drain.

SIMPLE SYRUP: To make simple syrup, boil 2 parts water to one part sugar for a short time (It can be used for many things, especially to mix with fresh fruit juices for drinks). For Hog's Ears, boil the syrup to the soft ball stage (may need to increase amount of sugar). Dip "ears" in hot syrup and place on platter and sprinkle with chopped pecans.

Martha J. Birchum (Mrs. J.W., Jr.)
Chickasha

"Grandmother Webster brought this Southern recipe to Oklahoma right after the Run, along with 5 children to gobble the Hogs Ears right up."

Carrie Lovell Reeves'

FILLED COOKIES

Filling: Make first and let cool   1 T. flour
1 cup chopped raisins   ½ cup sugar
½ cup nuts   ½ cup water

Mix all together, cook until thick, and cool.

Cookies:
1 egg   3½ cups flour
1 cup sugar   1 tsp. soda
½ cup shortening   ½ tsp. salt
½ cup buttermilk   1 tsp. vanilla

Cream shortening and add sugar. Add well beaten eggs, salt, milk, vanilla, and dry ingredients sifted. Dough should be soft. Put flour in gradually mixing. The softer the dough, the better the cookie. Use just enough flour to be able to roll dough very thin. Chill dough before using. Roll out very thin, cut with cookie cutter; cover one cookie with filling, then cover with a second cookie. Press edges together, bake 350° about 15 minutes. The secret of these cookies is to keep dough soft but roll very thin so you do not have too much cookie for filling.

Mary Evelyn Reeves Hogue (Mrs. Marvin Snell)
Kingston, Tennessee

It was about 1893 when young Dr. Henry Poindexter Lovell settled in Davis, Indian Territory with his wife and 10-year-old daughter, Carrie.

MOTHER'S LOVE-KNOTS

1 egg   1 T. milk
1 T. sugar   pinch of salt; pinch of nutmeg
1 T. butter   Flour to knead very hard

Roll out; then cut like a pipe-stem, tie in 2 or 3 knots, and fry in hot lard. Sprinkle with pulverized sugar while hot.

Mrs. V.C. Rosenstahl
Oklahoma City

"This was taken from Mother's favorite cookbook, printed in 1903."

DATE STICKS

1 cup flour	1 package dates
1 cup sugar	1 cup broken pecans
1 tsp. baking powder	3 eggs, beaten separately
½ tsp. salt	1 tsp. vanilla

Sift dry ingredients together three times. Cut dates fine. Add nuts to flour mixture, then dates and eggs. Spread thin in square pan and bake at 350° for 20 minutes. Just before cool, cut in sticks of finger length and roll in powdered sugar.

Ruth Vaught Thompson (Mrs. Wayman J.)
Oklahoma City

Prior to becoming a Federal Judge, Mrs. Thompson's father, Edgar S. Vaught, was Superintendent of Schools in Oklahoma City between 1902 and 1906.

Cookie Stamp

Bernice Mee's

OLD MISSION CRY BABIES

2 eggs	2 tsp. soda in cup of
1 cup molasses	strong coffee
1 cup white sugar	1 tsp. vinegar
1 cup butter	4½ cups flour
2 tsp. ginger	2 tsp. cinnamon

Stir well and drop on buttered tins. Bake in a medium oven.

Junior League Cookbook
Oklahoma City, 1929

Bernice Mee's father, William Mee, was an early-day banker in Oklahoma City and was prominent in civic affairs. He was a principal in the Security National Bank which through a merger became today's First National Bank.

Aunt Ellen Staton's

PEANUT COOKIES

1 cup chopped peanuts	¼ tsp. salt
1 cup flour	2 tsp. baking powder
4 T. butter	1 egg

Mix sugar and butter together. Add egg and beat hard, add peanuts. Mix salt and baking powder with flour. Add gradually in bowl, knead until smooth ball dough. Turn in floured board. Divide in 24 parts, roll each part into small balls, place on table, flatten with knife 1 8 inch thick. Place in greased pans ¼ inch apart, bake in moderate oven 10 minutes. Then pass around.

Mrs. Herbert D. Coulter
Meno

"Aunt Ellen Staton lived in Kansas, but her family came to Cleo Springs, Oklahoma Territory before statehood bringing some of her treasured recipes."

Mrs. Oscar Ruth's

PFEFFERNUSSE "Peppernut" COOKIES

2 cups sugar	4 cups flour
¾ cups shortening	1 tsp. cloves
4 eggs	1 tsp. cinnamon
1 tsp. soda	1 cup chopped nuts
½ cup sour cream	

Cream sugar, shortening, and eggs. Dissolve the soda in sour cream and add remaining ingredients mixing well. Make into finger shaped rolls. Cut in ½ inch pieces. Place on a greased cookie sheet and bake at 350° for 25 to 30 minutes or until light brown.

Helen and Kent Ruth
Geary

"These Pennsylvania German (sometimes called Dutch) cookies have been baked every Christmas since 1897 when the récipe was brought to Oklahoma, and they still are!"

Mrs. Eugene Dye's

JUMBLES

1 cup butter	⅔ cup sweet milk
2 cups sugar	4 even cups flour
2 eggs	3 tsp. baking powder

Beat the butter to cream with the sugar, add well-beaten eggs, then the milk and flour (with baking powder mixed in) by degrees so as to prevent lumps. Stir briskly for a few minutes. It will be quite stiff and must be made to stay up. Drop on a well greased pan with a dessert spoon and stick a raisin in the top of each.

1900 Stroud Cookbook

Mr. Dye, the Stroud miller, advertised "Nancy Hanks" brand of flour, a home product, as well as Corn Meal, Graham flour, and Chop. Mrs. Dye's comment: "A receipt we use in our family and all like."

Carrie Howell Abernathy's

FROSTED DELIGHTS

½ cup shortening	½ tsp. salt
1 cup sugar	1½ cups cake flour
2 eggs	1 tsp. baking powder
1 cup chopped nuts	½ tsp. vanilla

Cream shortening and sugar, add beaten eggs and sifted dry ingredients. Add vanilla; mix well and spread batter onto baking sheet (with sides) as thinly as possible. Cover with "frosting" before baking.
Frosting:
1 cup brown sugar folded into
1 stiffly beaten egg white
Spread frosting on batter and sprinkle with nuts. Bake at 325° for 30 minutes.

Carrie Abernathy Mothershead (Mrs. George L.)
Oklahoma City

"Shawnee was thriving in 1903 when Grandmother Carrie and her husband decided to make it their home."

186

Great-Grandmother Braidwood's
"SCOTCH" SHORTBREAD

Lightly butter a bakeboard of marble. Put ½ pound of butter on bakeboard to soften. Weigh out ¼ pound white granulated sugar and dump it on top of the butter. Work sugar into the butter by hand until thoroughly blended. Weigh out one (1) pound of white flour (1 quart) and work it by hand into the sugar and butter. If the butter is soft it won't be hard to work in. Work in all you possibly can of the one pound of flour. Dough will be very stiff but must be worked smooth. If impossible to work in all of flour be sure that at least ¾ pound has been, or it won't be shortbread.

Then pat out dough by hand on bakeboard (or lightly greased cookie sheet) until it is only ¼ to ½ inch thick. Do not use a rolling pin. Pat it out smooth with hand. With a fork, prick all over the dough and clear through. Score deeply in 1½ inch squares. Bake in moderate oven 350° for 20 to 30 minutes or up to an hour til color of lightly browned biscuit. Cut apart while still warm as it gets hard when cool (or can be broken as needed after cooling).

Robin Freeman Woods (Mrs. Pendleton)
Oklahoma City

This shortbread is rich and crunchy and beloved by all Scottish people. Helen Ralston married James Braidwood in 1854 in Scotland, later bringing a large family of children to America, where they founded the town of Braidwood, Illinois. This recipe was eventually brought to Indian Territory about 1900 by her son Robert Bruce Braidwood.

_C O N F E C T I O N S_

PEANUT BRITTLE

2 cups sugar
1 cup white Karo
1 cup water
2 heaping cups raw peanuts

2 tsp. soda
2 tsp. vanilla
1 rounded tsp. salt

Cook first three ingredients until it makes a brittle ball or spins a thread (approximately 15-20 minutes from the start of actual cooking). Add peanuts and salt. Cook til syrup turns a deep tan color (about 30 minutes) and becomes hard to stir. Turn off (or remove from) fire and add soda and vanilla.

Stir very well and pour out on three buttered cookie sheets (or marble slab). Pour kind of fast and divide evenly. As soon as it's cool enough, pull from the edges with the fingers and stretch as thin as possible, gradually working from the outer edge toward the center (which is the hottest part). It's best when pulled very thin. The outer edges will begin to break as you work toward the center and the edges cool sufficiently. When completed pulling, break all in uneven pieces. Don't cover until well cooled.

Ruth Vaught Thompson (Mrs. Wayman)
Oklahoma City

Mrs. Thompson's mother, Mrs. Edgar Vaught, like many fine cooks of her day, had a marble slab which she used for candy making.

Clara Rimpau's

TURKISH DELIGHT

1 box gelatin — soak in 1 cup boiling water
Boil together for 5 min. 4 cups sugar and 1 cup water
Juice and grated rind of 2 oranges
Juice and grated rind of 2 lemons

Add gelatin and juices and rind to sugar syrup, boil hard one minute. Pour over nuts that have been chopped into shallow pan or platter — to cover nuts. Let harden and cut into squares and roll in powdered sugar.

Helen Rimpau
San Diego, California

The early-day confectionery was a popular place for pioneer boys and girls to stop and spend a penny on candies. Dad could often get his cigars in the same shop. The Bon Ton Restaurant in Oklahoma City advertised in the 1900 newspaper: "Order Pineapple Snow, Ice Cream, Bread and cakes ... fresh confectioneries, cigars and tobacco."

Grandmother Braidwood's

CANDIED ORANGE PEEL

Cut as much of the inner white peel from the rind of the oranges as possible. Cut rind in narrow strips with scissors. Cover with cold water. Bring to a boil and continue boiling about five minutes. Pour water off and discard. Repeat boiling and pouring off four or five times to get rid of bitter oils in rind.

Make a white syrup by bringing to a boil twice as much sugar as water (i.e. 2 cups sugar to 1 cup water) depending on how much fruit you are preparing.

Put peel into syrup and cook until clear and syrup is almost boiled away and peel is candied. Dip peel out and roll in granulated sugar. Lay on platter to dry and cool.

Store in a covered jar to keep soft, but be sure it's dry so peel won't stick together.

Robin Freeman Woods (Mrs. Pendleton)
Oklahoma City

Lemon peel or grapefruit peel can be prepared in the same manner. This was a favorite confection in days past and could be chopped and used in fruit cakes, cookies, breads, or rolls.

Agnes Danler Christoph's

GLASS CANDY

2½ cups sugar   ½ cup water
1 cup white syrup

Boil until it cracks in water. Remove and add red, green, yellow or other colors and flavor with anise, winter green, cinnamon, or other flavors. Pour onto a greased cookie sheet or shallow tray. When hard, break into smaller pieces for eating.

Sister Mildred Christoph
Oklahoma City

"This 'receipe' is from my Mother's (Agnes Danler Christoph) hand copied 'Receipe' Book from Ellinwood, Kansas. Glass Candy made in various colors and flavors was our special Christmas hard candy from around 1900 to 1930 ... it was also a special Christmas gift sent to relatives in Western Kansas."

Mrs. Roberts'

DIVINITY CANDY

3 cups granulated sugar   whites of two eggs
½ cup Karo syrup   nuts
1 cup water   flavoring

Boil until it forms a soft ball in cold water. Pour slowly over beaten whites of two eggs. Beat until it is cool. Add nuts and flavoring while beating.

Raymond F. Long
Oklahoma City

This recipe was in a very old hand-written notebook of recipes which had been brought by his mother from Iowa many years ago.

Mrs. J.J. Evans'

COCOANUT DROPS

To 1 grated cocoanut add half its weight of sugar and beaten white of 1 egg. Mix thoroughly and drop on buttered white paper on tin sheets. Bake 15 minutes.

1900 Stroud Cookbook

Dr. J.J. Evans, Stroud physician and surgeon of 1900, advertised in the Presbyterian Ladies' cookbook that medicines were furnished and that he was located over Brogan's store.

WHITE TAFFY

Boil 2 cups sugar, 1 cup corn syrup, and ½ cup water, 1 T. vinegar. Cook without stirring until brittle in water — when done add ½ tsp. cream of tartar. Cool and pull. (Spreading the taffy out to cool works best.)

Mrs. Gerald B. Bremseth
Oklahoma City

This recipe which belonged to eighty-niner, Mrs. Holliday, recalls days when taffy pulls were among the most popular form of entertainment for young people and families in the years following the territorial openings ... Mary Lee Ervin recalls that even in later years her father was a fancy taffy puller, who would stretch it and flip it in the air in an arch, bewildering and amazing the small children in the household.

Mrs. J.R. Holliday's

MOLASSES TAFFY

1 cup molasses	¼ cup butter
1 cup sugar	

Cook until it forms hard ball in cold water — when cool, pull.

Mrs. Gerald B. Bremseth
Oklahoma City

Mrs. Ed McCarrel, who was two when her father staked his claim in the Unassigned Lands, recalls that he had a sorghum mill, "They would strip the cane in the fields, then press the juice and boil it down. This sorghum molasses was used in place of sugar, which was often hard to get and very expensive."

Aunt Kate's

DATE ROLL

3 cups sugar	1 lb. finely chopped dates
1 cup milk	1½ cups pecans or walnuts

In a pot, combine sugar, milk, and dates. Cook at medium heat until a few drops from your wooden stir spoon forms a medium hard ball in a cup of cold water. Remove from heat and let cool a bit. Then beat till the shiny turns to a creamy look. Add nuts, mix quickly. Turn out mixture onto a dampened (wet and wrung out) double layer of a clean, old sheet into a line about 15-20" and roll it up — smoothing from the center. Best to let stand overnight or longer. It will firm and keep well to be sliced rather thinly, on demand.

Judy Mideke Samter (Mrs. Pat)
Oklahoma City

Kate Jupe (Mrs. J.W.) recalls that in "nineteen-ought-nine", J.W. owned one of the first livery cars in Oklahoma City, a Moon with license # 3. His "stand" was across from the elegant new Huckins Hotel, where he was the choice driver of opera diva, Madam Schumann-Heink, who loved to take rides following her concerts, and Willie enjoyed her humming and singing as he drove.

Harriet Colcord's

DANDY CANDY

3 cups sugar	pinch salt
1 cup corn syrup	1 cup nuts
1 cup milk	1 tsp. vanilla
½ pound butter	

Put all except nuts and vanilla into pan and stir while cooking. When candy forms a soft ball in water remove and stir until thick. Add nuts and vanilla and pour into buttered dish.

Junior League Cookbook
Oklahoma City, 1929

Daughter of Charles F. Colcord, 1889er and early day leader, who was first chief of police and first Sheriff of Oklahoma County. Prior to the Run he had been a cow puncher in I.T. as early as 1876. Prospecting for oil at the turn of the century, he discovered the Glenn pool and became America's greatest producer.

PIONEER FRUIT CANDY

1 lb. raisins	Juice and whole rind
½ lb. figs	of 1 orange
½ lb. dates	1 cup walnuts, broken
1 cup stoned prunes	

Grind together fruits and orange rind and nuts. Shape into balls or into flat bars. Candy should be allowed to stand for 24 hours in order to ripen before eating. Dipping these fruit candies in melted milk chocolate makes them exceptionally tasty.

Linda Vee Anderson
Wilburton

Mrs. Gould's

CHOCOLATE CARAMEL

Put on fire in saucepan 2 pounds brown sugar, ½ pound chocolate broken in small pieces and one small cup cold water. Boil until it will harden in cold water. Stir into it 2 T. butter and 2 tsp. vanilla, turn into buttered pans and cut in squares.

1900 Stroud Cookbook

Mrs. Gould's husband, J.R., was the local Stationer and Printer in Stroud in 1900 and specialized in "Books, Stationery and School Supplies ... Subscriptions taken for all periodicals."

Mrs. Oscar Presson's

PEPPERMINT CREAMS

White 1 egg
equal amount of cream (before beating egg)
enough confectioners sugar to make thick

Beat egg. Pour in cream, stir in sugar until it is thick enough to roll out and cut. Use enough peppermint to taste.

1900 Stroud Cookbook

Mrs. Presson's husband was in business for himself in Stroud ... Oscar Presson & Co advertised: "Baking Day is a pleasure when your bread, cakes, and pies come from the oven light, white, and temptingly delicious. These good things are secured by using Blue Ribbon Flour."

CANDY LOAF

3 pints white cane sugar. Add water and boil to thoroughly dissolve sugar. Let this cook until thick like molasses. Add 1 pint sweet cream. Cook until it forms a soft ball, beat hard until it creams, then knead. Color half pink and leave half white. Add nuts to half and coconut to the other.

3 pints brown sugar, 1 pint cream, butter the size of an egg. Dissolve sugar with cream and cook until it forms a soft ball. Beat hard until it creams, then knead. Work in ½ pound nut meats. Use in layers with the white and pink and put melted chocolate between the layers.

Oil paper and line a loaf pan and put the candy in the pan in layers with the chocolate between. Chill, remove from pan and slice.

Dorothy Hensley Keys (Mrs. Mott)
Oklahoma City

This recipe belonged to Mrs. William Nelson Wheeler and was used for special occasions prior to statehood.

Mrs. Larrance's

POPCORN BALLS

Boil together without stirring 2 cups brown sugar, 6 T. water, a T. vinegar and piece of butter size of a walnut; when syrup will snap when dropped in ice water, pour it over 8 quarts popped corn, from which all unpopped or scorched grains have been removed; stir until cool enough to mold with hands, which should be rubbed with butter before forming into balls.

1900 Stroud Cookbook

One '89er reminisced about their family's first Christmas in Oklahoma Territory, "The Christmas tree was indeed a work of art. Father had brought a small blackjack tree home, and we strung popcorn while he wrapped each branch and twig with cotton; scraps of tinfoil from his tobacco made the icicles." Many other '89ers recalled using blackjacks that first Christmas, as pine trees were a rarity in much of the Territory.

NEAPOLITAN ICE CREAM

1 qt. cream	1 cup sugar
4 eggs	flavoring

Under this name may be included all the varieties made with eggs and cream. The foundation is the same for all, the varieties taking their name from the flavoring used.

Scald the cream; beat the yolks till thick and creamy, add the sugar and beat again. Beat the whites stiff, and beat them well into the yolks. Pour the hot cream into the eggs, and when well mixed, turn back into the double boiler and cook like a boiled custard. Stir constantly until the foam disappears and the custard has thickened enough to coat the spoon. Strain at once, and when cold add the flavoring and freeze.

Frosty Fancies (1898)

In 1898, the White Mountain Freezer Company, maker of the Arctic Ice Cream Freezer, published a booklet of recipes for use with the freezer, entitled Frosty Fancies. Mr. Raymond Long, Oklahoma City, has his mother's copy. Ice cream socials were popular in every community, particularly to raise money.

PHILADELPHIA ICE CREAM

1 qt. cream   Flavor to taste
1 scant cup sugar

This is a name generally applied in this country to all ice-creams made with pure cream and no eggs. There are three ways of making this ice-cream.

First: Mix the sugar and flavoring with the cream, and when the sugar is dissolved strain it into the freezer. This is the quickest and easiest method; the cream increases in bulk considerably and is of a light, snowy texture.

Second: Whip the cream until you have taken off a quart of the froth, mix the sugar and flavoring with the unwhipped cream, strain into the freezer, and when partly frozen add the whipped cream and freeze again until stiff. This gives a very light, delicate texture to the cream.

Third: Heat the cream in a double boiler until scalding hot, melt the sugar in it, and when cold add the flavoring. This is considered by many the best method, as the cream has a rich body and flavor, and a peculiarly smooth, velvety appearance. It also prevents the cream from turning sour.

Frosty Fancies (1898)

Oklahoma City boasted 7 Ice Cream parlors by June of 1889, just two months after the Run.

Mrs. Emmerson's

CAFE FRAPPE

1 cup ground coffee   12 ounces powdered sugar
1 pint water   1½ pints whipped cream

Allow the coffee to steep in the water all night. Beat the sugar with the whipped cream and mix with the coffee (stand the cream in a pan of cracked ice while you beat it) then put all in and freeze.

1900 Stroud Cookbook

As in most towns springing up in the Twin Territories, churches were an important part of life, providing inspiration as well as being the center for social activities. The First Presbyterian Church of Stroud had brush-arbor meetings in 1897 and within three years had enough devoted members to publish a cookbook.

Brookville Hotel

VANILLA ICE CREAM

4 eggs	3 cups heavy cream
2 cups sugar	1 T. vanilla
½ tsp. salt	2 quarts whole milk

Mix well and freeze in hand freezer til firm.

Florence Baxter
Oklahoma City

The Brookville Hotel in Kansas, has had among its famous guests Buffalo Bill Cody, according to Miss Baxter. Pioneers entering Oklahoma Territory from the north prepared for the run in Kansas.

Big Mammy's

VELVET ICE CREAM

2 quarts milk	6 lemons
4 cups sugar	4 beaten egg whites

Scald milk and sugar until bluish color (Do not boil). Pack and freeze for 5 minutes or until chilled. Add juice or lemons and egg whites beaten til stiff. Add choice of crushed fruit if desired, finish freezing. If fresh fruit is added be sure to sweeten to taste. Pineapple or fresh peaches are good.

Mary Evelyn Hogue (Mrs. M.S.)
Kingston, Tennessee

"My grandmother always made this ice cream and it is healthful today because it contains no egg yolks. Lemon juice gives it the velvety texture."

GRAPE ICE

2 lbs. Concord Grapes	1 qt. water
2 lemons	1 lb. sugar

Lay a square of cheese-cloth over a large bowl, put in the washed grapes, and mash thoroughly with a wooden masher. Squeeze out all the juice, and add an equal amount of cold water, the lemon juice and sugar. Use sugar enough to make it quite sweet. Freeze as usual.

Frosty Fancies (1898)

"Several distinctions have been made in water ices. The varieties made with fruit juice, water and sugar only are called water ices. Those with the addition of the white of egg are called sherbets. Sherbets which are of a smooth, fine texture, but only half frozen, are sometimes called sorbets."

Mrs. Dr. Burton's

ORANGE ICE

¾ pound sugar

1 quart water

juice and rinds 6 oranges

juice and rind 1 or 2 lemons

Boil sugar and water. When cool add orange juice. Steep rinds in a little water and strain and add. The lemons added is a great improvement when available. Freeze like ice cream.

1900 Stroud Cookbook

Dr. Burton was a physician in Stroud, and at the turn of the century the wife of a Doctor usually added his title to her own when signing her name ... the wife of a ranking Army officer might be referred to as Mrs. General Sumner.

Mrs. Dr. Evans'

FRENCH CREAM

3 quarts milk

3 pints cream

2 eggs

2 cups sugar

2 T. flour

Beat eggs and add 1 quart of the milk; cook in double boiler and when hot add the sugar with which the flour has been well mixed; let cook 20 minutes, stirring often so it will be smooth; cool, add remainder of milk and cream. Flavor to taste and freeze.

1900 Stroud Cookbook

The City of Stroud sits six miles south of the location of the Sac and Fox Agency established in 1870, on lands assigned to those tribes ... later opened for settlement in 1891. Dr. J. J. Evans was one of its first physicians and surgeons.

Mrs. Hornbarger's

LEMON SHERBET

Take one dozen lemons and make a rich lemonade with three quarts of water, make very sweet, put in freezer and when it gets to a freezing point have ready the whites of five eggs beaten to a stiff froth, beat very hard into the lemonade and freeze.

Capital City Cookbook
Guthrie, O.T., 1898

Ice Cream, Sherbet and Frozen Dainties were made to order at Mrs. M. A. Hornbarger's in Guthrie O.T., and were popular for serving at afternoon teas and other socials. Mrs. Hornbarger graciously shared some of her recipes in the Capital City Cookbook of 1898 and placed an ad as well.

Mrs. Hornbarger's

PINEAPPLE SHERBET

One can grated pineapple, the juice of six lemons, three quarts of water, make it very sweet and when partly frozen add the whites of five well beaten eggs.

Capital City Cookbook
Guthrie, O.T., 1898

One of the most pleasant chores of childhood was the Sunday duty of cranking the ice cream freezer. Brothers and sisters would trade off when numbness of the arm set in, but the treat was well worth the labor.

Grandmother's

SNOW ICE CREAM

Let snow fall several hours to clean atmosphere. Then place large clean dishpan or dutch oven where it will fill with falling snow. Bring snow into house and open can of sweetened Eagle Brand Milk. Punch hole in can and pour thin steady stream over the snow quickly before melting begins. Add a tsp. of vanilla or other flavoring. Stir rapidly and when milk and snow reach an "ice cream" consistency serve bowls to all the children and let them eat it at once.

Robin Freeman Woods (Mrs. Pendleton)
Oklahoma City

"The delicious flavor is only partly real since it is enhanced by the great excitement of gathering the lovely clean snow and magically turning it into food fit for the gods. My grandmother taught us to make this ... she loved the joyous experiences of childhood and never missed an opportunity to share them with us ... her grandchildren. Borden's Eagle Brand Sweetened Condensed Milk was developed in 1857."

Milk Wagon

PRESERVING & PICKLING

The Run

© Judy M. Samter '78

FRUIT BUTTERS

& JELLIES

GRAPE JELLY

Take garden grapes before they are fully ripe, pick them, and boil gently with a little water until the piece flows freely, and pulp dissolved. Strain through a thin Swiss muslin bag, pressing the pulp through, boil again fifteen minutes before adding the sugar, a pound of loaf sugar to every pint. Boil with the sugar 15 min. longer taking off any scum that may rise. Put in 'moulds' or glasses, and cover with egg paper. Wild grapes will make jelly, but not so firm as the cultivated ones.

EGG PAPER:

Soft, tough paper cut to fit jars, and dipped in a saucer of white of egg, put on steamed jars of fruit or preserves, will keep them better than all the late inventions. When the jars and fruit are scalded hot as possible, it will keep them nicely. For jellies and all kinds of pickles it makes a cheap, convenient cover. The paper must turn over the rim of the jar.

1877 Cookbook

One 89er recalled: "When my faithful nurse found out we were going to Oklahoma she advised us to make a lot of jelly and put in tin containers and pack it in a trunk as baggage, so we had plenty of jelly and could easily identify our trunk of jelly."

SPICED GRAPE BUTTER

1½ lbs. stemmed Concord Grapes
1 T. grated orange peel (optional)
1 cup water

2¼ cups sugar
½ tsp. cinnamon
¼ tsp. cloves

Wash grapes; separate skin from pulp. Cook pulp til soft; sieve to remove seeds. Add orange peel and water; cook 10 minutes. Add skins; heat to a boil; add sugar and spices. Cook til thick.

Linda Kennedy Rosser (Mrs. Ronald E.)
Edmond

In 1894, the Oklahoma Times Journal newspaper in Oklahoma City ran an ad offering 20 Concord Grape Vines free for every dollar in subscriptions to their paper.

Mormon

PEAR BUTTER

4 pounds ripe pears
6 cups sugar
½ cup orange juice

1 tsp. grated orange
  peel
½ tsp. nutmeg

Wash and cut up pears. Cook until soft, adding water as needed to prevent sticking. Press through sieve. Measure 12 cups pulp into kettle. Stir in sugar, orange juice, orange peel and nutmeg. Cook until thick. Pour into hot, sterilized jars and seal immediately.

Dona McLain
Oklahoma City

Members of the Church of Jesus Christ of Latter Day Saints were commonly called Mormons. The first recorded Mormon Sunday School in Oklahoma was in 1897, held in Indian Territory with 25 enrolled.

APRICOT CONSERVE

To every pound of halved and stoned fresh apricots, add ½ cup blanched, split almonds and 6 T. white raisins. Weigh this mixture and add equal weight of white sugar. Stir the conserve over low heat until sugar dissolves, stirring now and then. Cook til thick. (When cool, brandy is added by some.)

Pearl Ogden Pemberton, 1889er, has made apricot conserve for many years. This recipe is similar to her method, though she may not have added the raisins. She often used dried apricots in place of fresh ones.

SAND PLUM JELLY

In early July pick sand plums from roadside thickets, both ripe pink ones and partially ripe ones (for natural pectin). Wash well, barely cover whole plums with water and boil til fruit is soft and juice is bright pink. Strain carefully (for jam, press pulp through). Bring juice to boil and add equal amount of sugar gradually, stirring. Boil rapidly until jelly dropped on cool saucer barely runs.

Linda Kennedy Rosser (Mrs. Ronald E.)
Edmond

When the gun sounded at high noon that spring day in 1889, Lava Smith's daddy was among the throng racing to stake a claim. Now Mrs. Ed McCarrell, she recalls that during those first years, jelly was made from wild fruits such as sand plums, blackberries, and elderberries when expensive white sugar could be obtained. The little wild plums are smaller than domestic ones and are too sour to be eaten fresh.

Mrs. D. N. Collins'

PEACH BUTTER

Peel nice ripe peaches, mash with hands. To every quart of fruit stir in one pint of sugar, put on stove and boil until clear, stirring all the time. This is also good for apples, berries, and grapes.

1900 Stroud Cookbook

"The purest of extracts and drugs. Nice line of holiday goods, toilet articles, stationery, school supplies and finest line of Perfumeries in the city. Call and see us," advertised D. N. Collins at the People's Drug Store in 1900.

Mary Ellen Davis'

APPLE BUTTER

Take ten gallons of sweet apple cider before it has fermented. Put it in a brass kettle; if the kettle will not hold all of the cider, put in part of it, and set it a-boiling; skim it, and as it boils away keep adding until you have put in all the cider; boil down to about five gallons. For the ten gallons of cider, take half a bushel of quarters of apples; part quince gives it a fine flavor.

Now wash and drain the apples and put them in the boiled cider, and when they are soft, it must be stirred constantly until finished. It requires a stick formed in such a way as to keep moving on the bottom of the boiler to prevent the apples from sticking and burning. Have a slow fire, and attend carefully to the stirring of the bottom of the kettle. If for winter use, from one to two hours after the apples first begin to boil is sufficient. Before taking it from the fire, season with cinnamon and cloves to taste. Remove from fire, dip the apple butter while hot into well glazed crocks or stone jars; then set aside to cool. When cold, cut paper covers for each crock; soak it in apple jack, lay it inside of the vessel on the apple butter, cover and close.

Mrs. J. H. Warram
Oklahoma City

"Grandmother Davis raised her own fruit in Lehigh, Indian Territory, where my grandfather was a master mechanic in the mines of Choctaw County. I fell heir to her daughter Maggie's cookbook, published in 1878, and this is the way they made apple butter in those days."

Josephine Giles Davidson's

CANTALOUPE BUTTER

Pare the melon, removing seeds and cut into small pieces. Cook and rub through a colander. To every gallon of the pulp of the melon, take one qt. of sugar and ½ cup of good vinegar. Add spices, cinnamon and cloves or nutmeg (1 tsp. of each). Do not use too much water cooking melon.

Mrs. Oletha Anderson Hinton
Altus

I still have the handwritten copy of grandmother's recipe, which is over 100 years old. She was born in Dover, Iowa in 1854, to Elizabeth Taylor Giles, who was the daughter of Betsy Ross of Philadelphia.

205

Grandmother Davidson's

RED WATERMELON PRESERVES

Remove the seeds and white portion of a firm, ripe watermelon. Weigh and allow half as much sugar as melon pulp. Use grated rind and juice of two lemons to every six pounds of melon pulp. Put all together in large preserving kettle and cook slowly until thick as desired. No water is needed, but be sure it does not scorch. It will be thickness of jam.

> Mrs. Oletha Anderson Hinton
> Altus

"There was little choice of food in those days, but good melons were raised on my grandfather James Davidson's farm near Lone Wolf, Oklahoma. Three families came to Oklahoma from Van Buren County, Iowa in 1902; Silas Anderson, John Anderson and James Davidson.

Mrs. Scroggins'

WATERMELON RIND PRESERVES

Select melons with thick rinds. Peel off all green portion using only the white part of the rind. Cut into small dice. Soak in mild salt water overnight (⅓ cup salt to 1 gallon water). Remove from the salt water and cook in clear water about 30 minutes or til tender. Drain well. For 4 pounds of the melon rind, make a syrup of 9 cups sugar, 8 cups water, 2 lemons sliced, and add 4 teaspoons stick cinnamon, 4 teaspoons cloves (tie spices in cheese cloth bag). Boil the syrup and spices 5 minutes before adding the rinds. Add rinds and cook until transparent and clear. Remove spice bag, pour into sterilized jars and seal.

> Mrs. Edna E. Foster
> Oklahoma City

"All the 'old-timers' made watermelon rind preserves!"

PRESERVED APPLES

Use sweet apples that will keep their shape well, drop in quarters into a thick boiling syrup made of white sugar and water, and when they are cooked clear, remove and pack them in a glass jar. Add to the syrup for each quart of apples, 10¢ worth of pine apple extract used by dealers in soda water to flavor their soda; pour this syrup while hot over the apples and seal. These are almost equal to the canned pine apple.

1900 Stroud Cookbook

It was on Sac and Fox lands, opened to public settlement in the run of September 22, 1891, that James W. Stroud homesteaded, and by the following summer he had applied for a post office and opened a general store on the northeast corner of his farm.

PICKLES

&

SAUCES

PICKLED ONIONS

Peel and scald in strong salt water, and take out. Cover with boiling hot vinegar. Strew over whole peppers, white mustard seed. When cold put into bottles and cork closely.

1897 Chickasaw National Records
Volume on Choctaws in Chickasaw Nation

The Chickasaw and Choctaw Tribes were two of the Five Civilized Tribes (others were Cherokee, Creek, and Seminole) their way of life was much like the white man's with large plantations, schools, and a tribal government.

PICKLED PIGS' FEET

Scald, scrape and clean the feet very thoroughly, then sprinkle lightly with salt and let stand for 4 to 8 hours. Wash the feet well in clean water. Place them in hot water and cook until tender but not until meat can be removed from bones. Pack the feet into clean jars, filling the jars to within ½ inch of top with a boiling spiced vinegar. Process jars in water bath for 90 minutes. Vinegar Solution:

2 quarts vinegar	1 tsp. whole black pepper
1 small red pepper	1 tsp. whole allspice
2 T. grated horseradish	1 bay leaf

Mix all together and bring to the boiling point.

Mrs. Edna E. Foster
Oklahoma City

Pioneers did not waste any edible portion of the hog. Sometimes less desirable parts, such as the feet, were given to poor neighbors in return for their help with the fall slaughter.

Annie Henthorn's
PICKLED CORN

Gather corn fresh from the field in morning. Shuck and clean. Have a tub of boiling water on the wood range. Build a very hot fire under this tub. Drop whole ears of corn into this tub of boiling water. Fill tub loosely so it can be stirred and adjusted, so all will get scalded. When water boils again it is time to take corn out. Have another tub of cold water ready. This can be done out in the yard in an old iron kettle near the well; have fire tongs ready to pick out the ears of corn and place them in the cold water. Have a 10 gallon crock jar sterilized and ready, an outside table close, and a sharp butcher knife. When corn has cooled enough to handle, cut the corn from the cob and scrape the cob and put in the crock jar. When all has been cut (enough to fill up to 6 inches of top of the jar), then prepare the brine. Mix enough salt in hot water to float an egg. Pour this brine over the corn. Place a clean flour sack over this and a large plate weighted down with a clean brick. Tie another clean flour sack over top, and have someone carry it to a cool place (in back bedroom). When cold weather comes, push the ice off it, dip out as much corn as needed, wash several times, then cover with water. Put on back of stove to simmer over night. Next morning wash several times again, pour enough cow's cream over it to cover, and simmer for dinner. The milk can be squeezed out of the kernels, it is so fresh.

Nita Lemon
Oklahoma City

This 129 year-old recipe belonged to Annie Houghland Henthorn (born 1864), a pioneer in Hennessey.

Estella Kariker Hedrick's

CHILI SAUCE

12 large ripe tomatoes	1 cup sugar
1 red and 2 green peppers	1 tsp. ground cinnamon
4 onions	1 cup vinegar
2 tsp. salt	

Chop all vegetables fine. Do not put through food grinder. Mix with dry ingredients and vinegar. Simmer 1½ hours. This makes about 6 pints. Do not double recipe or texture will not be satisfactory.

Elsie Hedrick Ferguson (Mrs. David B.)
Oklahoma City

Kingfisher County was the destination of the Kariker family that month of May, 1889. With them was their 8 year-old daughter, Estella. Her great-grandfather had fought in the Revolution, and now like other colonial descendents, they were braving new adversity in the young West. Mrs. Hedrick now lives in Oklahoma City.

Mildred Paul Orbach's

CHILI SAUCE

50 tomatoes	1 tsp. cloves, ground
10 onions	or whole
4 red peppers	1 tsp. cinnamon, ground
4 green peppers	or whole
1 qt. vinegar	3 cups sugar
1 bunch celery	2 T. salt
1 tsp. allspice, ground	1 tsp. nutmeg
or whole	

Grind all vegetables after peeling and washing. Mix together. Bracketed spices may be tied in a bag and dangled while cooking. Cook 2½ hours and seal in sterilized jars.

Harriette Rosenthal Orbach (Mrs. Robert L.)
Oklahoma City

"Bob and his mother made this every year, and so do we. Mildred Paul came to Oklahoma City in 1900 from Indiana with her family. This was a recipe of her family. Bob's uncle, G. A. Paul, was County Attorney in 1905."

Agnes Jupe Mideke's

CHILLI SAUCE

36 tomatoes (medium)	1 tsp. cloves
3 green peppers	1 tsp. cinnamon
3 red peppers	1 tsp. allspice
6 small red peppers	1 tsp. nutmeg
3 onions (medium)	½ tsp. chilli powder
6 cups vinegar	½ tsp. powdered red
6 cups sugar	pepper
(½ white, ½ brown)	½ tsp. paprika
3 T. salt	

Cook 3 hours. Let it boil slowly.

Judy Mideke Samter (Mrs. Pat)
Oklahoma City

"Mother, Grandmother, and my aunts used to gather in the kitchen once a year and make many jars of chilli sauce, strawberry jam and catsup. Mother was a very small girl when she arrived in Oklahoma City shortly after the turn of the century."

Alice Gordon's

GREEN TOMATO PICKLE

1 peck green tomatoes	1 doz. onions
½ peck ripe tomatoes	½ doz. green peppers
3 heads cabbage	½ doz. ripe peppers

Cut it all up fine. Sprinkle with one pint salt, let it stand all night, drain well through a colander in the morning, then put in a kettle with 3 lb. sugar and one teacup grated horseradish, cover with vinegar, while boiling, add 1 tablespoon black pepper, 1 white mustard, 1 of cloves, 1 of mace and 3 of celery seed and boil one hour.

Kathy Bearman (Mrs. Charles H.)
Oklahoma City

"My husband's grandmother, Mary Ellen Bearman, recorded this recipe in her account book and dated it October 30, 1894."

Choctaw

TOMATO CATSUP

1 gal. skinned tomatoes, 4 T. salt, 4 T. pepper (black), half spoon allspice, 8 pods red pepper, 3 large spoons ground mustard; boil together one hour. Strain; when cold, bottle for use.

1897 Chickasaw National Records
Volume on Choctaws in Chickasaw Nation

The Five Civilized Tribes contributed greatly though their expertise in government and tribal organization in the formation of Indian Territory and later the State of Oklahoma. The name of Oklahoma was derived from two Choctaw words: "Okla", meaning people and "Humma" or "homma" meaning red ... Red People.

Half Dugout

Mrs. J. R. Holliday's

CHILI SAUCE

2 doz. tomatoes	1 T. each of ground cloves,
3 green peppers	nutmeg, ginger and
3 onions	allspice
½ cup sugar	1 qt. vinegar
2 T. salt	

Scald and peel tomatoes, cut in small pieces and put all ingredients into a granite (heavy) saucepan. Cook slowly for 3 hours. Bottle and seal.

Mrs. Gerald B. Bremseth
Oklahoma City

"This recipe of Grandmother's was brought into Oklahoma from St. Louis shortly after the run of 1889. I use it today, and it is excellent as a meat sauce."

Grandmother Phelps'
GREEN TOMATO PICKLE

1 peck green tomatoes	1 tsp. ground allspice
(1 bushel = 4 pecks)	2 qts. vinegar
1 doz. medium onions	½ box pickling spice
1 doz. sweet green peppers	1 tsp. mustard seed
1 or 2 hot green peppers or	2 sticks cinnamon
some small red ones	2½ pounds brown sugar
2 tsp. ground cloves (in	2 tsp. celery seed
a bag)	

Slice tomatoes, peppers and onions. Cover with water and 1 pint of salt. Let stand overnight. Drain few at a time in colander. Boil vinegar, spices and sugar and add vegetables and cook until tender, but not mushy. Let stand overnight and taste for salt and sugar. Reheat and seal in jars.

Marta Frost Reynolds (Mrs. A. D.)
Oklahoma City

When Charles Phelps moved to Oklahoma City with his parents from Arkansas before statehood, he was already engaged to a beautiful girl named Betty Blake; but a new neighbor won his heart as they went for long buggy rides. Breaking his engagement in 1906, he married the girl next door, Carrie Warren ... Betty Blake later married Will Rogers, another Oklahoman!

Mother's
DILL PICKLES

Wash cucumbers well. Leave whole. Pack vertically in clean jars. Boil 1 gallon water, 1 quart vinegar, one cup salt. Pour this boiling mixture over the cucumbers. Add 1 T. plus of peeled garlic pods. Stuff fresh dill heads and a couple of fresh grape leaves in each jar. (Mary doesn't know why grape leaves are important but they are!) Seal immediately. Wait 4-5 weeks before opening. These will be crisp and delicious if instructions are followed exactly and cucumbers are fresh.

Mary Miles Clanton
Oklahoma City

The secret of her family's excellent dill pickles is that they must go from garden to jar within two hours. Use any variety of cucumbers, gathered when they are approximately 4 inches long. Mary recalls sitting by the fireside at the foot of her grandmother's rocker listening to stories of meals prepared on the Georgia plantation for 50 to 60 people.

Mrs. John H. Shirk's

MIXED MUSTARD PICKLES

Large head cauliflower	6 colored sweet peppers
1 qt. large cucumbers, cut up	2 heads celery, cut coarse
2 qts. small cucumbers	2 qts. wax beans
1 qt. small white onions	1 can kidney beans

Pour boiling salted water over cucumbers and let stand in a crock overnight. Pour salted boiling water over chunks of peppers and let stand for 2 hours. Boil each vegetable separately in salted water until vegetable is just tender. Scald onions. Drain the vegetables and mix together being careful not to bruise vegetables. Add 1½ cups of sugar to 2½ quarts of vinegar and cook until sugar is completely dissolved. Place vegetable mixture in jars, cover with vinegar, seal. If a mustard pickle is desired, add 2 T. flour and ½ lb. dry mustard very slowly to the vinegar.

Lucyl Shirk
Oklahoma City

George H. Shirk, Lucyl's brother, was Oklahoma's greatest historian, doing more to preserve the heritage of this state than any other individual. He served as President of the Oklahoma Historical Society for 20 years, was the state preservation officer, was a trustee of the National Trust for Historic Preservation, and founded the Oklahoma City Preservation Commission. Through his guidance, Heritage Hills was preserved for future generations.

BRINE TO PRESERVE BUTTER

To three gallons of brine strong enough to bear an egg, add ¼ lb. loaf sugar and 1 T. of salt "petre". Boil brine; when cold, strain. Pack butter in small rolls and place in small jars, cover closely, after brine is poured over to the depth of 4 inches.

1897 Chickasaw National Records

This recipe was found in the Indian Archives of the Oklahoma Historical Society, the Volume of Choctaws living in the Chickasaw Nation. By 1833, eleven thousand Choctaws had arrived in the new country and implemented a constitutional government which was still in use in 1897. Part of their lands were assigned to the Chickasaw Nation in 1855, following twenty years of sharing their country.

GREEN TOMATO CATSUP

Equal parts of cabbage and apples, a few more tomatoes than cabbage and apples, peppers to suit. Grind all, cover with vinegar and cook til good and tender. Seal.

Billye Gaines
Holdenville

Mrs. D. W. Greene's

PICCALILLI

Mix 2 gallons chopped green tomatoes, 1 cup salt and let stand overnight. In the morning drain through a sieve, then take 3 qts. weak vinegar, let it come to a boil, put in the tomatoes, scald them through and drain again; throw away vinegar, then add 1 gal. of cabbage, chopped fine, 1 pt. grated horseradish, 2 T. black pepper, 2 T. mustard seed, 2 T. cinnamon, 1 T. celery seed, 1 doz. sweet peppers chopped fine, ½ doz. little red peppers, and 1 doz. onions chopped fine, 1 gal. of good cider vinegar, ½ gal. brown sugar; scald well, pour over the whole, mix well and put in a jar. It will keep without sealing and yields 33 pints.

Mrs. Earnest Taylor
Thomas

"This recipe was taken from Great-grandmother Greene's cookbook entitled 'To The Cupboard', published by the Society of Christian Church Workers, Barry, Illinois, in 1896. I've used this recipe many times."

Mrs. Selkins'

BREAD AND BUTTER PICKLES

1 gallon cucumbers	5 tsp. regular dry mustard
1 qt. vinegar	3 medium onions
2 cups sugar	1 tsp. celery seed
2 T. salt	1 tsp. tumeric
5 tsp. whole mustard	

Mix all ingredients together, let come to a boil and can.

Mrs. Edna E. Foster
Oklahoma City

"A lady ... should never consider it extravagant to supply herself with the best cooking utensils — egg-beaters, sugar-sifters, double-boilers, etc., and, if a good housekeeper, she will find both pride and pleasure in her jars of home-made pickles and preserves," (From an old cookbook belonging to Mary Lee Ervin.)

Cam Golt's

HOT RELISH

18 red & green sweet
  peppers, seeded
12 medium onions

6 hot peppers (remove
  stem but not seed)

Grind the above and mix thoroughly and let stand 10 minutes; drain and add 1 tsp. celery seed and 1½ T. mustard seed. Mix thoroughly and let stand 10 minutes. Fill sterilized jars loosely to within ¾" of top. Boil together: 2 T. salt, 1½ tsp. sugar, 2 cups white vinegar until sugar and salt dissolve. Pour liquid in each jar to within ¼" of top and seal. (Make more liquid if necessary to fill jars). Add more hot peppers if desired. Let age 2 weeks for best flavor.

Paul Lyon
Geary

"My father-in-law, Cam Golt, made this for years, and the recipe from Georgia or East Texas would have to be at least 75 years old."

Mrs. Travis F. Hensley's

HORSE-RADISH AND BEETS

2 cups grated horseradish
2 cups boiled, chopped red beets

1 scant T. salt
1 tsp. sugar

Moisten mixture with strong vinegar. Pack in wide mouth jars.
To prepare fresh horseradish. Scrape the roots like carrots and cut into cubes, then grind or grate. Use white or distilled vinegar as cider vinegar turns it dark.

Dorothy Hensley Keys (Mrs. Mott)
Oklahoma City

Travis Hensley was called a double pioneer: into the Cheyenne-Arapaho lands in 1892, establishing the first newspaper there, the El Reno Democrat; and the following year into the Cherokee Outlet. Working for the Department of the Interior in the Territory prior to 1889 must have given Hensley "Oklahoma Fever," as it was commonly called — that urge to join thousands heading for the Indian Territory, about to be opened for settlement.

Mrs. W. W. Morrison, Sr.'s

UNCOOKED CHOW-CHOW

½ bushel green tomatoes	1 large stalk celery
8 large green peppers	2 T. celery seed
(1 or 2 red)	1 scant T. cloves
½ gal. onions	2 or 3 sticks cinnamon
1 large head cauliflower	8-10 lbs. sugar (to taste)
1 large head cabbage	3 qts. to gallon vinegar

Grind tomatoes, cabbage and onions, separately cut; salt each well and let stand overnight. Next morning squeeze all juice out of each, especially tomatoes. Mix well with the ground peppers, celery and chopped cauliflower. Heat vinegar, sugar and spices to a good boil — pour over above, mixing well. Pack in a 3 or 4 gallon crock and weight down. To seal in jars, reheat mixture to boiling point after vegetables are added to vinegar mixture.

Mary Ila Morrison (Mrs. Ward, Jr.)
Geary

Favorite family recipes were often carried in the minds of the pioneer women as they crossed the continent. That is the way this was brought to Oklahoma from West Virginia (via Kansas) in 1902 by Mrs. Morrison's mother-in-law, Mary. It was first written in 1942, when a neighbor desiring the recipe, came to the Morrison home and wrote down measurements of ingredients and procedures while Mary made the chow-chow.

Mrs. C. E. Hensley's

TURNIP KRAUT

Grate or chop raw turnips. Pack into quart jars firmly. To each jar add 1 teaspoon sugar and 1 teaspoon salt. Fill with boiling water. Watch carefully and keep lids tight until it is through making. I wait at least 2 or 3 weeks before using. It can also be put in crocks if jars are not available. Be sure to cover tightly and have a weight on the lid.

Dorothy Hensley Keys (Mrs. Mott)
Oklahoma City

Mrs. Hensley's recipe included this notation: "My family made turnip slaw and kraut when we lived in a sod house in Kansas, arriving too late to plant a crop and again in Oklahoma when it was too late for a crop."

STONE JAR SAUERKRAUT

40 to 50 lbs cabbage   Large stone crock
salt

Prepare cabbage by selecting firm, good-sized heads. Let them stand at room temperature one day after picking. Wash carefully and core. Working with only 5 lbs. at a time, shred cabbage with knife or slaw cutter to about one-sixteenth or one-eighth inch thickness. Pack firmly and evenly with a potato masher into a stone jar (or crock) that has been washed in soapy water, rinsed and scalded. Repeat shredding and salting cabbage until jar is filled to within 5" from top. Press firmly (do not pound) with masher to extract enough juice to cover cabbage by the time jar is filled. Keep cabbage covered with juice. Cover with two or three layers of white, clean cloth, tucking edges down against inside of jar. On top, place a scalded, heavy plate that just fits inside the jar, or a paraffined board. Weight it down with a fruit jar filled with water (or with a stone-not limestone-or paraffined brick), so that juice comes over plate. Fermentation will begin the day following the packing. It works faster but is more likely to spoil at a high temperature. The best quality product is made at room temperature (70° F.). Give the kraut daily care. Remove the film as it forms and wash and scald the cover cloth as often as necessary to remove mold and film. When bubbling stops in 2 or 3 weeks (4 weeks in cold weather), tap jar or crock gently. If no bubbles rise, fermentation has ended.

Laura Ambrose Long (Mrs. Raymond F.)
Oklahoma City

"If you eat sauerkraut often and will use your supply before winter ends, it will hold in the stone jar in a cold room (55° F. or lower)." The Ambrose family had a cool cellar and kept the sauerkraut there in the huge crocks that Laura loves to tell about "pounding" full of the shredded cabbage when she was a child.

Laura Ambrose came to Oklahoma City as a child in 1889 and grew up on Choctaw Street where the Union Station was later constructed. As a teen-ager barely out of high school, she went to work for the Brock Dry Goods Store, which later became the John A. Brown Company. She served many years as controller and upon the death of Mrs. Brown was elected President, serving until the sale of the store to the Dayton-Hudson Company.

Mother's

KRAUT

Put double handful salt in barrel, cut heart out of cabbage and throw in barrel; take a nice clean spade and chop up what is in barrel. To every 10 common-sized heads sprinkle on a double handful of salt until barrel is full. Put on a board that just fits inside of barrel, Weigh it down and set in cool place.

Viola Gulick Krob
Aline

1898 Dining Room

MISCELLANY

SNACKS, etc.

Couch Family

WHIZZ

Whizz is a mixture of soft butter and honey whizzed together. (See Whole Wheat Sticks)

Edna M. Couch
Norman

Another 89er recollected: "Butter was very scarce as there were so few cows in Oklahoma at that time, so my husband, Mr. Wahl, sent to Illinois for 50 lbs. of butter packed by some of his old customers. We dug a hole on the north side of the home and kept this butter as fresh and sweet as possible until it was all used."

Ellen Gulick's

EGG BUTTER

One pint sorghum molasses; bring to a boil. Have ready 2 well-beaten eggs. After adding a bit of allspice or cinnamon, stir in the eggs, stirring constantly until it thickens, which will be as soon as it boils up. We prefer to add a gill (½ cup) of water or sweet milk as it takes away the "too strong" or "rich" taste. This is fine for children's lunch in spring when fruit gets scarce.

Viola Gulick Krob
Aline

"This is from Mother's cookbook, over 70 years old."

220

CHEESE BARS

Make these on "pastry day" from the pieces left over from pies. Cut strips 3 inches long and 2 inches wide. Cover the upper side thickly with grated cheese and the merest dust of cayenne pepper, and fold the pastry lengthwise over this, sift cheese on top and bake quickly. Eat hot.

Viola Gulick Krob
Aline

According to Mary Lee Ervin's old cookbook: "Wednesday is devoted to baking part of the cake, bread, and pies that will be needed during the week. In this work the mistress helps by washing the currants, stoning the raisins, beating the eggs, and making the light pastry. Often a lady who has a taste for cooking makes all the desserts, cakes, and pies."

Mormon

PIONEER SYRUP

1 cup corn syrup   ¼ cup water (or less)
2 T. molasses

Combine corn syrup and molasses. Heat, but do not boil. If a thin syrup is desired, add water.

Dona McLain
Oklahoma City

One of the early Mormon missionaries to Indian Territory was Father Parley Pratt, who travelled through the area around Fort Gibson in the 1850's and died in defense of his faith in western Arkansas.

Mrs. Harry Coil's

CORN COB SYRUP

Cut off musty ends of 12 clean cobs, and wash until free from grit, put in large kettle with enough water to cover, cook for about 1½ hours. Remove cobs and strain liquid.

1 cup white sugar, 1 cup brown sugar, 1 cup of strained liquid and 2 T. white corn syrup. Cook all this til thick as desired. The corn syrup keeps it from crystallizing. Put remaining liquid in glass and put it in refrigerator to use when needed. Try this on hot cakes, waffles, or biscuits.

Lucile McManus (Mrs. John)
Oklahoma City

"This was always made in the fall on the farm northwest of Geary, where Grandfather raised corn and wheat."

WHITE SAUCE

1 T. butter
1 T. flour
1 cup scalded milk

¼ tsp. salt and a few
grains of pepper

Melt butter in saucepan, add flour mixed with seasonings, and stir until well blended; then pour on gradually while stirring constantly hot milk, bring to the boiling point, and let boil two minutes. A wire wisk is the best utensil to use in making sauces.

Irene M. Fallon
Mountain View

To scald milk, put in top of double boiler, having water boiling in under part. Cover and let stand on top of range until milk around edge of double boiler has a bead-like appearance. A good cook had to know how to make a good white sauce as it was basic to so many dishes.

Grandmother Couch's

KUSH

Left-over cornbread
1 or 2 tsp. of butter
   to each slice of
   cornbread

Milk

Melt the butter in a heavy sauce pan or skillet. Cut cornbread into chunks and add to melted butter. Turn over a little but not enough to break the chunks. Pour in a little milk and stir again lightly. Cover with a lid, turn off the heat, let it set for a minute. Serve from a bowl. Eat with a fork like spoonbread.

Edna M. Couch
Norman

"We made Kush out of left-over cornbread for as long as I can remember, a custom handed down from Cynthia Gordon Couch. Sometimes a left-over baking powder biscuit might be cut up with the cornbread. About 1916 my Aunt Irene taught school in New Mexico and, as was the custom, lived with a family. The mother and daughter put on their best cooking skills for the benefit of the new school teacher, but the father said, 'I'd rather have Kush.' Irene said, 'I would too.' "

Laura Matthews Rennie's

PANADA

Take stale bread (broken in bite size pieces). Dot with butter. Sprinkle with sugar and cinnamon. Sprinkle on just enough hot water to make palatable.

Laura Rennie Hamilton (Mrs. Wm. A.)
Anadarko

"Mother's mother made it for her as an afternoon snack when nothing else was available. This is delicious if served by loving hands to a hungry child!"

LUMPY DICK

Take water or milk, add a little butter or grease, then enough flour and salt to make lumpy when mixed. Cook in a skillet until done.

Elva Lindsey Jacobson (Mrs. F. Conover)
Oklahoma City

"This was liked by Mormon pioneers who came to Indian Territory. My children and grandchildren still love it. My great-grandfather Ray came to Blanchard, Oklahoma from Louisiana and his wife from Mississippi. Their old house still stands ½ mile south of the Blanchard Cemetery."

PARCHED CORN

Shell yellow field corn into a heavy iron pan and parch in the oven of the wood stove all day or til centers of the kernel turn a golden brown. Grind in coffee mill and serve with cream and sugar.

Grace Smith (Mrs. Myles F.)
Oklahoma City

Mrs. Smith says their day started at 4:00 a.m. and by 10:00 they needed a "pick-me-up" . . . this was excellent and very tasty. A very interesting person in her 80's, Mrs. Smith wrote a book, "Freckles and Feather Beds," about growing up on an Oklahoma farm.

Eugene Couch's

CRYSTAL WHEAT

Wash whole kernels of wheat. Cover with water and simmer for 3 or 4 hours until a wheat berry is soft all the way through. Spread the cooked wheat out to dry. My grandmother had a dryer made for this purpose. It might take several weeks to cook and dry a large quantity of this wheat. We might have a whole bushel when we took it to the mill to be ground. That would supply our winter cooked cereal.

Bring ¾ cup water to a boil. Add ¼ cup Crystal Wheat and salt as desired. Lower the heat to a simmer and allow to reconstitute for about 15 minutes in a covered sauce pan. Eat with milk, cream or buttered like grits.

Edna M. Couch
Norman

"This recipe was from my father's cooking school lessons. We made our own cereal as long as I can remember, more than 70 years. Mother always placed this in the warm oven of her wood stove. When I first discovered Taboli Wheat (very similar), I asked my Aunt Irene if she remembered Crystal Wheat. 'Yes, I'd sure like to have some.' I gave her a pound of Taboli Wheat and reminded her how to cook it. She is now 89 years old, still does her own cooking."

Eugene Couch was 12 years old when his father led homesteaders into the Unassigned Lands called Oklahoma Country in 1889. He and his mother were still living in Kansas waiting for the house to be built while William Couch served as provisional Mayor of Oklahoma City.

BLANCHED ALMONDS

Almonds are blanched by pouring boiling water over them. The skins will then rub off easily. If one application is not sufficient, another will be. The skin is tough and hard to digest.

Harriet Rosenstahl (Mrs. V. C.)
Oklahoma City

Mother's
CORN MEAL MUSH

Bring to boil 4½ cups water and mix in a bowl 1½ cups corn meal, 1 tsp. salt, 3 T. flour and mix to a smooth paste with 1½ cups cold water, then immediately stir into the boiling water stirring constantly so that it doesn't lump or scorch at the bottom. Bring to a boil, lower the heat and simmer for about 10 minutes. Serve warm.

Florence Isaacs
Ada

"When I was just a girl my mother would make a big pot of mush for supper on cold evenings. Served with a big glass of sweetmilk, it was so delicious and filling. If any was left she put it in a bowl to cool overnight and the next morning she would slice it into about ½ inch slices and dip in flour and fry until brown on each side and served it with butter, syrup or jelly."

Mrs. J. C. Hudman, of Oklahoma City, whose parents were pioneers of Greer County, recalls: "The old-timers all grew corn, and some of it would always be taken to a mill for grinding. When the seasons made other foods scarce, one staple always available was corn meal. Mush was very popular with Pioneers and was a nutritious food. My parents were Mr. and Mrs. Eli Delsworth Maddux." Her mother used milk and 1 T. of sugar in mush.

Mama's
BROWNED CORNMEAL MUSH

Place cornmeal in a dry skillet on low heat. Stir the cornmeal constantly until it is light brown. Make cornmeal mush as usual.

Edna M. Couch
Norman

In 1883, William L. Couch was wagonmaster of the Boomer invasion of Camp Alice (near Jones), with over 200 wagons to oversee. Ms. Couch's grandfather was elected leader of Payne's Oklahoma Colony, commonly called the "Boomers," following the death of Captain David L. Payne in 1884. He led over 200 men to Stillwater Creek attempting to settle it in December, 1884.

Due to the persistence of the Boomers, led by Captain Couch, Congress agreed in 1889, to pay the Creek Nation two million dollars and the Seminoles almost the same for their claims to the Unassigned Lands.

Mrs. Zenn's

SLANG-JANG

1 qt. canned tomatoes,
mashed or chopped
1 8 oz. can cove oysters,
coarsley chopped and
drained
½ cup diced celery
1 T. minced or chopped
onion

½-¾ cup finely shredded
or chopped cabbage
1 tsp. Worcestershire
6 drops of Tabasco
1 T. vinegar
1 T. Pepper sauce —
more if desired
Salt and Pepper to taste

The right amount of Pepper sauce seems to be the secret to this recipe. Chill before serving. If you like taste of oysters, add drained juice.

Paul Lyon
Geary

"This has been served for 75 years each Thanksgiving and Christmas along with or prior to eating, in a small bowl. Very good for in-between snack. Also good hangover cure."

1901 Style

GRAPEFRUIT

"In 1901 Dawson introduced Oklahoma City to something new ... the grapefruit.

Dawson ordered two boxes from Florida. He sent a half box to the Chickasha branch house. The dealer sent them back — said he couldn't use that stuff. He must have tried one himself.

Dawson got to thinking about a way to market the grapefruit ... He had learned Oklahoma City would eat bananas, once it got started. Grapefruit ought to go the same way — although it was bitter. The women were called in, and a recipe for sweetening and serving evolved. The recipe became popular, and grapefruit was served at many parties. They were served after an overnight soaking of sugar and wine."

Oklahoma — The Beautiful Land
Reminiscences of the Eighty-Niners

1835

HONEY VINEGAR

To one quart of clear honey, put eight quarts of warm water; mix it well together; when it has passed the acetous fermentation, a white vinegar will be formed, in many respects better than ordinary vinegar.

James Neill Northe
Oklahoma City

CLOVER BLOSSOM VINEGAR

Pick clover blossoms only. Put one peck of blossoms in a stone crock, add 2 quarts brown sugar, 1 quart molasses and 4½ quarts boiling water. When cool add 1½ pints hop yeast. Mix well, cover with white cloth, and let stand in cool place 14 days. Strain the vinegar off and seal in jars.

Mrs. Charles M. Godfrey
Cushing

Mother Treeman's

BAKING POWDER RECIPES

No. 1. Sixteen ounces corn starch, eight of bicarbonate of soda, five of tartaric acid; mix thoroughly.

No. 2. Eight ounces flour, eight of English bicarbonate of soda, seven of tartaric acid; mix thoroughly by passing several times through a sieve.

Mrs. R. W. Treeman
Perry

"When I married in 1916, my mother-in-law made her own baking powder, which was new to me because my mother swore by Royal Baking Powder and would use nothing else. Both of these recipes were in my mother-in-law's cookbook."

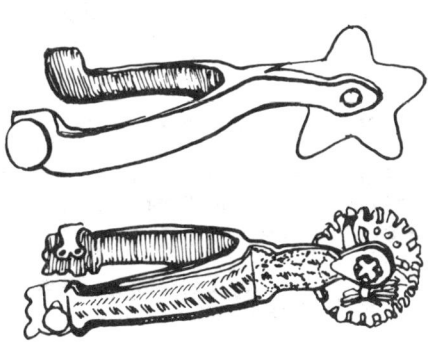

ᏰBEVERAGES

O. O. Martin, Sr.'s

BOILED COFFEE

(Camp Coffee)

For each cup of coffee:
1 heaping T. of freshly
   ground coffee
1 cup water, boiling

1 egg shell for the pot —
   or a whole egg (wasn't
   always available while
   camping)

Scald the coffee pot, if possible. Put in the coffee and pour over it the boiling water, add egg shell. Cover closely and boil 3-5 minutes. Place the pot where it will stay hot but not not boil. Pour out one cup of coffee and return to pot — this is to clean the spout. Then add 1 cup of cold water and let the grounds settle for 5 minutes.

Mary Lee Martin Ervin (Mrs. John W.)
Oklahoma City

"My father, O. O. Martin, Sr., came to Oklahoma in Territorial days from St. Louis — a big city even then — and became an immediately devoted citizen of the territory and state. He was a great campfire cook, could make biscuits using a Dutch oven on a camp fire. The cast iron 'oven' was buried in the coals and coals heaped on the lid — it worked when you had the 'know how' which he did, and I don't."

Mrs. Col. Soward's

COFFEE

Select good coffee, look over carefully, removing all impurities and worthless kernels, and roast evenly to a light brown. (A few burnt berries will spoil the mess.) Grind just before making, very fine. Rinse the coffee-pot with boiling water, then fasten a flannel bag in the top by means of wire hooks or staples, turn in the coffee and pour boiling water on, cover and let it leach through. When the necessary amount of water has leached through, remove the bag and send to the table immediately. Be particular and not allow the coffee to boil, as this destroys the peculiar aroma which is the charm of a good cup of coffee.

Anita Ellis (Mrs. Marvin)
Guthrie

Colonel Thomas E. Soward's wife, Libby, brought an 1879 cookbook with her when they came to Guthrie in the Run of '89. He became the first mayor of "East Guthrie", one of four original settlements which would eventually be incorporated into Guthrie, the first capital of Oklahoma.

Old-Fashioned

LEMONADE

¼ cup fresh lemon juice   1 cup water
4 tsp. sugar (or to taste)

Mix well with ice.

Linda Kennedy Rosser (Mrs. Ronald E.)
Edmond

When the beautiful Overholser Mansion was completed out on N.W. 14 in 1904, a reception was held for their friends. Children and young people attending were served lemonade in the third floor ballroom, where they danced to the music of a gramophone.

Aunt Kate Jupe's

LEMONADE SYRUP

Combine two cups of white corn syrup with the juice of nine medium lemons. This will keep in the icebox for several days in a covered jar. Use 3 T. syrup and crushed ice to each glass. Add a few halved strawberries, whole raspberries, or pitted cherries to each glass for fancy.

Judy Mideke Samter (Mrs. Pat)
Oklahoma City

The Zero Ice and Cold Storage Company was well-known in Norman. The Jupe and Oderman families first had ice companies in Oklahoma City. It was the custom to deliver ice by horse-drawn wagon to homes and businesses who placed their ice cards in the window!

Mrs. J. O. Severns'

CHOCOLATE

One tablespoon cocoa to each pint of water, as much milk as water, sugar to taste. Rub cocoa smooth in little cold water. Have ready on fire one pint boiling water, stir in grated cocoa paste, boil twenty minutes. Add milk and boil five minutes more. Sweeten to taste.

Capital City Cookbook
Guthrie, O.T. 1898

On November 16, 1907, Oklahoma celebrated statehood with a mock wedding of the "Twin Territories" between a young white man representing Oklahoma Territory and an Indian maiden in buckskin representing Indian Territory. The "marriage" took place on the steps of the Carnegie Library in Guthrie, built in 1902, and was followed by the inauguration of the first Governor of Oklahoma, Charles N. Haskell.

SASSAFRAS TEA

1 tsp. Sassafras root per cup of water. Boil ten minutes. Sweeten to taste and drink hot. (Root bark may be re-used several times.)

Mrs. Viola Gulick Krob
Aline

Mrs. Krob says, "Sassafras Tea was a hot drink in spring, to build up body for the hard spring and summer work."

Ellen Marsden Braidwood's

OLD ENGLISH FRUIT WASSAIL

2 qts. sweet apple
   cider (or fresh apple
   juice)
2 cups orange juice

1 cup lemon juice
1 stick whole cinnamon
1 tsp. whole cloves
sugar or honey to taste

Combine ingredients and bring to a simmer. Strain and serve hot.

Robin Freeman Woods (Mrs. Pendleton)
Oklahoma City

Ellen Marsden was born in England about 1870, and when her parents brought her to America as a young girl, they brought with them many traditional English recipes.

Grandmother's

HARVEST DRINK

One quart of water, tablespoon sifted sugar, half pint vinegar.

Mrs. R. W. Treeman
Perry

Mrs. Treeman sent an interesting old quote: "A neat, clean house, a tidy table and well-cooked palatable meals are safeguards against the evils of the ale-house, the liquor saloons, and the gambling table."

Julia Amanda Vandiver's

EGG NOG

16 T. white sugar, added 1
at a time to
16 egg yolks, well beaten
2 dashes of cinnamon
2 dashes of all spice
2 tsp. nutmeg
1 qt. whiskey, added gradually

1 qt. milk, added slowly
1 cup rum, added slowly
1 pt. whipped cream
1 qt. vanilla ice cream
folded in
16 egg whites, beaten stiff
and folded in

Martha J. Birchum (Mrs. J. W., Jr.)
Chickasha

"In early days in the South, ice for the ice cream was brought to the plantation by boat and stored in caves. Served twice a year, Christmas and New Years, this was my great-grandmother's recipe from Atlanta."

Phil C. Kidd Sr.'s

EGG NOG

Beat the yolks of 6 eggs and gradually beat in 1 cup sugar. Add 1 pint whiskey (less if "corn") to egg yolk mixture. (Important — it cooks the egg yolks.) Add 6 egg whites beaten stiff and 3 pints of whipping cream. If desired not so thick, add a little milk. If serving in punch bowl, use 1 quart frozen egg nog to keep chilled.

If you want to freeze egg nog recipe, do not whip cream first and only use 1 cup whiskey and add it gradually while freezing or it won't freeze.

Mary Lelia Kidd Holmes (Mrs. W. M.)
Norman

This was always served on Christmas morning and frozen, too, for Christmas dinner ... references to "freezing", such as this, usually referred to the use of an ice cream freezer and does not imply an updating of the recipe.

CLARET PUNCH

A pint bottle of Claret
A gill of French Brandy
4 T. powdered sugar

Juice and thinly cut rind of lemon
A lump of ice
1 pint of water

1877 Cookbook

On March 10, 1900, "Mesdames George Gerson and B. B. Pollack" entertained at a Black Cat Party in Oklahoma City, serving their guests claret punch, and amusing them with games and prizes following the Black Cat theme.

Zella Mendenhall's

ELDERBERRY BLOSSOM WINE

Steep 3 pints of elderberry blossoms in 1½ gallons of water for 1½ hours, then strain through fine cloth.

Add 2½ pounds of sugar for each gallon of water and ½ cake of dry yeast per gallon of water (for 5 gallons of wine use 3 cakes). Then grate or grind 3 lemons, pulp and all, put in bottom of jug. Add enough water to make out the 5 gallon jug of water to finish the working. Let work until all pulp has worked out.

In adding water, do not bring additional water above the bend line of jug. Be sure to burn hole in the cork correct size for hose. Then seal with parafin. Drive finishing nail thru hose so that when the wine starts working the hose is not blown out. Hang hose at least 5 feet high then bring remaining hose down to floor level and put in water bucket for gas escapage.

Adalene Mendenhall Coleman
Oklahoma City

Born in a dugout in Cowley County, Kansas, in 1888, Zella Smith was brought to O.T. after her father, James R., made the Run of '89, later settling in Blaine County west of Geary in 1890. As County Commissioner, Mr. Smith supervised construction of the original courthouse ... his name was in the cornerstone.

Sarah S. Goldberg's

GRAPE WINE

Add one-half as much sugar as grapes, by weight. Crush fruit either first or after fermenting. Let it work until it quits before bottling. (Fruit will settle to the bottom.) Cork lightly. Put aside in cool place.

Harriet Goldberg Carson (Mrs. Joel)
Oklahoma City

"One of my favorite spots to play as a little girl was under my grandmother Goldberg's grape arbor in Hartshorne. She grew several varieties of grapes. When you opened the door to the cellar, you could smell the wine, mixed with the smell of crocks of home-made pickles."

QUICK BEER

14 qts. of cold water   1 qt. hop yeast
1 qt. of molasses   4 T. ginger

Mix it well, strain through a fine sieve and bottle it immediately. In 24 hours it will be ready for use.

1877 Cookbook

Prior to statehood, the only laws regarding alcoholic beverages pertained to the sale of such to Indians. Saloons were common in most towns in the Twin Territories.

Grandmother Bearman's

BLACKBERRY CORDIAL

To 2 qt of juice add 1 lb white sugar, ½ oz nutmeg, ½ oz cinnamon and ½ oz cloves, all pulverized. Boil all together a short time. When cold add 1 pt brandy. Dose from a teaspoonful to a wine glass, according to the age of the patient.

Kathy Bearman (Mrs. Charles H.)
Oklahoma City

The 1880 account book of Mary Ellen Bearman contained this "receipt", transcribed as written.

CREMEDIES

&

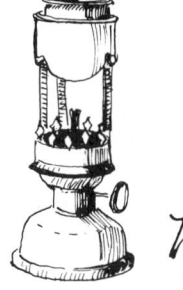

Vaporizer

CHOUSEHOLD HINTS

Leonard Family

VEGETABLE ELIXIR

Take 1 gallon of best 4th proof Brandy. Add 1 tt of Gum Myrrh pounded fine. Shake them well together every day for 5 or 6 days and the Elixir is fit for use.

This Elixir is useful in all cases of pain. Taken inward or applied upon the outside it is one of the most valuable medicines in the known world.

Alice Everett (Mrs. Mark R.)
Oklahoma City

This New England remedy has been in the family since about 1800. Mrs. Everett's copy is in the original hand.

Mrs. Miller's

REMEDIES

Watercress: for scurvy
Carrots: for asthma
Turnips: for nervous disorders
Lettuce: for insomnia
Blackberries: for diarrhea
Bananas: for diarrhea
Cayenne Pepper: increases digestive power of weak stomach
Weak solution of salt water: for prevention of hair loss

E. B. Morgan
Dallas, Texas

Mrs. Ellis'

REMEDIES

Itch Remedy:

½ lb. lard (melted)
1 dram ammoniated mercury
1 dram sulphuric acid
1 oz. sulphur

1 dram benzoic acid
1 dram oil of bergamat
2 dram nitrate of potassium

Stir constantly until cold. For itch, lice, and sores. A very old remedy and very effective. ("looks like peanut butter ... ingredients are now hard to find")

Cough Syrup:

1 cup whiskey
1 cup strained honey

1 cup gylcerin
1 gram menthol crystals

Dissolve crystals in whiskey before adding other ingredients. Put into bottles and do not seal for 24 hours. Sealed, it keeps indefinitely. Take only a taste, not even a full tsp. "Mother still makes it every year, keeps some on hand, and gives the rest away."

Joe Ellis

Ellen Gulick's

REMEDIES

Sore Throat: Take off your stocking when going to bed, place the foot part next to throat, pin it around neck and leave until morning. Be sure to put it on before stocking gets cold.

Colds: Mix turpentine and lard together. Rub on chest.

Coughs: Mix ½ vinegar and ½ sugar. Place slices of onion in a small kettle and pour sugar over and let set out on just a warm spot on stove until the sugar becomes onion syrup.

Snake Bites or Insect Bites: Slice onion, and hammer in all the salt it will take and wrap on bite. As soon as onion and salt turn green, make another and put on until it doesn't turn green. I still use this for bites.

Summer Complaint: 2 T. castor oil.

Viola Gulick Krob
Aline

NAVAJO REMEDY FOR ARTHRITIS AND NEURITIS

2 lbs. alfalfa seed

Use ¾ cup seed and 2 quarts water. Boil slowly 20 minutes. Cool. Then strain. Press seed to get out juice. Place in dark bottle. Keep cool.

Dose — 5 T.: Drink before meals; known to relieve conditions of arthritis in 5 to 10 days.

Kay Oliver (Mrs. Gates)
Oklahoma City

George T. Webster's

COLD REMEDY

½ gallon jug filled with rock candy, then covered with whiskey. In winter, use for colds 1 T. at a time.

Martha J. Birchum (Mrs. J.W., Jr.)
Chickasha

"Grandfather Webster brought this remedy from his home in Kentucky when he made the Run and staked his claim north of Norman."

Grandmother Jupe's

ASAFETIDA BAG

Use one teaspoon of asafetida gum (buy at apothecary), wrapped carefully — for it is quite sticky — in a double layer of soft cotton material to make an amulet about the neck of a child. It is said to ward off contagious diseases (and everyone else), as it has an odor stronger than garlic. It will surely prevent many things.

Judy Mideke Samter (Mrs. Pat)
Oklahoma City

"Mother had to wear this as a child and dreaded the strong odor."

Fred B. Champion's

ALL PURPOSE REMEDY

Pure gum spirit turpentine (from the drug store): use on scratches, nail injuries, etc.

Mrs. John E. Burley
Oklahoma City

"Papa invented a new strain of corn on our Kansas farm. He always soled the children's shoes himself."

Maria Goodrich's

CURES AND PAIN RELIEVERS

For splinters or for those times when children stepped on nails: with a doctor miles away and inaccessible try putting on a poultice of fat meat with pepper covering it. Within 48 hrs. this poultice would usually draw the infection from the wound and relieve the pain.

For splinters, or other painful spots: shave off a bit of soap from a bar of "Crystal White" laundry soap, dampen, sprinkle with sugar, and put on a cloth which is then bound on the sore place. It usually brought relief in 24 or 48 hrs. and prevented infection from gaining ground.

Sprains: always soaked twice a day in warm water put into a pan along with 2 T. of Epsom salts.

Mother's remedy for colds: In a sauce dish she would slice an onion and sprinkle it with sugar, and the cold sufferer was supposed to take a teaspoon of the syrup thus formed 2 or 3 times a day. This was efficient enough in relieving the cold that it was later used on the grandchildren.

Papa's remedy for colds: Papa always had a can of pine tar around — it came in a can about the size of condensed milk. He would bring it in from the shed and pour a little of it over about 2 tablespoons of sugar in a saucer. We were instructed to go by and take a pinch every little bit. It did help our cough and I guess the cold, too.

Irene Nation Van Sandt
Ruth Nation Jerkins
Oklahoma City

Mrs. Cora Nation, our mother, came to Oklahoma in 1902. Our grandmother, Maria Smith Goodrich, was the nurse for a Kansas doctor, and whenever Dr. Emerson was not available she carried on his work with a free hand. Few nurses in that day had training, and she mixed folk medicine and scientific medical practice with ease. Her 'cures' and 'pain relievers' came down to us through our mother, Cora Nation, but all of these were from the 'Grasshopper' period in Kansas. Our father, Mark Nation, brought his cold remedy from Indiana."

HOME REMEDIES

Skurvey: Take Red Oak bark, Persimmon bark, bark of red Sassafras root, yellow percoon root, also sum sugar, also sum alum and sweeten with honey.

Nueralgia and Toothache: 1 oz. best alcohol, 1/8 oz. landunum, 5/8 oz. chlorophorm, 1 drm. oil of lavender and ½ drm. oil of cloves. Used as liniment.

Bowel Disease:

1 T. castor oil	2 or 3 drops Landunum
1 T. weakeye (perhaps whiskey by another name)	In case of blood, add 2 or 3 drops turpentine

Take in a tablespoon every 3 hours.

Ida Robertson
Clinton

"From a Day Book kept by Grandfather Vowell, a Civil War Veteran, begun in 1875 when he started on a cattle drive from Henrietta, Texas, these remedies were copied as he had them, spelling and all. The Day Book include lists of distances covered each day, hand-drawn maps, and supply lists."

Grandmother's

RED WOOL FLANNEL COUGH REMEDY

Soak a red wool undershirt in hot oil (boiled out of the hogs) and turpentine. This long sleeved shirt, buttoned down the back, was required when appearing to take a cold — worn next to the body as Mother and Grandmother had done. Normal clothing was worn over it and children were sent to school as usual, itching and in agony all day. The shirt was resoaked at night and worn under a long flannel nightie. You were not permitted to remove it until all signs of cough and cold had gone.

Mary Miles Clanton
Oklahoma City

Mary says she turned purple before she would cough in front of her mother ... as her whole tummy and chest would be red and blistered when at last the shirt was removed.

AN OLD FASHIONED RECIPE
FOR HOME COMFORT

Take of thought of self one part, two parts of thought for family, equal parts of common sense and broad intelligence; a large part of the sense of the fitness of things; a heaping measure of living above what your neighbors think of you, and twice the quantity of keeping within your income; a sprinkling of what tends to refinement and beauty, stirred thick with Christian principle of the true brand and set-to-rise.

Capital City Cookbook
Guthrie, O.T., 1898

Mrs. Belye's

SURE CURE FOR DIPHTHERIA

To The Household:

I will give a recipe that I know has been tried and cured without fail by my mother. She learned it when she was a little girl. I have known her to use it on an infant 2 months old. The doctor had given it up to die and it was easy and asleep in a few minutes after my mother applied the poultice. I have often wished every family in the world knew this remedy and its value. It is a certain cure, no doubt about it, until death has them in its clasp.

A POULTICE FOR DIPHTHERIA: One tablespoonful each of common salt, sulphur, turpentine and coal oil, the yolk of one egg, beaten together. Put in a flannel cloth, put it to the throat and tie the cloth on top of the head. The wash to use after is sassafras tea, vinegar, honey and alum. I know it would be a good rule if all doctors would make a habit of using this remedy.

Polly McGaughey Sutton (Mrs. C. W.)
Oklahoma City

"Brought to that part of Oklahoma which is now Altus in 1902, by my father's cousin, Knox D. McGaughey."

1896

COOK'S POEM

We may live without poetry, music, and art;
We may live without conscience and live without heart;
We may live without friends, we may live without books;
But civilized man cannot live without cooks.

Mrs. Ernest Taylor
Thomas

Grandma Dobbs'
SAYINGS

"Children are natural mimics — they act like their parents in spite of every attempt to teach them good manners."

"When love is doing the work, expect a masterpiece."

"Never miss an opportunity to do kindness, speak a true word, or make a friend."

"Next to God, we are indebted to women; first for life and then making it worth living."

"When you have lots of chores to do, peel the little potatoes first and the big ones won't be so hard."

Ova S. Hull
Oklahoma City

A RECIPE FOR HAPPINESS

2 Heaping tsp. Patience   A dash of laughter
1 Heartful of Love   1 Headful of understanding
2 Handsful of Generousity

Sprinkle generously with kindness. Add plenty of faith. Mix well. Spread over lifetime — And serve to every one you meet.

Nita Lemon
Oklahoma City

HOUSEHOLD HINTS

To tell if an egg is boiled or raw, place it on its side and spin. It will not spin if raw, but will spin like a top if cooked.

Dip the bottoms of metal cannister sets, cleaning powder cans, etc. in paraffin wax and they will not make rust marks or rings on your shelfs.

Mix 1 tsp. cornstarch in egg white when making meringue for pies and the topping will not weep.

Do not grease the sides of cake pans. "How would you like to climb a greased pole"?

Shortly before taking cup cakes from oven, place a marshmallow on each for frosting.

Rub a little meat of a pecan or walnut on little scratched places on dark furniture.

Do you know why moths eat holes in your rug? "To see the dirty floor show." Carpets should be kept clean.

Mrs. M. C. Minton
Duncan

1894 VALUABLE FACTS

Ants are great pests to the housekeeper at certain seasons of the year. Coal oil is used quite effectively to keep them away, but a very simple remedy is a heavy chalk mark made on the shelf completely surrounding the sugar box or cake dish, etc. If the line is complete they will not cross it.

Brooms dipped for a minute or two in boiling suds once a week will wear much longer. It makes them tough and pliable.

Elizabeth Patterson (Mrs. E. W.)
Oklahoma City

ROSE BOWL

Rose leaves (red are the best)
Sprinkle with table salt (NOT iodized)
 and leave in sun one or two days.
Layer of rose leaves
Layer of lavendar
Powdered orris root
Cinnamon and nutmeg
Oil of bergamot / lemon / bitter almond,
 a few drops of each
Any sweet scented leaves such as Rosemary balm

James Neill Northe
Oklahoma City

BEAUTY TIPS

Face Powder: Take of wheat starch, one pound; powdered orris-root three ounces; oil of lemon, thirty drops; oil of bergamot, oil of cloves, each fifteen drops, and rub thoroughly together.

Pearl Water For The Face: Put a half a pound of best Windsor soap scraped fine into a half a gallon of boiling water; stir it well until it cools, add a pint of spirits of wine and a half ounce of oil of rosemary; stir well. This is a good 'cosmetique' and will remove freckles.

Wrinkles In The Skin: White wax, one ounce; strained honey, two ounces; juice of lily bulbs, two ounces. The foregoing melted and stirred together will remove wrinkles.

Ann Lee Byrd (Mrs. Jerome)
Oklahoma City

"These are contained in the cookbook of my grandmother, Mrs. Charles Orson Gose (Anna Covington), wife of Dr. Gose, Hennessey. The book was published in 1890."

Anna Essary's

RECIPE FOR KEEPING COTTONS FROM FADING

2 T. salt	1 T. turpentine
1 T. ammonia	1 gallon warm water

Dip cloth in solution and dry without rinsing. Wash as usual.

Louis Schoenleber
Bethany

1884 Method

TO TEST THE HEAT OF THE OVEN

Put a spoon of flour on an old dish and set in the oven. If it browns in 60 seconds the heat is right for bread. If it browns in less time, the heat must be lessened. But if it is not browned, the oven is not hot enough. The oft-repeated rule to hold the hand in the oven long enough to count so-and-so is no accurate test, on account of the varying ability of different persons to bear heat. If stoves had a thermometer attachment for the oven door, by which the degree of heat could be seen at all times, the invention would be of incalculable benefit.

Harriet Rosenstahl (Mrs. V. C.)
Oklahoma City

Humidifier

CASTOR OIL SOAP

1¼ cup lye	2¾ cups olive oil
4 cups water	2¾ cups coconut oil
1 cup castor oil	2 lbs. lard

Elva Lindsey Jacobson (Mrs. F. Conover)
Oklahoma City

This was a mild and soothing soap which made a rich lather. Mrs. Jacobson, historian of the Church of Jesus Christ of the Latter Day Saints in Oklahoma City, tells that early Mormon pioneer ladies used cornstarch for face powder, rainwater to wash hair, and mutton tallow for cold cream.

Mrs. William Wheeler's

HARD SOAP

2½ pints of rain water   1 can of lye
5 pounds of clear grease

Melt the grease and let it cool just so it will pour out. Dissolve the lye in the rain water and let it cool, then pour the grease into it stirring until well mixed and no more. Make it in a vessel it can stand in until ready to cut out. This is a fine good soap. I use a small strong muslin bag and slice or shave the soap and put it in the bag.

Dorothy Hensley Keys (Mrs. Mott)
Oklahoma City

Anne Stout's

LYE SOAP

5 lbs. fat   1 T. vinegar
1 can lye   ½ cup rain water
1 qt. cold rain water   ¼ cup ammonia
3 tsp. borax   1 T. salsoda (washing soda)
1 heaping T. salt   (I added ¼ cup clorox)
  (2 T. sugar, optional)

Mix original 1 qt. rain water with original 1 can of lye and dissolve. Set aside. Mix next 8 ingredients and mark.

Heat grease, strain and let cool but not cold; mixing all other ingredients together, start stirring in a one way motion and pour in very small stream the grease. Keep a steady stirring; not fast or slow. It will start to thicken. Let it set a few minutes and pour in hearth pan, like a dishpan, with a few layers of absorbent cloth to absorb the water.

Louise Schoenleber
Bethany

This 100 year-old recipe of Anne Stout's was a common way of making a good, strong soap. Rain barrels were a common sight next to early homes, and water could be collected easily and stored. The water was not pure enough for drinking purposes, but because of it's softness was fine for bathing, washing hair, watering plants, and making lye soap.

GLOSSARY OF TERMS

CALORIC: A type of cooking-warming oven. (See Soup Chapter.)

CRACKER DUST: Fine cracker crumbs.

CROCK: A pot or jar made of earthenware, often used for pickling and preserving.

CURD: The caseine substance obtained from milk by coagulation, used for making cheese.

BRINE THAT WILL BEAR AN EGG: Water with enough salt added to float an egg.

BUTTER THE SIZE OF
A BANTY EGG: Equals approximately 3 T.
AN EGG: Equals approximately 4 T.
A HICKORY NUT: Equals approximately 1 T.
A WALNUT: Equals approximately 2 T.

CHUCK WAGON: The trail cook's wagon on cattle drives containing all supplies and equipment.

CIDER VINEGAR: Vinegar made from apple cider, sweeter than regular vinegar.

CLABBER: Thick, sour milk.

EXTRACTS: Concentrated, pure flavoring taken directly from the source, such as vanilla from vanilla beans, almond, peppermint, etc. They were sold in drug stores or pharmacies. Today artificial flavorings are more common.

GEM PAN: Similar to, but more shallow than, a muffin tin.

A GILL: Equals ¼ pint or ½ cup.

GRUB-BOX: Storage box for food during wagon travel.

GRUB WAGON: One wagon used in common by members of a wagon train for food storage.

INDIAN MEAL: Corn meal.

ISINGLASS: A pure, translucent form of gelatin.

JELLY ROLL PAN: A baking sheet with sides, similar to a cookie sheet.

LARD: The rendered fat of hogs. (Substitute shortening.)

LARDER: Stock of food supplies.

LEACH: To cause water to percolate through something, such as coffee.

OVEN TEMPERATURES:
  SLOW: Warm, 250° -300°
  MODERATE: 350°
  QUICK: Hot, 400° -450°

PASTE: Dough, early word for pastry.

QUINCE: The hard, yellowish, acid fruit of the small quince bush or japonica.

RECEIPT: Early word for recipe, also receipe.

A SAFE: A cabinet where breads and cakes were kept "safe", sometimes with screen or perforated tin doors and sides.

SALERATUS: Baking Soda (Sodium bicarbonate).

SCALDED MILK: Heated to just below the boiling point, when tiny bubbles form at edges of pan.

SORGHUM: Common name for dark syrup, sorghum molasses, made by grinding fresh sugar cane stalks, extracting the juice and boiling it down. Used as a substitute for refined sugar.

SPIDER: A long-handled skillet on legs used over hot coals or open fire.

STONED RAISINS (or other fruit): Raisins from which seeds have been removed.

SUET: Hard, fatty tissue from around kidneys and loin of cattle left after slaughter.

SPONGE: Basic yeast mixture used for bread, prior to adding final flour and kneading.

TALLOW: Hard, coarse fat from cows, sheep, etc. often used for making candles or as grease.

WHEY: Milk serum, separating as a watery liquid from the curd after coagulation.

WORK: To ferment, as with bread yeast or alcoholic beverage.

YELK· Early word for yolk.

Cherry Stoner

INDEX

CONFECTIONS (Candies)

COOKIES

CHEESE and EGGS

FISH and SEAFOODS

FROSTY FANCIES (Ice Cream)

FRUIT BUTTERS and JELLIES

GAME

MEATS

2E79

PIONEER COOKERY AROUND OKLAHOMA
c/o Bobwhite Publications
P.O. Box 14641
Oklahoma City, Oklahoma 73113

Please send me _____ copies of PIONEER COOKERY AROUND OKLAHOMA at $9.95 per book, plus $2.00 per book shipping and tax.

Enclosed is my check for $_____ payable to Bobwhite Publications.

Name _____

Street_____

City_____ State _____ Zip _____

Trade Discount Available For Retailers and Non-Profit Organizations. Write For Details.

2E79

PIONEER COOKERY AROUND OKLAHOMA
c/o Bobwhite Publications
P.O. Box 14641
Oklahoma City, Oklahoma 73113

Please send me _____ copies of PIONEER COOKERY AROUND OKLAHOMA at $9.95 per book, plus $2.00 per book shipping and tax.

Enclosed is my check for $_____ payable to Bobwhite Publications.

Name _____

Street_____

City_____ State _____ Zip _____

Trade Discount Available For Retailers and Non-Profit Organizations. Write For Details.

2E79

PIONEER COOKERY AROUND OKLAHOMA
c/o Bobwhite Publications
P.O. Box 14641
Oklahoma City, Oklahoma 73113

Please send me _____ copies of PIONEER COOKERY AROUND OKLAHOMA at $9.95 per book, plus $2.00 per book shipping and tax.

Enclosed is my check for $_____ payable to Bobwhite Publications.

Name _____

Street_____

City_____ State _____ Zip _____

Trade Discount Available For Retailers and Non-Profit Organizations. Write For Details.